Best wishs

Kathir Wei

楊

小

燕

魏
小 楊
燕

SECOND DAUGHTER

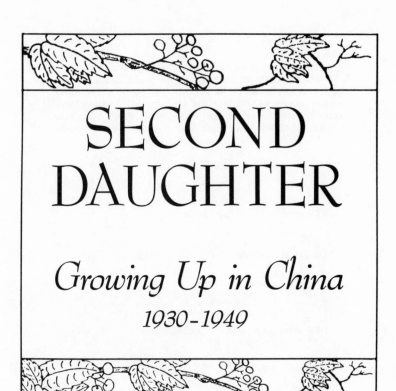

SECOND DAUGHTER

Growing Up in China
1930-1949

Katherine Wei and Terry Quinn

LITTLE, BROWN AND COMPANY • BOSTON • TORONTO

Second Printing

The names of some of the people mentioned in this book have
been changed to protect their privacy.

LIBRARY OF CONGRESS CATALOGING IN PUBLICATION DATA

Wei, Katherine.
  Second daughter.
  1. Wei, Katherine. 2. China—Biography. 3. Chinese
Americans—United States—Biography. 4. China—Social
life and customs—1912–1949. I. Quinn, Terry, 1945–
II. Title.
CT1828.W435A37 1984   951.04′2′0924 [B]   84-5727
ISBN 0-316-92811-9

RRD

Designed by Dede Cummings

*Published simultaneously in Canada
by Little, Brown & Company (Canada) Limited*

PRINTED IN THE UNITED STATES OF AMERICA

To my husband, Charles,
for never failing to believe in me

To my wife, Jane,
for inspiring me to write

Authors' Note

We wish to thank Maimie Lee, Dick Frey, and above all our editor, Genevieve Young. Without their advice, helpful contacts, and countless technical suggestions, it would have been futile to attempt a realistic rendering of events that took place thirty-five to fifty years in the past and, to a great extent, in settings that have been lost to history.

CONTENTS

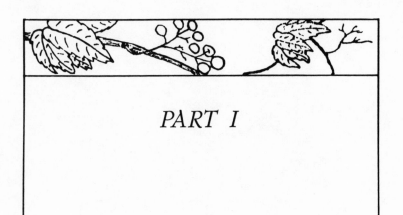

PART I

Hankow

I knew my father was dying. I had seen too many deaths to fail to recognize the signs: the lightless eyes, the faint yet piercing odor of papery skin. I turned in anger toward my mother, who chattered like a parrot in a corner of the room. The scene was too preposterous. Oblivious to her husband, and to me, who had not seen her in thirty-two years and must return to the United States the next morning, Mother entertained two of her friends with the dozens of Polaroid photographs she had prevailed upon me to take the day before. All of them shots of her, proudly exhibiting the quantities of goods I had brought her from Hong Kong. Mother in the western clothes she had had me buy for her in America. Mother pointing toward her massive, crated shipment of appliances and gadgets (a refrigerator, two toasters, a color television set, a stereo, a camera, two watches, a large calculator, and a sewing machine) that, once the lot had been installed, scarcely left any room for Father and her in their tiny Hankow apartment.

How well she had calculated my influence as a wealthy American citizen, who had for years funneled large sums of currency to my family in the People's Republic. Most of that money, I now learned, had been turned over to the State authorities, for there was nothing to spend it on in their humble city one thousand miles inland, where necessities were in

3

scarce supply, and luxuries nonexistent. "Bring everything listed below," she had written. "Our commune leader has made inquiries on our behalf. He says that the articles will pass customs at Canton, and that a portion of the hundred percent import tax will be waived." She had been correctly informed.

It is not entirely accurate of me to ascribe these words to my mother. The letter in which they appeared, the first direct communication I had received from my parents since I had flown to the safety of America in 1949, arrived in the spring of 1981 and was written in my father's hand. Nevertheless, it was in every other respect Mother's letter, and bore her sting. I received it on the morning of May 3, the date my husband's newest ship was to be christened and launched in Orange, Texas. We had invited one thousand guests to the festivities, and I am certain none of them noticed the bitterness I felt on what should have been a day of joy and triumph. In my youth I had been trained to mask emotion. That morning and afternoon I must have seemed absorbed in the ceremonies, yet all I wished to do was to be left alone and to read that message over and over. I was feeling the pain of a long-forgotten wound. Once again I had come within the grip of Mother's power.

For three decades I had heard nothing from her. Not when I had sent money and requests for news; not when I had written of my three children's births. Nothing from her, and nothing from Father — whom, I suspect, she forbade to write until she chose her time. It was Alice, my older sister, who had written me about the family's health and who had acknowledged receipt of the money. Seven letters before the Cultural Revolution, and as many since the political thaw — brief, courteous letters filled with expressive silences. Yet this plea in my father's still beautiful calligraphy — this two-page message that weighed like a stone in my pocket — held nothing graceful, or even the least respectful. "You must come now to our home in Hankow," it read. "It's shameful for a parent to have to beg not to be neglected by his child, but I am going to die soon, and I want to see my Second Daughter, who, judging from what her dutiful sister tells us, has flourished so in the

West." I had only to read a few words to understand with whom I was dealing. It was as if Mother had sat me down forcibly in a chair and begun lecturing me in her grating voice. She was wise not to have written the letter herself. I might not have returned.

Instead Mother had hit on a masterstroke by threatening the most precious memory I had of my China days, the love between my father and me. On the day before we parted, he had talked to me alone of that bond. It was his soft voice then, his face at that moment, that I had wanted always to remember him by, and not his moments of weakness in the face of Mother's relentless will. This letter was designed to look like a betrayal of our love.

There was an enclosure. Had Mother not thought to include a photograph of my father, she might have failed to lure me homeward. On the day of the ship launching, I had pored over that haunting likeness at every spare moment. I had seen what she had wanted me to see — the clear indications of imminent death. My father, so tall for a Chinese man, so brimming with health as I remembered him at the age of fifty-four, looked as shriveled as a fallen leaf. She would not let me preserve my idealized picture of him; that and the illusion that I had broken cleanly and forever with the pain of my years spent in China. Father's shoulders were rounded, and his bloodless lips were twisted into a pathetic smile. His hair was fairly thick, pure white in hue, but matted on the left side, as if he had been propped up in his sickbed just long enough to sit for this travesty of a portrait. He looked diminished in size and in spirit. When I knew him he was a brilliant man, renowned throughout China for his teaching and writing. His shoulders were broad, his skin fair and unwrinkled, his smile engagingly subtle. Mother had counted on this physical degeneration, no doubt, as her trump card. Yet ironically it was my father's eyes that persuaded me to return — the one feature of his that had not changed in any way.

On the afternoon of the launching, I had excused myself from the gaily striped luncheon pavilion and, in the privacy of a restroom, scrutinized again the youthful eyes that stared out from that photograph. There was the same blend of warmth and melancholy. There had always been a distant look in Father's face that seemed to say he had been let down by someone or something. It was a look of metaphysical detachment, which, I realized, must always have been concentrated in those soft brown eyes.

In my youth I could read meanings in Father's eyes that no one else saw or bothered to interpret. And he would talk with me at times about what I saw. In the photograph, there were clear indications not only of suffering and shame, but also, and what intrigued me most, a kind of quiet triumph. I envied Father his look of self-acceptance, his apparent victory over his past. For I had repudiated my own past, not conquered it. I had begun a new life when I came to America and shielded from my mind's sight all that had gone before. The wisdom I saw in Father's eyes chastened me and made me consider another course. Now, perhaps, I was strong enough to come to terms with everything I had fled from at the age of eighteen.

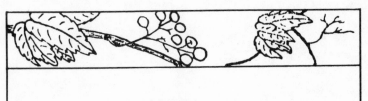

PART II

Peking

1

"ALICE, come down, please, and play something for our friends," Mother called in English. Although she had never set foot outside her native China, my mother had made my American-educated father drill her in the idiom of her Promised Land until she spoke nearly as fluently as he did. "And, Li-Ma, bring Katherine along." Li-Ma, my nursemaid, understood only Mandarin; yet she, no less than any of us, knew what was expected of her that evening. At the prearranged signal she straightened my stiff-collared, western-style blouse, pulled a brush twice through my hair, then hustled me into line at the top of the stairs behind my older sister, Alice, and her amah, Hsu-Ma. We descended.

I know that the year was 1935 — the year Mother changed Erh-Ma's name to Li-Ma — but this could have been any one of thirty such parties, for the sights and sounds and smells did not vary enough to allow me to distinguish among them. The first floor of our house was always afire with candles and jewelry on those nights. Colleagues of Father's, local Kuomintang leaders, European and American diplomats, all milled about before dinner in our spacious parlor, their fancily dressed wives suffusing the atmosphere with a heady mixture of western perfumes. Before sitting down at a dinner table set with starched napkins and silver, they sipped the cocktails and nibbled the hors d'oeuvres our servants brought around, and browsed through Father's collection of English novels or chatted over the big-band music playing softly on my mother's phonograph.

We lacked for no comforts in Peking. Father lectured in sociology at Yenching, one of China's three major universities. In those years professors enjoyed high status. In addition, Father was the dean of his department. We were given a house on campus and maintained a staff consisting of a cook, a maid, a gardener, and an amah for each of the children. We ate the finest foods, dressed in the most expensive materials, furnished our house lavishly, and, each weekend, entertained members both of the Peking academic community and of the Kuomintang — the Nationalist Republic political party, which my father had joined in 1913 shortly after its formation by Sun Yat-sen.

Yet what distinguished our household from others in Peking was not its wealth so much as the extent to which it resembled a home in the West. Since Yenching was founded by an American educator and statesman, supported by American contributors, and, in large part, staffed by American-born faculty members, Mother had access to an ever-renewable supply of books and magazines describing clothes then popular in the United States, as well as house furnishings, customs, recipes, music — in short, a compendium of 1930s Americana. A professor and his wife who had lent us a *Better Homes and Gardens* one month might well spend a Saturday evening at our home the next, sipping Manhattans and listening to Artie Shaw recordings while seated in a living room arrangement recommended by their magazine; later they might dine on a dish described in that very same issue's recipe section.

The Americans, I remember, openly admired my mother's ingenuity, or at least sank into that pseudo-western ambience in an attitude of grateful nostalgia. Mother brought off her imitative effects with such energy and panache, and was so openly eager for approval, that our foreign-born guests were invariably effusive in their praise. Still, I cringe now to think of what my father's Chinese colleagues must have thought. How it must have set their teeth on edge to sit in furniture not aligned with the vertical or the horizontal, a fundamental principle of Chinese decor, but rather in chairs and couches set on the diagonal near the center of the living room or tucked into corners in such a way as to relieve the right angle. How peculiar it must have seemed to them, Christians though they may have been by birth or education, to recite grace in common and then to take Hong Kong–bought silverware to a rack of mutton that my mother had cajoled the Mongolian butcher into fashioning along the lines of a crown roast of lamb, having herself that afternoon painstakingly cut out of parchment paper sixteen frills to decorate the rib ends. What could our Chinese guests have made of Mother's smoking habits? That she smoked at all was a sign of her emancipation, but beyond that, she spurned all the local brands, claiming she could tolerate only Lucky Strikes, for which she had a Peking-based specialty tobacconist as a source. Mother's insistence that English be spoken during her soirees and that the male guests wear western-style suits probably worked no cultural hardship on her native-born guests, since anyone connected with the university was used to such practices. But what could those people have thought when Alice and I were trotted out in our tartan skirts and patent leather shoes to provide the after-dinner entertainment? Mother would smile and dismiss our amahs, then turn toward her guests and present us. She would walk back to her armchair during the ground swell of approving comments, trailing one arm behind her, in the manner of a distracted actress. My sister and I would curtsy and take our positions. While Alice, a musical prodigy, could have played any number of traditional Chinese melodies on her lute, and while I would have been able to perform the Hopei Province folk dances I had learned at the Yenching grade school, this would in no way have suited Mother's plans. Instead, Alice would walk directly to the spinet and rap out "Jeepers, Creepers," to which I would do a frantic Charleston, incorporating every last one of the knee-gripping, arm-flailing, and heel-slapping bits Mother had studied in some 1920s film. She had taught me the routines verbally, never hazarding a single step herself, but making me guess at how each one was executed until I got it right.

Few scenes seem stranger or more incongruous to me now than those dinner parties in Peking: the spacious parlor with its overstuffed sofas, its walls hung with European prints side by side with Chinese scrolls; the flush-faced Americans, hooting with delight as I capered up and down the carpet; the Chinese guests sitting erect, their true feelings, whatever they might have been, hidden behind cordial smiles. I see Father standing proudly behind my mother's chair, tugging at his belt or at the underarms of his too-snug suit, and Mother, dressed splendidly in a *ch'i-p'ao,* coral earrings, and satin pumps, her beauty marred only by the tightness of her facial muscles; Mother nodding her head in wooden time to the piano beat; Mother accepting the applause as if the performance had been her own — which, in a sense, it had been. Just as she lived through my father and his professional successes (or, as she once privately phrased it, through the professional success she had made of my father), she lived through her daughters' minor triumphs as well.

My mother, born to a Shanghai merchant family in 1903 and named Chow Hsu-hue, was a woman to contend with. I have never known a person of stronger will and have never met anyone more skilled at controlling the people around her, or at parlaying a middle-class upbringing into an aristocratic life-style. She lived through us all and, with a martyr's appetite for recognition, sacrificed herself for our sakes. She was a woman of prodigious intelligence, energy, passion, ambition, but a woman born decades too early. Had she not been raised during the last years of the Ch'ing dynasty with its petrified social conventions, she would certainly have excelled in a profession. As it was, she had snatched at every liberating opportunity within her reach in the early days of the first revolution.

She had begun with an advantage. My maternal grand-mother's feet had been bound, but she did not make my mother submit to what was still, in the first decade of the twentieth century, a fairly widespread practice. At the age of eight, in 1911, Mother cut off her Manchu pigtail and success-fully pleaded with her father to enroll her at a Christian school in Shanghai, where she would be assured of a modern sec-ondary education. At a time when marriage brokers were still employed by parents to arrange their children's matches, she persuaded her brother-in-law, Ling Tso-ren, dean of admis-sions at Shanghai University, to introduce her to Professor Yang K'ai-tao, whom she married one year later.

She adopted Christianity, less from any religious conviction than from her agreement with the strong stand Protestant mis-sionaries were then taking against foot-binding and concu-binage and in favor of equality of the sexes. Having joined the ranks of the first generation of emancipated women in 1920s China, she entrenched herself in her household as the arbiter of her family's fate.

Secure in that position of domestic strength, Mother flouted a good number of the unwritten laws still hindering the free movement of women in a China that proclaimed itself a re-public but was actually a loose confederation of fiefdoms. She gave her daughters Chinese names: Hsiao-hue, Hsiao-yen, Hsiao-ying, and Hsiao-ch'ing, but western names as well: Alice, Katherine, Victoria, and Joan. She spent a fortune on our education, while managing my father's rise to prominence. She decided where Father should teach, when he should pub-lish, what promotions he should seek, accept, or decline, what political and academic contacts he should cultivate, which Kuomintang responsibilities he should take on or avoid.

Part of my mother's effect, I now realize, lay in the fact that she possessed none of the physical traits commonly associated with dominance. She was four feet ten inches in height, more than a foot shorter than her husband. She was thin, light-boned, delicate. Her skin was pale, almost white — a sign of status in China, where laborers were browned by their work in the sun. Her fingers, always bejeweled, were long and slender. Her whole appearance suggested frailty. However, for those acquainted with her mastery of language, her volatile moods, her innate understanding of emotional dynamics, Mother's presence in a room was so compelling as to inspire an excitement that bordered on fear.

Mother was not above the use of crude psychological devices. She would scowl at us children to show her disapproval. If she considered the stakes high enough, she would resort to a falsetto whine, or even to fainting spells, in the course of an argument with my father. Still, her true power resided in her fierce belief in herself.

The image she presented was one of awesome self-assurance that, at its most effective, bore all the trappings of theater. Mother walked slowly, almost regally, and availed herself of the sorts of broad gestures calculated to project an actor's emotions to the most distant seat in the house. Like other ladies of her class, Mother rarely went out to the shops, but instead granted appointments to the merchants of Peking, who would lug their blue-cloth bundles to our house. Mother would let them display an enormous inventory before her, discouraging their chatter with pointed silence and allowing them to set no more than two or three objects aside in an hour's time. In the end she would announce an offer in a tone of voice that conveyed absolute disdain for further negotiation. The figure was always startlingly low, but the merchants' protests seemed to lack a certain vehemence, and the ensuing bargaining was seldom protracted. I believe Mother's imperious manner cowed the merchants into accepting a price they would have rejected out of hand in less well-managed circumstances. It was as if they realized they were paying, dearly yet fairly, for a show.

Little that Mother did was done without show. In our Peking days my sisters and I were seldom with her, since child-rearing responsibilities fell chiefly to our amahs. Often we would not see her until the main meal every evening. Those occasions, too, she often tried to transform into semisolemn rituals, although my father always lightened the tone with his slouching, casual presence and quiet clowning. Otherwise, sporadically scheduled, carefully orchestrated events represented our best chance of spending time with her. Once Alice and I were led by our amahs into my parents' bedroom, where a gaunt, sallow-skinned man was kneeling before Mother and repeatedly piercing her fully clothed body with needles. (Acupuncture patients did not disrobe then, nor were the needles sterilized, as they are now.) Several were so long that they would enter her abdomen and protrude from her back. The man worked quickly, his wrist and hand aiming, rearing, striking, while Mother maintained a posture of silent stoicism. No one explained anything to my sister and me. We were not told that this was a doctor treating Mother's ulcer. It was theater, and effective theater at that. My memories of Mother in those earliest days take the form almost exclusively of some impressive tableau.

Given though she was to histrionics, Mother could not fairly be described as lacking substance. She held firm moral views relating to social justice and the dignity of the individual, yet even those tenets were often decked out in theatrical raiment. One day before my youngest sister, Joan, was born, I recall her gathering Alice, Victoria, our amahs, and me for what amounted to an emancipation proclamation. As we children sat on our stools with our nursemaids ranged behind us, we were informed that the age-old custom of referring to the family amahs as Ta-Ma, Erh-Ma, and San-Ma (big nurse, number-two nurse, number-three nurse, depending upon which child the particular woman in question happened to be assigned to) would be abolished. We were told that from that day forward our nurses' surnames would be used. "Ta-Ma," Mother intoned, "here you will be called Wu-Ma. Erh-Ma, here you will be called Li-Ma . . ." and so on. Having spoken her piece, she strode from the room, leaving three confused children and as many vaguely grateful employees, the latter weeping and bowing in her wake.

Then there was the breast-feeding ceremony, during which

theater and conviction were once again seamlessly interwoven. Just as Mother had insisted on hospital births, scarcely a common practice at the time, she decided as early as 1929, when she bore Alice, that she would forgo the services of a wet nurse and breast-feed her children herself. This was just not done by the ladies in Mother's circle. In our house it was done, and done with style. Alice and I witnessed a nursing session the day after Mother returned from Yenching Hospital with Victoria. We were summoned to the family room, where Mother, wearing a spotless white smock, was seated in an armchair. She directed us to sit at her feet, then signaled Chang-Ma, the family maid, who first carried into the room a basin and alcohol-soaked sponge — with which Mother cleansed her hands — then the child, swaddled in a satin coverlet. Mother made awkward small talk with us, asking in her thin, sharp voice what music Alice had been practicing and what games I had been playing. Much of this has faded from my memory. But what I have not forgotten, and was not intended to forget, are the more formal words she spoke that morning. "When you're older," she began, "you may hear people ridicule me for nursing my own children. They may say things like, 'Ah, the wife of Professor Yang thinks she's superior to the rest of us and must do things in her peculiar way,' or, 'Oh, she wouldn't think of tainting her offspring with a common woman's milk,' and other such raving." She fed the baby as she talked, yet held her in such a way at the opening of her smock that we never caught so much as a glimpse of her breast, and were not at all sure of what exactly she was doing.

"The reason why I do this is just the opposite." Mother went on to explain that there was little grazing land in China, and so, few cows and a scarcity of milk. It was unfair, she said, to take the milk of a wet nurse, who might then not have enough for her own newborn child. It was wrong for the rich to take advantage of the poor. To interrupt Mother was out of the question, yet I did not have the slightest idea of what she was talking about. I saw no logical link between my new sister, Victoria, and the state of the nation's grazing lands. I had made no connection yet between female breasts and milk. (In fact, Chinese women's bosoms are small enough, and the fashions concealing enough, and the rules of modesty strict enough, that I was not then aware of any significant anatomical difference between my father's and my mother's chests.) Nor did I understand why the presence of wet nurses, several of whom I had seen in the homes of my schoolmates, constituted taking advantage of the less privileged. What I understood was that my mother, to hear her tell it, was the talk of the neighborhood, and that she preferred it that way.

I knew Mother reveled in her difference from those around her and enjoyed being regarded as a spirited modern woman, free of the conventions that others unthinkingly accepted. Still, from time to time her carefully controlled facade would crack. When that happened it became painfully clear, even to a child, that she was not entirely free of the bonds of tradition. For example, when I was six I learned that Mother felt a wrenching personal shame at having failed to bear my father a male heir. I cannot believe Father ever gave her the impression that he was disappointed at not having a son. Even so, there came a time, one winter morning, when the psychic pain she must have suffered for years became so acute that it burst from her in a terrifying way.

2

My youngest sister, Joan, was born in February 1936, at a hospital affiliated with Yenching University. Two days after the birth, Father and I went to visit Mother. Alice had not even asked to come along. She had a superstitious dread of sickness and death, and would not so much as go near a hospital or a grave. Her absence pleased me greatly, because it meant I would have Father to myself. He always seemed so carefree and relaxed during our times together, so alive with jokes, teasing comments, and puns that I would sometimes scheme to bring about just the sort of private interlude that fell to me that day by accident.

The hospital was only a half mile from our house. Hand in hand, we walked silently at first, our breath smoking in the cold air. We crossed bridges that spanned the campus's stream, at that time of year a glistening ribbon of ice, and walked briskly beneath the eaves of the nine-story pagoda and past No Name Lake. We slowed down once we reached the traditional garden with its bare acacias and willows, and its snow-laden artificial hillocks whose south-facing slopes were so brilliant with reflected sunlight that I could not look at them without squinting. In summer the campus seemed almost oppressive to me; too athrob with human bustle, the rush of moving water, the color of countless banks of flowers. It was quiet, intimate, on a wintry Sunday morning. The snow blanket muffled what few sounds there were and presented to the eye a calming white prospect.

Had I not been so curious to know the circumstances surrounding my mother's delivery, I might have savored that silence throughout the course of our walk. Our young, brash family cook, Lao Chang — the husband of our maid, Chang Ma, and my principal source of information in those years — knew little about the birth other than that Mother had borne yet another daughter. I had an interest in the matter. Mother had made it known throughout her pregnancy that this time she was certain she was to bear my father the heir who would further the family name, and whose birth, Lao Chang had once whispered to Alice, would redeem Mother in the eyes of her peers. No one had paid more dearly than I for what she saw as her one failure. In the Chinese culture, it is no tragedy if the firstborn is a female. There is time yet for a son to come. As the proverb states it, "First the blossom, then the fruit." The First Daughter and her mother are granted a dispensation. And in our family's case, Alice, my mother's decided favorite, was born in the Year of the Dragon, the most coveted in the cycle of twelve; the royal year, in which prospective dynastic emperors had been required to be born. Beautiful, artistic Alice, so like Mother in temperament and physique, was never blamed for not being male. It was I, the Second Daughter, who bore the stigma. Mother lavished affection on Alice alone, treated my younger sister Victoria with a kind of indifferent civility, and singled me out for resentment.

"Father," I asked, "was Mother happy last night?" Since he seemed not to have heard me the first time, I repeated my roundabout question. He answered almost mechanically, still lost in his thoughts.

"Yes, Hsiao-yen, of course she was happy. Very happy."

"What did she say?"

He glanced at me searchingly. When he spoke again it was with more animation. He said that Mother had smiled when the doctor had shown her the child, then said she was weary and wished to sleep. "And when she fell asleep, it was with that smile still on her lips." He squeezed my hand and smiled himself, before retreating once again into his private world.

We walked on in pleasant silence until I happened to make a comment on the peacefulness of the scene. Hardly had I spoken than Father shook his head and said, "The time will come, Hsiao-yen, when this place won't be peaceful at all." My father was almost six feet tall and had large eyes of a rich brown hue — eyes that looked at once warm, even embracing, and startled, as if by the complexity he saw in everything. That morning as he talked in the most general terms about what he knew was an inevitable war, his shoulders drooped and his eyes looked less piercing than usual. I asked him a question about some tree or bird, trying to distract him, but he talked on, as though he had not heard me. "Someone once warned me that these times would come," he said. I could not tell if he was talking to me or to himself. "A man named Leonard Hsu, a very good friend." He glanced at me and smiled wistfully. "He said, the year before you were born, that I should take your mother and sister and go with him to America . . . to live our lives in America."

"But you didn't want to go?"

"No. I'd left China once, and I won't ever again. I wanted to live right here in this most beautiful of all cities, Hsiao-yen. But who can tell how long we'll be able to stay now? Not long, I'm afraid. Not much longer at all."

I did not know how to react. I could hear tension in his voice, and that was the first suspicion I had that we were living in a dangerous place. Lao Chang had said the things my father was saying, and more, during long summer afternoons when he would take Alice and me on picnics. Yet there was nothing very menacing in his diatribes against Generalissimo Chiang Kai-Shek. More than anything else they sounded like bluster and bravado; fairy tales about how if he were not bound by loyalty to his master, he would drop everything and join the Communist guerrilla cadres of Mao Tse-tung and Lin Piao and fight the Japanese to the death. Whatever Cook's true personal beliefs might have been, I felt he had been playacting for children then; and if I had hung on his words and gestures, it was solely for their entertainment value. Now it was the opposite. I tried to ignore what Father was saying, and he himself tried to mask his fear behind a matter-of-fact tone of voice. Yet that fear seeped through the skin of his palm. I pretended I was listening while he droned on in the manner of a man trying to talk away his worries. It was a compromise we hit upon by instinct.

As soon as we reached the lobby of the hospital, the day's mood changed. The netherworld lighting, the antiseptic smells, the people in white walking briskly in every direction made me nervous. I recall counting up consolations. I would see Mother, after more than two days of separation, and the baby for the first time. And there would still be the walk home with Father. There were no restrictions prohibiting children from visiting the maternity ward, and we walked up one flight of stairs, then the length of a linoleum corridor, passing two western doctors and a nurse — all of whom greeted my father respectfully.

Mother was lying in bed when we entered her room. The covers were drawn to her chin, and she was smiling placidly. It was strange to see her looking truly happy. She held out a hand when she saw I was there and stroked my cheek, a show of affection so uncharacteristic of her that I almost recoiled involuntarily. Still, as much as I felt compelled to shrink back, I wanted to grasp her hand and keep it in contact with my face. She whispered "Hsiao-yen," and my Chinese name, no less exotic than a foreign phrase on her lips, seemed all the sweeter. Mother cupped the left side of my face in her hand as a nurse carried the baby into the room. I felt freed of a burden.

Joan was swaddled in a brown cotton blanket. Her eyes were closed in apparent sleep, but her tiny hands twitched. The nurse held her out for my father and me to see and touch. Her skin was white as talc with little red blotches on the cheeks and forehead. There was the merest wisp of black hair. The nurse laid the bundle next to Mother before withdrawing into a corner of the room. Father just kept nodding his head slowly and smiling. It was Mother who spoke first.

"Isn't he a fine-looking one?" she said, and the spell was broken. Father flinched beside me.

"Not he, *she*, Mother," I heard myself saying. Her lips smiled still, but her gaze turned cold and piercing, so that her mouth and eyes looked horribly unconnected.

"What do you mean?" she whispered with only a trace of edge in her voice. "Why do you call my son 'she'?"

I stood there openmouthed, unable to speak. The muscles of my calves began to quiver. Father pulled me away from the bed.

"Don't be upset, *t'ai-t'ai*," he said to her in his low, calming voice, as he reached toward the waking infant. "Hsiao-yen, wait outside," he added more firmly.

"Stay where you are," Mother commanded, and I stayed. There was no disobeying her when she summoned all the dynamism of her will and concentrated it, as she did now, in a raw, tremulous tone of voice and in a look so accusatory that one felt shot through with guilt and remorse. She thrust Father backward with one arm and was now sitting upright with the baby in her lap, roughly undoing its robe while keeping Father and the nurse at bay with her withering stare. "A *son*, Katherine," she kept repeating. "Not a daughter but a *son*."

Her loose clothing and unbound hair gave her a wild look. "See!" she cried. "See, Katherine!" but when she saw the baby naked she shrieked and dropped her to the mattress. The nurse lunged forward and scooped up the crying infant, fleeing at once from the room. A heavyset American doctor materialized and began guiding Father and me toward the door. "That's not my son!" Mother screamed. "What have you done with him? Where's my son?" Father tried to force his way back into the room, but the doctor was adamant. Soon two more men rushed in and unintentionally knocked me sprawling to the floor. I looked up and saw Mother glaring at me. She was still screaming, though I could hear no sound. Spiky tresses framed her face. And her hand, with one finger outstretched, pointed toward my forehead, as if to impart a curse.

In some ways I am not free yet of the force behind that gesture, and have thought a great deal about the anger that inspired it. It must have galled Mother to live in a culture where, even in her childhood, daughters of peasants were seen as such economic liabilities to their parents that often they would be drowned in their infancy, or sold in their teens to men of wealth as concubines. Where middle-class parents made every sacrifice to educate their sons, who represented the family's hopes for future security, while the formal education of any girl fortunate enough to receive one would consist almost entirely of instruction in the art of household management. Where a woman, upon marriage, left her parents' home forever and "belonged" to her husband and his family. If Mother tried to resist those pressures by embracing western ways, she did not quite prevail. Her failure to give birth to a son — the first requirement of a Chinese wife — came as a blow she could not parry; a personal ordeal that had begun at the time of my birth in October of 1930, and that took on the nature of an indelible mark against her on that chill day six years later.

As the tides of her own psychic turmoil pushed Mother one way or the other, those of us under her control were in turn affected. I was constantly on guard. At the worst times, the tension would leave me dry-mouthed, with a sharp metallic taste beneath my tongue. At the best times, I would be carried along by her energy and high spirits.

Our last December in Peking was to be one of those best times. That was when we celebrated our first truly American-style Christmas. Mother was not, however, its sole architect.

In years past we had observed the celebration of Christ's nativity by attending a special service at the campus chapel on the morning of December 25. We would then congregate at the home of J. Leighton Stuart, the university's founder and president. Surrounded by the elite of Peking's academic and diplomatic communities, we would have a ham and roast chicken banquet. At night Alice and I, as members of the children's choir, would make the rounds of the faculty houses and student dormitories, and sing carols. When the group reached our house, my mother passed out gingerbread elves to the choristers. All of that strikes me as sufficiently out of the ordinary and, as far as I can recall, considerably more enthusiastic an involvement in a Christian feast day than was demonstrated by any of our Chinese acquaintances. And yet in 1936, the year my maternal grandmother joined our household, our Christmas celebration reached an unprecedented level of fervor.

Grandmother was almost as slight and almost as beautiful as Mother. She shared Mother's passion for ritual and her hunger for all things modern, and she too bore herself with an air of combative self-belief. If she had not had bound feet—and so been reduced to tottering about or, at times, being carried— she might have looked like Mother's double from a distance, so white and smooth was the skin of her face and hands, so black and shiny her hair. Upon closer inspection, however, one noticed another clear difference. Grandmother possessed that rarest of physical traits among the Chinese: her eyes were blue.

In 1934, at the age of fifty-seven, Grandmother had converted to Roman Catholicism. To understand what such a choice represented, one must realize that while thousands of Christian ministers, priests, nuns, and religious laymen founded churches, hospitals, and schools in China's major cities following the nineteenth-century Opium Wars, they never succeeded in attracting more than a small percentage of the native population away from its amalgam of Confucian, Buddhist, and Taoist beliefs. For decades, rival missionaries from Europe and America spread the gospel and performed charitable works, striving to dissuade their Chinese flock from worshipping deceased ancestors or from practicing concubinage and foot-binding—long-accepted customs that the proselytizers labeled heathen abominations. It was only when the 1911 Revolution and the fall of the Ch'ing dynasty brought about a gradual retreat from ancient habits and an interest in transforming feudal China into a modern, mechanized nation that the missionaries gained a foothold among families like my own. Motives for converting abounded. In my father's case, the reason was strictly a professional one: the Christian university system presented him with a far broader scope for his research, writing, and lecturing than would have been available in a traditional academic environment. Mother's choice was prompted by a social dynamic: as a Christian woman her gender did not shackle her.

Grandmother's reasons for converting were considerably purer. Given her nearly total ignorance of the English language, her fifty-two years of Buddhist observance, and her bound feet, she must have represented the capstone in the evangelistic edifice of the Shanghai-based American priest who converted her. ("He is a saint," she gushed on the day she arrived at our home.) There was nothing spurious about Grandmother's faith. From the moment of her conversion, until her death, she pursued the way of Christ with a piety bordering on the fanatical.

One of the rules that remained unchanged in China even during the turbulent second decade of the twentieth century was that a wife was not permitted to leave her husband. She exposed herself to scandal and the direst of legal recriminations if she did. Nevertheless, Grandmother left her husband, a wealthy Shanghai coal merchant, on the basis of religious scruples. For seventeen years Chow Chung-lan had kept a series of concubines. Upon becoming Catholic, Grandmother issued him an ultimatum: he must choose between marriage and sin. "I quoted him the Sixth Commandment," she told me many times. "'Thou shalt not commit adultery.' That, Hsiao-yen, is the law of God and cannot be trifled with." In addition to this concession, he was to dismantle their home's Buddhist altar with its heathen idol and its spirit tablets inscribed with the names of his forebears. ("'I am the Lord thy God,' says the Bible, Hsiao-yen, 'thou shalt not put strange gods before me.'") For two and one half years they battled, he proposing a host of compromises, she dismissing his offers with the words of Revelation: "I know thy works, that thou art neither cold nor hot; I would thou wert cold or hot. So then because thou art lukewarm, and neither cold nor hot, I will spew thee out of my mouth." When he did not reform, she deserted him and sought refuge in the home of her youngest daughter. During her year with us, she attended Sunday Mass at a Catholic church in northern Peking, fingered the beads of her jade rosary three times a day, cited the Scriptures at every turn, insisted on leading us in grace before meals, and orchestrated our observance of Lent, Easter, the Ascension, the Immaculate Conception, and Christmas.

The family's religious life was the one sphere that my mother allowed Grandmother to influence significantly. (Mother had a masterful knack for neutralizing threats to her control by channeling others' energies into areas that were important to them, but relatively unimportant to her.) This charge my grandmother accepted with relish and, beginning in late October, managed to involve all of us but Father in a flurry of meticulous Christmas preparations. Exotic foodstuffs were ordered so that Lao Chang might bake a western-style fruitcake, a treat that Grandmother had tasted two Christmases before at a church-sponsored party in Shanghai. That delicacy was doomed to disappoint, owing to Grandmother's hazy recollection of the ingredients, the inappropriateness of our kitchen equipment for baking, the substitution of delicate plum wine for a hearty brandy or rum, and Lao Chang's thinly veiled attitude of disdain for the entire enterprise. (At soaking time each week he greeted the loaf-shaped cake as his "little mummy" before extricating it from its cheesecloth winding-sheet, embalming it with wine, then re-interring it in the depths of our ice chest.) The gardener was to make arrangements to procure a pine sapling and to fashion from its lowest branches two wreaths, which he was to hang on the wall of our family room. He was to build a bamboo stand for the tree, as well, and see that the whole affair was in place by December 20.

Hired tailors were instructed to sew for each family member the new set of clothes one traditionally received months later during the New Year celebration. (A mere holiday, not a holy day, as Grandmother pointed out.) There was a blue silk *ch'i-p'ao* for her; for Mother, one in green, her favorite color; a gray *chan shan* for Father; and for each of the children, a red velvet dress with a hoopskirt and white cotton collar that made us look very much like members of an ice-skating troupe. We were instructed to make little presents for one another and to rehearse those carols that Grandmother approved as nonsectarian.

In late November we began observing Advent, a four-week vigil that, when managed correctly, can heighten one's anticipation to the point of fever pitch by the time Christmas dawn finally comes. This Grandmother accomplished through the use of an Advent calendar, sent her by her former confessor in Shanghai. Each night, beginning the fourth week before Christmas and ending on Christmas Eve, one of my sisters or I was privileged to open a set of cardboard double doors that concealed an illustrated religious scene. The portals were arranged in ascending pyramidal fashion, so that one would open the pair at the apex on the evening before Christmas.

In the weeks before the big day, Alice and I also crafted ornaments. Under Grandmother's watchful eye we spent hours producing paper decorations, tracing them from Christmas issues of Mother's magazines, then cutting them out and coloring them with crayons and waterpaints. Alice eventually tired of those materials and objected to working from predesigned patterns. She took a block of soap and a whittling knife, and shaved and gouged until the likeness of an angel rested in her palm. Mother exclaimed over it and gave her the entire household supply of soap, sending an amah out to buy still more. I burned with envy as my sister set to work in earnest. After she had a batch of rough-hewn figures, she took a needle and refined the angels' features so that each one came alive with character. Grandmother's satiny white hands sifted through Alice's work pile each evening and winnowed out the dragon or phoenix invariably hidden among those pious miniatures.

In that carefree season of religious and artistic endeavor, Father's frequent absences were hardly noticed. None of us children knew until later that he had begun attending nightly Kuomintang meetings related to Japanese maneuvers in Manchuria. Mother and Grandmother did not let on that there was cause for alarm, and Lao Chang said nothing. Either he was sworn to silence by Father, or he paid as little attention to the threat of an enemy invasion as did the great majority of the citizens of Peking. At the very time Father was engaged in secret war-preparedness efforts, Mother, Grandmother, Alice, and I were stringing our decorations and making brightly colored paper loop-chains for the tree.

On Christmas Day itself there was such an explosion of sights, sounds, smells, and tastes in our home that even Father was coaxed out of his month-long dour mood. As for church obligations, a compromise was struck. My parents attended services at the university chapel, where Father's absence would have proved an embarrassment, while Alice and I went to Catholic Mass with Grandmother. We trimmed the tree with our handmade decorations in the early afternoon, using as a model a photograph of a Christmas tree that appeared in a year-old issue of the *Saturday Evening Post*. And we ate Christmas dinner at home, Mother gamely trying to duplicate Dr. Leighton Stuart's American repasts in the face of Lao Chang's subtle sabotage. In the evening, Mother sat down at the piano and, following Grandmother's direction, sounded the chords for "Silent Night," "Oh, Come, All Ye Faithful," and "Good King Wenceslaus." Father, Grandmother, Alice, and I sang, while Joan and Victoria looked on in wonder.

The caroling done, we turned to the ill-fated fruitcake and a goat's-milk disaster meant to approximate eggnog. My sisters and I did not care how awful those things tasted, for we were distracted by the gift exchange, which was to take place next. None of us realized, either, that Father had disappeared from the group at the end of the music, so that when he burst into the family room wearing a white beard and a monstrous red suit and lugging a burlap bag on his back, we were struck dumb for several seconds. We had seen enough magazine illustrations of the North Pole workshop and had heard enough stories from Grandmother about "Old Saint Nick" to identify the figure who was supposed to be visiting us. We knew, too, who lurked behind the cotton beard and cushion-bloated stomach. But we could not put those two ideas together. We stared at the apparition, and he at us, while Mother rushed back to the piano and Grandmother kept prompting "Ho ho ho" in a cackling soprano. At last Father picked up that jolly chant, stamping about, more or less in time with Mother's playing. Twice he made the rounds of the room, then plumped down in our midst and gave out all the beribboned presents that lay at the bottom of his sack.

It was a wonderful end to the evening. Once Father relaxed, everyone did, and we began to make jokes about the lower half of his costume, which, with its pant legs tapered at the ankles and its silk slippers instead of bulky black boots, looked more like the elves' getups than the master's. The amahs, the maid, Cook, even the gardener, were summoned once Father had changed into a *chan shan*. They were all given gifts and new clothes by my parents. Then they bowed and retired, but not before stealing a glance at the weird trappings that by now littered the room. Lao Chang, more than any of the others, seemed out of his element — he who, when alone with us children, always boasted that he had seen and experienced everything. He kept smiling weakly in the direction of the tree, which appeared to be rooted in the floor itself, its branches barely visible under all the decorations we had made for it. Nothing could have been more expressive than Lao Chang's smile, which hid none of his confusion, disapproval, or amusement.

3

I had no friends in Peking, save for Cook. Our life on Yenching campus was so circumscribed by the scope of Mother's tastes and beliefs that I was exposed to very few outside influences in those years. There were playmates I would see during school hours, and neighbors whose sons and daughters Alice and I were occasionally permitted to entertain in our home. Yet we were never given enough freedom from our amahs' supervision to relax with the children we knew and develop anything approaching genuine friendship. Our health, cleanliness, and safety fell within the province of the nursemaids' responsibilities, and so those women hovered over us like ewes over newborn lambs. My amah, Li-Ma, spoke with me often, but never as a friend or confidante, something that she would have regarded as unpardonable presumption on her part. That is just the sort of class discrepancy Lao Chang refused to recognize, at least while he was alone with us children. He saw himself as our equal.

Lao Chang was a scamp. So many of the lessons Mother tried to instill in us with threats and sermons were undermined by his wit and comic sketches. He would not make so bold as to cut up in her presence; nor did he ever once indicate during his many outings with Alice and me that she was the butt of his lampoons. Yet it did not escape us that Cook's warped story morals and Mother's preachments often contrasted like the opposite faces of a coin.

Lao Chang, it must be said, was ugly. His back and head were both slightly misshapen — the fleshy hump behind his left shoulder curiously balanced, as it were, by a far smaller but considerably more noticeable protrusion on the right side of his forehead. Though he was of average build, his skin always looked puckered and flaccid, as if instead of bone, there was only cartilage beneath it. His hair, often redolent of day-old cooking odors, was mottled with unruly, mouse-gray patches, which at times gave him a maniac's air. His fingers, though adept at creating out of the medium of thin air the most lifelike shapes imaginable, were, at rest, an unsightly collection of gnarled stubs, generously flecked with the pale, shiny reminders of knife and cleaver nicks. His two bottom front teeth were solid gold — he called them his personal bank account. All the rest were brownish-yellow and leaned this way and that, like little gravestones. This much can be said in favor of Cook's appearance: his eyes were exceptionally fine. They were very large and of a cocoa hue; cloudy, soothing, spellbinding eyes. I would watch him closely and would see that in the presence of his master and mistress, he did not call upon his full range of resources. He appeared to veil his eyes in some way. When he was with Alice and me, it was different. He met our gaze straight on and enticed us, spiderlike, into his weave of "story-truth." ("Yes, but is that true?" Alice once inquired when Lao Chang concluded an account of the fall of the T'ang dynasty with an apocryphal twist. "It is," he said solemnly. "Didn't you ask me to tell you what the Emperor Hsüan-T'ung was like? Well, that was just the sort of thing he would do. Just that sort of thing.")

There was no refuting Cook's words, no resisting his personality, when he singled me out and blanketed me with a stare, silently pleading with me to consider both what was spoken and what was left unspoken in the impromptu playlets he was forever presenting. Whether his subjects were contemporary politicians, relatives, acquaintances, long-dead historical figures, or the ghosts of legend and myth, he summoned forth the very soul of his characters and imprinted on one's mind the attributes that distinguished them from all others. I would learn from my teachers what was factually true, or thought to be true, about the assassination of Kublai Khan's minister Achmach Bailo, and what was pure fabrication on the part of Lao Chang. I would learn which victories of the eighth-century general An Lu-shan were legitimate, and which were bogus. There was nothing the least disillusioning in this. It was as though the figures were glass vessels that might be filled with any of a variety of colored liquids. I did not care about the details. And, except insofar as they might enhance the portrait of his hero or villain, neither did Lao Chang.

Just as Cook never displayed the breadth of his powers in my parents' presence, so he seldom seemed very animated when with his wife, Chang Ma. She was a very queer woman. She seldom spoke to anyone but her husband, and to him only in quick, breathy phrases hardly louder than a whisper. Chang Ma must once have been beautiful, but she was no longer. There were signs of vanished delicacy in her body and face. Misfortune had weighed on her and bent her over, drained her eyes and mouth of all life. She was like a wraith, never speaking, gliding silently about the house in her gray cotton slippers, hardly seeming to notice us when her vacant gaze met ours. She had what were called re-formed feet, a grisly physical trait that tied her to a specific historical period. I was six years old when Cook told me Chang Ma's story, speaking, as he did so, in somber tones unaided by any play of the hands or eyes. He summarized, instead of elaborating; and for once, I assume, he hewed to the factual truth.

Chang Ma was born in 1901 to peasant parents who could not afford to feed and clothe a daughter. "She was, however, a child of great beauty," Lao Chang said proudly. "And in those days poor families often gambled that so lovely an infant daughter might some day fetch a high price as a concubine. Do you understand what that word means, Second Young Mistress?" I did not, and so he explained. There were few things

Lao Chang ever shrank from explaining to me. "They scratched together what money they had to pay a tutor for her education and to dress her in fine clothing. They bound her feet when she was four years old." It confused me when he said that, for although there was a strange catching motion in Chang Ma's walk, she did not totter about, nearly helpless, the way Grandmother did. Cook, always alive to the moods of his audience, must have noticed that I was puzzled. "Yes, wrapped them in bindings until the bones were reshaped. A rich man wasn't likely to take into his home a 'little wife' whose feet were not bound. Still, she was never bartered away to some country lord. No, the New Order came, and customs changed. For me, this posed no great problem. My mother lopped off my pigtail and sent me out into the modern age. But for girls in Chang Ma's predicament, it wasn't such a simple matter. A doctor had to re-form her feet by breaking and resetting the bones. That's why she walks the way she does."

I did not want to think about the breaking of the bones. I quickly asked a question, to keep that thought away. "Is that why Chang Ma won't talk with us, Lao Chang? And is that why she seems so sad?"

Cook smiled and shook his head. "That isn't why. Chang Ma's sadness is another tale. One I don't think I'll tell you."

In all the time we lived in Peking, I can hardly ever recall leaving the university enclave with Mother, Father, or Grandmother. But during our last two summers in the North, Cook took Alice and me on dozens of expeditions to the Forbidden City, or to the grounds of the Summer Palace in the Western Hills. Victoria and Joan, too young to come along, stayed at home in the care of the amahs. The three of us would walk to the campus gates, then travel by rickshaw either to Central Park, a grassy public area inside the walls of the once-sacred Purple City, or to the Imperial Lakes on which China's rulers and their favored courtesans once sailed in magnificent barges. I loved those sallies into Peking, a riotous bazaar bursting from morning till night with colors, odors, and raucous sounds so foreign to our well-ordered neighborhood. Yenching was a sanctuary whose walls defined an environment sculptured to the needs and tastes of a fastidious biracial population. There was much that was comforting and nurturing about living there as a child. And yet, we were isolated from the roiling currents of civil strife and the threat of war with Japan that both menaced and enlivened the metropolis we shunned. Every three weeks or so Mother would go to one of the White Russian beauty parlors to have her hair done, but she never took us. Nor, except on one occasion, was I ever taken into the city by Father. Only by Cook, who had been born in central Peking, and who was drawn there like an addict to his den. There was no day when Lao Chang did not travel into the business district to cull the best vegetables and fruits in the marketplace at dawn, to settle an account, or to run some other real or fabricated errand that would take him back to the crowded streets and shops he so loved.

On each of our glorious, carefree outing days, Alice and I would alight from our rickshaw in a different sector of Peking (the Tartar City, the Chinese City, the Imperial City), then alternately hike and ride through narrow, bustling streets and along the broad avenues that led to the gates of the Forbidden City. We saw grotesque, foul-smelling camels delivering coal to residences, and all sorts of human traffic entering and leaving street gates: ragged, pockmarked beggars being apportioned a dole of rice by the stewards of wealthy homeowners; head-shaven Buddhist monks and gaunt Taoists in their hollow hats and protruding topknots, soliciting food and alms; droves of fleet-footed messengers brandishing their chit books and seals as they scuttled from one house to another, mongering gossip along with supposedly confidential communications.

In the markets, everything from currants to gigantic live pigs was for sale. There were donkey-driving vendors armed with portable stoves who prepared and sold steamed meat dumplings, succulent crabs, wheat-flour noodles, pungent sausage, almond tea, confections made of spun sugar, bitter-prune soup. Blind men moved laboriously through the throng, striking low-pitched gongs to announce their passage. Occasionally a funeral or wedding procession wound through the city's thoroughfares. I never felt more a part of Peking than when I took a place among its insatiably curious citizenry and gazed with them openly at a funeral cortege: at the hired chief mourner leading the way in his unhemmed white garment, supported by a manservant who held a bowl before his face to catch his tears; at the men bearing the curtained catafalque; or the women weeping and shrieking from horse-drawn carriages. Those lugubrious parades affected me deeply — those, and the lavish wedding trains resplendent with peacock splashes of embroidered silk and eagle-feather fans, and bursting with the lovely racket of firecrackers, trumpets, and drums. Those stylized displays were my first exposure to the China my parents had put behind them, the China that had flourished for millennia and that would survive little more than another decade.

Once we entered Central Park, Lao Chang, Alice, and I would eat before doing anything else. For our very first picnic, Cook had prepared a meal my sister and I enjoyed so much that we pleaded with him to bring the same thing each time, and he did — a practice that heightened the special air of ritual suffusing those long summer days. We would start with eggs hard-boiled in tea soy sauce, the shells having been cracked in the cooking process so that the flavor might seep into the whites. There would be fruits, nuts, and ginseng tea purchased from lakeside vendors. But the main course would always be round, sesame-topped wheat cakes stuffed with seasoned Mongolian lamb. We would eat this meal on the park grass — or, if we were at the Summer Palace, on the deck of the marble boat that lay stationary on the shore of Kunming Lake. Then, at Alice's request, we would sit quietly for a time, staring out over a shallow, tree-encircled lagoon and contemplating the purple hills to the west of Peking.

In our childhood years my sister and I were never closer than during those interludes alongside the water, when we gazed together at the calming horizon for what seemed to me ages. Alice did quiet, meditative things like that by nature. For me it was a case of trying to imitate her perfect grace and composure. People would stop and stare at my sister, perched on her stool like a porcelain statuette, hands folded in her lap, a faint smile of pleasure on her lips. Alice was a mystery to me. She would sometimes go for days scarcely speaking, and when she did speak, she never raised her voice. You could not hear her when she walked. A chance touch of her hand or arm, something she did not consciously allow, gave one the sensation of brushing against the chill smoothness of jade. Still, though she was moody at times, she was seldom forbidding, the way Mother was. There was a genuineness of expression behind her movements and stillnesses that Mother lacked. With the exception of certain times when she feigned sickness, there was nothing of the pose in her behavior. Then too, while the themes of Mother's tableaux were almost always contemporary, Alice struck all who saw her as a reminder of the days when artistic talent and sensitivity radiated a special aura of authority. "Ming Princess" was Father's nickname for her.

There on the park lagoon, it was precisely that artistic authority, that precocious inner vision, that my sister so effortlessly projected. In imitation of her, I would interlace my stubby fingers, straighten my back, and try to conjure up some semblance of her otherworldly smile until the muscles of my cheeks cramped. However, when Cook would finally fold up the newspaper or political pamphlet he had been reading, stick it in his pocket and tell us, in far simpler language than he was used to affecting, that he was going to start back home that minute if we did not quit boring him to death, I gladly threw over our vigil in anticipation of livelier entertainment. There would follow a moment even quieter than the ones that had preceded it; then Alice would sigh from the depths of her being and turn toward Lao Chang. He would make some face or simply stare back at her in his bugeyed way until her smile broadened, and the spell she had cast was dissipated on the breeze. From then on, Cook set the mood for the day.

Passersby must have thought he was demented. The man

had not a shred of the Chinese instinct for decorum. He would saunter along, flailing his arms like a bumpkin, pointing out, but never slowing down to appreciate, the beds of narcissus and orchids, or some statue of a full-bellied Buddha. He would drag us through museum halls in search of some access to the maze of dilapidated courtyards and tortuous alleys that the Imperial Eunuchs once walked and that were now closed to the public. It thrilled me, and mortified Alice, to sneak thief-like into that cobwebbed realm of the past, to scoot after Lao Chang down those ghostly lanes where, at most, we might run into some grizzled caretaker or a scholar there by special leave. These men Cook would hail in his brash, democratic manner, seldom receiving any greeting in return. We could not have looked more out of place: Alice and I in our mock-American outfits and Lao Chang in one of the navy blue, high-collared cloth jackets made popular by his revolutionary hero, Sun Yat-sen. And yet no one ever challenged this humpbacked servant whose air seemed to suggest that the place belonged to him.

No matter which off-limits area we entered, we usually ended up in one particular courtyard that, for reasons I cannot fathom, had captured Cook's fancy. That spot, though offering the charm of total privacy, was in every other respect a study in death. Its marble benches were chipped and felted with soot. Weeds and strangling vines overran a patch of brittle bamboo. A fish pool, drained years, perhaps decades, before, was half filled with rotting quince blossoms. An untenanted shrine and the branches of a withered plum tree threw spectral shadows over the very bench on which Lao Chang would seat us, once he had swept away the loose dirt with the aid of his newspaper. In the distance, the rose parapets and mustard-yellow roofs of the palaces showed majestically, and the sunlight glimmered on the tops of the varnished lintels and on the green tiles capping the Western Gate. Little more was needed to evoke a phantasmagorical, nimbus-ringed past.

The teachings of Lao Chang encompassed history, literature, ethics, religion, and philosophy. They were, by turns, pro-

and anti-dynasty, pro- and anti-Buddhism, pro- and anti-Republic. He proclaimed himself a supporter of Mao Tse-tung, but would have opened a vein before submitting to the ordeals of the Long March. He idolized the late Sun Yat-sen, but often seemed equally enamored of the same imperial regime that patriot was responsible for toppling. In short, Lao Chang was a breathing object lesson in inconsistency. If he ever practiced what he preached, it was through inadvertence; and he regarded the settings for his historical tales only as conveniently maneuverable vehicles for the presentation of an oblique life view.

"They are here in my kingdom. . . . They slither about like maggots. Like pale, bloated maggots. . . ." That was the start of the lesson I remember best. Lao Chang had suddenly begun declaiming in a voice not his own, once Alice and I had settled ourselves on the courtyard bench. In an instant we recognized the Empress Dowager Tz'u Hsi, the Imperial Concubine who ascended the throne as a regent in the middle of the nineteenth century and who reigned intermittently until her death almost fifty years later. (Lao Chang would take on any role, male or female. He would play emperors, peasants, heroes, outlaws, foreigners, patriots, or traitors, and especially warmed to such characters as Tz'u Hsi, to whom several of those labels applied.) We could have identified the Empress with our eyes shut. Had we not heard that self-pitying whine before? That deceptive whimper intended to put one off guard? It was the voice Cook had used when enacting the Dowager's plot to slay the followers of her nephew Kuang Hsü, the last obstacle to her sovereignty. "They dare to come again. To defile our soil with blood-encrusted boots and violate the sanctity of a city forbidden to them."

My sister and I were transfixed by that voice and by the sight of the figure seated at the opposite side of the courtyard. Lao Chang had transformed himself into the Empress and conveyed us back to the start of the century, just after the suppression of the Boxer Rebellion, when the armies of the West sought vengeance. He sat unmoving on a bench beside the empty pool. His face was paler than normal. The muscles surrounding his eyes and mouth were pinched; his forehead, creased. His neck was so relaxed as to produce the impression of slack flesh. His shoulders drooped. Foreshortened arms were supported by the rests of an imaginary throne, while hands trembling with paranoic rage kept worrying the jade knobs at the ends of those supports. His knees were raised slightly so that his feet were suspended eight inches above the ground, where they remained so still that they appeared not to hang but rather to balance on the tall ivory columns of the Empress's Manchu clogs.

"Ch'ien Yu-wei," she cried. (This was the name of a man I remembered from past stories — the gaunt, resourceful leader of the Imperial Eunuchs.) The Dowager's head remained motionless, but she lowered her eyes, then slowly raised them again as her subordinate kowtowed before her. "Ch'ien Yu-wei, this time the round-eyed vermin will not plunder the choicest riches of the kingdom. I saw them come before. I saw them rape, murder, and desecrate. We are still too weak to resist them. But they will not make off with the finest of my treasures. I will deceive them this time." Her head gently nodded and a smile appeared on her lips. There was no wisdom in her unfocused stare, no warmth in her grin. Her face showed only a vise-sure craftiness, a reservoir of calculation as cold, deep, and surface-still as a tarn. "Choose five of your most trusted men," came the command, "and lead them to the Courtyard of Peaceful Old Age. There I will reveal to you a secret of the Ming heretofore shared only by the members of the Imperial Family."

For half an hour Lao Chang dramatized how the Empress Dowager concealed from the western invaders the court's most precious adornments, and how she murdered Ch'ien and the five other eunuchs who had learned the location of the hidden vault. Her smiling face was the thread that bound the tale together. At first the look seemed merely cunning. But by the end, it had been developed into a searing self-indictment, a mirror clearly reflecting the woman's cruelty and limited vision.

Lao Chang heaved a deep sigh. Immediately we began putting questions to him. Alice wanted a full description of the Empress's robes and jewelry. She asked too about the age and estimated value of the articles hidden from the marauders. I wanted to know exactly what a eunuch was. By then we had learned not to bother asking Cook what parts of his story were true. And so, on that afternoon we were left with a vivid impression not only of the historical Ch'ing dynasty ruler, Tz'u Hsi, and of a documented instance of her ingenuity, but also of an Imperial Eunuch who, in fact, never lived; who existed only in the imagination of Lao Chang and in a courtyard lost in the labyrinths of the Forbidden City.

The lesson completed, Cook would rouse us from our reveries with a double clap of his oversized hands and hustle us back through the pavilions and courts toward the main gate. Once in the surrounding Imperial City, we would stop at a restaurant to have peanut candy and special-cut wheat dumplings cooked in broth. It was as pleasurable to watch that latter dish being prepared as it was to eat it. A bald chef would stand in full view of his customers with a long, sharp knife in each fist, a boiling soup caldron in front of him, and a wad of dough resting on his shiny pate. Tilting his head forward, he would blindly slash at the dough with a crisscross motion of his blades until ten or so dumplings had plopped into the broth and started cooking.

By late afternoon we were back in our Yenching neighborhood, a world away from the hubbub of central Peking. Lao Chang would slip back into his grown-up mode, respectfully saluting my parents and beginning the preparation of the evening meal, while my sister and I took baths.

"Alice," I once said after such a day, "do you love Cook?" My sister looked at me the way an elder will regard a child who understands nothing. "What do you mean, 'love Cook'?" she asked, greatly amused. "Lao Chang is skilled enough at what he was hired to do. What more can be said?" I disagreed. I loved Lao Chang. I loved the food he cooked, the tales he told, and the whole idea of story-truth. I loved the way his clothes and zany walk told the world he was worth at least as much as the next fellow; and I learned from that. I loved the way he made his abacus rattle when he wanted to let the whole household know that he was doing the accounts, and his habit of walking the streets with a newspaper sticking conspicuously out of one jacket pocket as proof that, though he was a servant, he could read. I loved him too, for the respect he showed Alice and me. In our Confucian culture, in which deference to one's parents, one's elders, one's governmental authorities, and one's ancestors formed the cornerstone of a well-ordered state, it was rare indeed when an adult spoke and listened to children the way Lao Chang spoke and listened to us. He geared his humor and advice to a level I could appreciate, and he did so without patronizing me. Unlike many of my teachers, he taught me lessons that sparkled with point of view, and he never failed to keep an ear attuned to my feelings and moods. From those earliest years, it was always Cook who made it possible for me to vent my frustration, satisfy my curiosity, express sorrow or joy. Not Mother, who gave the impression she did not care. Not Alice, who felt such different things from what I felt. Not Grandmother, who would reshape what one said to her until it fit some preconceived religious mold. Not even Father, who was at work or meetings so much of the time. Lao Chang was my only true friend.

4

O NE evening less than a month after our last summer picnic stands out in my memory as the most wonderful
and, at the same time, most traumatic experience of
my childhood. It was the night Father took me to the opera,
and the night war came to Peking.

No one had taken sufficient heed when in 1937 the Japanese
increased from two thousand to seven thousand the number of
troops that the Boxer Protocol permitted them to maintain in
the environs of Peking. And everyone had dismissed as a
meaningless skirmish the Marco Polo Bridge incident when, on
July 7 of that same year, Japanese soldiers precipitated a gun-
fire exchange with Chinese militia — an exchange that would
soon serve the enemy as a pretext for invasion. For years
Chiang Kai-Shek himself had turned a blind eye to Japan's
hostile maneuvers in Manchuria while investing finances,
manpower, and precious time in a futile attempt to annihilate
his Communist countrymen, the one political faction that recognized the need to oppose the Japanese with military force. In
the summer of 1937, the citizens of Peking still trusted in the
notion, gainsaid often enough by history, that the walled
perimeter of the city where the Son of Heaven once dwelt was
impregnable.

Mother, Father, Alice, and I were all to have dinner at a

restaurant in the Imperial City, then go to the Kuang Lo Ho — the Pavilion of Extensive Knowledge — Peking's most famous theater, for an opera performance. We were celebrating my father's forty-first birthday. One of the few things Father ever insisted on during the eighteen years I knew him was that there be some sort of fuss made every July 29. He and Mother had always gone out for dinner on that date; this was the first year Alice and I were invited to join them. I had never been to the opera before, but Cook had often told me that a Peking troupe in full regalia, re-creating *The Snow Woman, The War of the Monkey King,* or some other classic drama, was the most dazzling sight there was to be seen. Thanks to Lao Chang's own renditions of those operas, I knew fifteen or so of the plots by heart and all the major character types, such as the *ch'in i* (poor woman leading role), *tao matan* (female warrior), *hua tan* (vivacious female), *hsiao sheng* (leading male role), *wen wu hsiao sheng* (young male warrior), *lao sheng* (bearded scholar), and *chou chiao* (clown). Naturally there were several dimensions lacking. When Lao Chang acted out an opera for Alice and me, there were none of the trapeze stunts, thrilling music, or precision choreography, and one had to imagine the fabulous silks, jewelry, feathers, and multicolored makeup. That evening we would not have to content ourselves with his pantomimes of a landlord sheepishly searching out a prowler in a darkened room or a blind man making his way across a heavily trafficked road, or with his frantic battle scenes complete with somersaults, handsprings, cartwheels, and flips. We were to see the finest troupe of the many that performed the traditional repertoire in the city. And we were to witness the spectacle in a theater constructed during the reign of the Emperor K'ang Hsi in the late seventeenth century. The seating areas and lighting equipment had been renovated in the modern style, so Cook told me, but the building's facade and stage were no different from the way they had looked in the days of the Ming. The excitement was so overwhelming that when it came time to bathe that afternoon and put on the blue dress and white shoes Mother had bought for me that very morning, I broke down in a fit of sobs.

At the restaurant I could manage only to pick at a bowl of rice and sip some tea. I might even have been too tense with anticipation to enjoy myself later that night, had it not been for one of Alice's attacks. We were no more than halfway through our meal when Alice fell prey to one of her mysterious headaches, whereupon Mother created, as was her practice in such emergencies, the most disruptive scene imaginable. She began by loudly announcing my sister's distress, which caused all the other diners to turn toward our table, and the restaurant manager and staff to congregate around us. She called for cold water, a fresh napkin, and a cup of plum wine, the last of which she thrust beneath my sister's nose.

"Come, Hsiao-hue, what's the matter?" Father asked.

"'What's the matter?'" Mother echoed. "Can't anyone see what the matter is? The child is ill."

"Perhaps one of the capsules," he suggested, referring to a vial of specially prescribed herbal medicine.

"Nonsense," Mother snapped. "We must take her home immediately." Not just what she said but her peremptory way of saying it gave me a sick feeling in the pit of my stomach. I knew, all of us knew, what it meant when Mother spoke in that tone of voice. I was sure I was not going to get to see the opera.

It was at that point that Father pronounced, in barely audible tones: "Well, as for myself, I'm going to the theater." Mother and I, as well as the stricken Alice, looked at him dumbly for a moment or two before he turned to me and asked with soft-spoken gallantry: "Would you care to accompany me, Hsiao-yen?" I was only able to stare at him speechlessly.

"You won't be coming back with us?" Mother inquired calmly enough.

"No. No, I don't think so."

"Ah." Mother was livid. It showed in the tightness of her lips and the intensity of her stare. (Grandmother, who, on her daughter's account, often had occasion to rein herself in, would glare like that too, in suppressed rage, and one would notice more than ever the azure hue of her eyes.) A second later, however, Mother's features seemed to thaw, then regroup into a mask of irony. Her eyebrows arched ever so slightly, and her lips quivered, as if in stifled amusement. She was beating an orderly retreat. This was, after all, Father's first mutiny, and she could see that she had been caught out of position. She ceded ground, sensing instinctively, perhaps, that the victory she could surely have forced on the spot would cost her more dearly than a temporary withdrawal from the field. We all assumed, in any event, that Father's act of defiance would not go unavenged.

And so, it was as if I had written a script for the way the evening should develop. The restaurant manager called for a sedan chair and carriers to conduct Mother and Alice home, while Father and I stole away into the night like a pair of shiftless conspirators.

We arrived late at the Kuang Ho Lo because of the scene at the restaurant. I had to run the distance between our rickshaw and the theater in order to keep up with Father, who was no less excited than I was. As we entered the hall, a play entitled *Pai-shih ch'uan,* or *The White Snake,* was already in progress. I knew the story well. The beautiful White Snake Spirit takes on human form and marries the youth Hsu Hsien. Hsu, however, dies of fright when his bride reverts to her serpentine form after taking a draught of realgar wine. At the time of our arrival, the heroine had reached the Enchanted Mountain and was fighting the celestial deer and storks, the guardians of the magic herb that could restore her husband to life. Father and I were immediately separated by a pair of attendants who were hurrying down the dark aisle with a steaming tea service. I was so enthralled by the light and sound and movement emanating from the stage that I did not even notice I was alone. Brass, strings, pipes, and percussion resounded in the wings as the whirling Snake Spirit, hemmed in by a quartet of horned and feathered assailants, repelled the barrage of spears being hurled at her — now fending them off with the springy shaft of her own weapon; now knocking them back, one or two at a time, with her ankles or hands; now ducking one aimed at her head and kicking it with the back of her calf, so that it rebounded to the enemy who had thrown it. The faster and louder the music got, the more frenzied became the juggling, yet not one of the five bamboo shafts ever touched the platform on which the battle was being fought. I had never before seen such colors. Olive, maroon, magenta silks, all embroidered in gold. Green- and brown-plumed headdresses. Chalk-white makeup against which eyes and mouths stood out as black and fiery red accents. As a girl of less than seven years, I could not gauge the subtlety of the actress's weapon play or chanting. What affected me far more deeply was the quality of Pai-shih ch'uan's love and fearless determination. She was a thrilling model of female power: strong or tender, gentle or menacing, straightforward or clever, depending upon which trait was needed at the time. She could wound or heal. In the seats and aisles, there was a constant flurry of activity. Still, nothing intruded to the core of my consciousness, where that woman danced and did battle.

"Hsiao-yen!" Father called from the darkness, five paces away. I did not move, could not, until the Snake Spirit had vanquished her foes, wrested the herb from its niche in the mountainside, and performed her wild dance of triumph. Father stood beside me in the aisle until the dance was completed, then ushered me to my seat, where, my mouth still dry and agape, I watched the rest of the drama in undiminished awe.

Only after savoring what I had seen, and thinking so hard about Pai-shih ch'uan that I would never forget the way her body moved, only then did I become aware of how much noise the audience was making during the intermission, and had made throughout the whole first opera. People chatted openly in midperformance and felt free to cheer, clap, or hiss as the music, songs, dances, acrobatics, and stylized posturing pleased or displeased them. Everyone in the theater, it seemed, was an expert and had seen the program offerings on many

past occasions. And most of them made it clear by their behavior that they held the actors accountable for every traditionally prescribed pitch or leap or twist of the head. The
Snake Spirit's singing, for example, often drew shouts of *"Hao!"*
(Good) and *"Ding hao!"* (Excellent) from ten or twelve men
who, Father said, were recognized connoisseurs, while moans of
pleasure rose from the pool — the most densely populated section of the theater. Many people sipped tea and smoked
cigarettes throughout the evening. And everyone ate melon
seeds, so that the theater air was alive with a constant tattoo of
brittle pops. The atmosphere could not have been more different from what I had witnessed at Mother's soirees. Everyone
was relaxed, and there to have fun. Even though I could not
get my nerve up to shout out my own appreciation of the main
actress's feats, it was exhilarating to be a part of that carefree,
vociferous group.

"Isn't it wonderful?" I said to Father, whose face was
radiant.

"Yes, Hsiao-yen, it's splendid, just splendid. And, you
know, I was just reminiscing. It's so curious. The first opera I
ever saw was performed in this very theater, twenty-three years
ago to the day. I was en route to America and had come by
way of Peking to see the sights of what was then the capital of
the new Republic. On my birthday, I treated myself with a
ticket to the famous Kuang Lo Ho." He smiled and pointed
toward the stage — a raised, square dais covered by an ornate
canopy that was supported by four wooden pillars. "Everything looked the same," he went on abstractedly. "The
balustrade, the red satin draperies, the varnished wooden tablets inscribed with the calligraphy of masters. I didn't sit in the
pool, if I remember, but in one of the balcony boxes, and
from there watched Mei Lan-fang, an actor who has no peer.
That night he played Lady Yu in *The Emperor's Farewell to
His Favorite*. The experts in the audience could not cry out
often enough."

"Will he sing tonight?" I asked, anxious to see this man
whom Lao Chang and Father both held in such esteem.

"No, he left Peking for Shanghai, long before you were old enough to gad about the city like a society lady. Last year he and his troupe moved again, I believe, from Shanghai to Hong Kong."

"Why?" I asked.

"Because," he said in a tone meant to end the conversation, "he has more sense than your father."

The second opera, *The Sword of the Universe,* did not begin on time. The audience became restless, then loud and surly as they waited for the emergence of the actors. All the hissing and shouting seemed to amuse Father, whose patient smile soothed my own anxiety. But soon a nervous-looking man dressed in street clothes scampered onto the stage, bowed to the audience, and asked for silence. He announced that there were as yet unconfirmed reports that Japanese troops were moving against the city. As once before, at Yenching Hospital, I was aware of tension in my father's body and became afraid. At first the words of the man onstage meant little to me. I did not absorb them quickly enough to understand why Father scooped me up at once in his arms and carried me toward the rear of the hall. Only a handful of other patrons followed in our steps. Hardly anyone, it seemed, believed what had been said. From my perch on Father's shoulder I saw the announcer get hooted off the stage. By the time we reached the lobby, the string players had sounded the next play's opening strains. At first the massed instruments drowned out the insults, but the taunts returned in full force, and the once-sturdy musical structure gradually weakened at its foundation, then collapsed beneath an onslaught of deafening jeers.

Father bulled his way through the crowd that was gathering in the lobby, and set me down on the marble threshold just inside the Kuang Ho Lo's lacquered doors. "Don't be afraid," he said over and over as he led me outside, but I was terrified. The squeals of the theatergoers were still echoing in my ears. We hastened down the gloomy street, searching for sedan chair carriers. Father kept muttering self-recriminations, and his hand trembled terribly. There were signs of panic everywhere. Despite its lack of a widespread telephone or radio network, Peking was athrob with rumors of the coming attack. Merchants carted away their wares. Entire families streamed toward the main railroad station. Servants and heads of families alike hauled sacks of household possessions.

The crowds grew denser and the traffic almost impenetrable as we made our way north to Yenching campus, yet I could sense a weird stillness behind all the commotion. When I first drew back the curtain of our sedan chair, my eye caught only the sight of people fleeing. In time I looked closer at the fugitives—for the most part, affluent citizens and foreigners—and saw among them the artisans, beggars, monks, and laborers of Peking who, whatever happened, would be staying in the city. They stood mutely on the walkways and watched, often grinning at the sight of the elite, who were scurrying about so unceremoniously. They congregated as at a parade, buying steamed shrimp or pieces of pungent sausage from street vendors, then settling down to observe and to wait.

It took us nearly an hour to reach home, where all was in a state of paralysis. No one, not even Mother, knew what to do. It was nearly ten o'clock. Joan and Victoria were asleep. The four amahs, Lao Chang, Chang Ma, and the gardener huddled nervously in the kitchen while Mother, Alice, and Grandmother stood like mannequins in the family room. Everyone had heard the news. Cook came into the hall to meet us when we arrived. There were tears on his cheeks.

"Have the amahs wake the children. Tell them to gather in the family room," Father ordered. "And bring me the small cedar box that lies on the floor of my wardrobe." He handed Cook a key, then led me inside.

"Cato!" Mother cried when we entered. That name sounded so strange. I had never heard her use anything but the title *hsien-sheng*, or husband, before, just as Father always called her *t'ai-t'ai*, or wife. He smiled reassuringly and said something to her, but spoke so low that I could not make out what it was. The words brought a short-lived calm to Mother's face. Soon the gardener and Chang Ma straggled in. Then came the four nursemaids, two of them carrying Joan and Victoria, still asleep, against their breasts, each of the other two toting an armful of blankets. Last came Lao Chang with the hand-worked wooden box. Chang Ma stood there, stolid as ever. The amahs and the gardener must have known that Cook and Chang Ma would flee with us, for Lao Chang was considered by my parents to be indispensable. They, on the other hand, would certainly be left behind. Their lot was a difficult one. They were not well enough off to relocate in the South, and yet they had become used to a comfortable existence, and were ill-prepared for the leveling of status that would occur once the enemy took over the administration of the city. The poor had little to lose; the servants of the rich, everything.

Their judgment came swiftly. Father asked Cook for the box, from which he extracted five packets of paper currency. He handed them each a parcel and explained what they already knew. The gardener kept nodding his head and smiling incongruously. The amahs covered their faces with their hands and moaned, as if at a funeral. Father dismissed them with words of gratitude for their service. He told them where we expected to be living and encouraged them to try to get in touch with us if they were ever in need. The sleeping children were surrendered. Then those five people whom I had known for all of my childhood retired to the servants' quarters to pack their few belongings and disappear forever.

Grandmother sat despondently on a sofa in a corner of the room. Her eyes looked faded and resigned. Everything was out of her control. In less than a year's time, her life had fallen into ruin. She was completely at the mercy of others' decisions — she who had made such a point of her independence. Alice's face, too, bore a vague expression. She seemed content to sit quietly, scarcely listening.

"What are you doing, Cato?" Mother challenged. Though she fixed Father with her eyes, there was something irresolute in her gaze. They must have discussed this contingency plan before; she might even have been largely responsible for devising the logistics. Still, I believe it was important to Mother that she wash her hands of all responsibility for the decision to flee from Peking.

"We must leave, *t'ai-t'ai*," Father said. "Tonight. This very hour."

"Leave? Leave our house and all we own? What are you saying? What is he saying?" she cried to Alice and Grandmother, thrusting out her palms in supplication. She started to swoon, and Father quickly advanced to support her. He walked her to an armchair and told Lao Chang to bring water, linens, and medicinal salts, the customary accompaniments of Mother's fainting spells, when she suddenly rallied. "No, I'm all right," she gasped. "I'll be all right. Go, do whatever you like."

"Very well," Father said. "Lao Chang, Chang Ma, you're free to go if you wish, and I've provided for you, should that be your decision." He held up a thick envelope, though the couple kept staring timidly at the floor. "I would ask you, though, to consider . . ."

"We'll stay with you," Cook blurted out, his voice cracking. It was clear that he had spoken out of turn only because he might not have been able to speak at all, had he waited.

Father nodded and replaced the envelope in the box, then pulled out two smaller ones, which he handed to Lao Chang. "We'll travel to Tientsin tonight," he said, naming the first major city to the south of Peking. "The rest of us will take temporary lodging there while you make your way to my family's home in Hunan Province. There you'll deliver this message to my father and wait for his reply. Do you understand?" Lao Chang nodded. He took the message and the second packet, which I assume contained money.

Father instructed Cook to engage five carriages, and next turned his attention to Grandmother. *"Yüeh-mu,"* he said, using the term of respect for one's mother-in-law, "I hope you'll accompany us to Hunan and share the hospitality of my father. His land is in the mountains, far from the enemy's path. You'll be safe there."

"I'll go with you to Tientsin," Grandmother replied. "From there, I'll travel back to my husband and home in Shanghai." Mother began groaning and rocking from side to side in her chair, perhaps taking her mother's words as a personal rebuke.

"Yüeh-mu," Father pleaded, "I'll see that you reach your home safely, if that's where you still want to go once we arrive in Tientsin. But Shanghai will surely fall. Shanghai and all the coastal cities. Allow me to say that you'd be safer with us."

"I'll return to my husband and home," she repeated, gazing straight ahead, her blue eyes focusing on nothing.

Lao Chang hurried back into the room and bowed quickly to Father, indicating that all was in readiness. Mother rose from her chair. "There are things we cannot leave behind," she said.

"That's been taken care of, *t'ai-t'ai,*" Father answered her. He told Cook to have the sedan chair coolies carry down from the master bedroom a chest filled with jewelry, money, carpets, robes, accounts, and documents that he had packed weeks, perhaps months, before. Within minutes we were all bundled into the hired carriages and en route to the railroad depot.

The ride was a bumpy one, for Father had paid the carriers an incentive to speed our way. All the curtains were tightly drawn, and until my eyes adjusted to the darkness, I could not see a thing. It was like hurtling through the night air in a casket. I sat beside Chang Ma, who carried Victoria swaddled in a blanket. My sister was awake now. Her dazed eyes were open wide with fear. Chang Ma, as always, kept silent.

I felt weary, nearly exhausted. Everything seemed alien and confused. Though it was summer, a night breeze sent cold drafts through the carriage. I was nestled in a blanket and still had on the new dress I had worn so long ago to the opera, yet I was freezing. Beyond the curtains, voices crackled—loud voices distorted by the speed of our passage. They were not all Chinese. There were shouts and curses in any number of tongues, harsh, cruel words whose meaning I could not comprehend. After a time our forward motion slowed, then ceased altogether. The carriage began to jostle from side to side. I heard our coolies, front and back, shouting oaths at those around them and orders to one another. Nothing happened. We were like flotsam at the mercy of great fluid masses. The swaying made me feel nauseous. I leaned over, expecting to vomit, but only a raw, retching noise escaped from my throat. I looked up sheepishly at Chang Ma. She did not seem to care, or even to have noticed. She just sat there — as Victoria sat in her lap, as Grandmother and Alice had sat in the family room — blankly staring before her. I felt cut loose and abandoned in that cold, raucous darkness. I wanted to scream at Chang Ma and make her react to me. I pulled at the sleeve of her jacket but she shook herself free. It irked me all the more to see that she had not been immobilized by fear; that she was alert, and had ignored me out of choice. I screamed once, when it seemed the walls of the sedan chair were pressing against my chest and sides. Chang Ma said nothing still, did nothing. Nor did my sister so much as flinch. I sat still for a moment. Then, when I could stand it no longer and was about to yell out again, the carriage crashed to the ground and Father yanked open the door. "Come quickly!" was all he said, yet the sound of his voice and the pale, golden glow of the streetlights of Peking were such welcome sensations that the simple command only bewildered me. Seconds later Chang Ma and Victoria were gone, and Father was lifting me bodily from the compartment. Before I knew it, my arms were wrapped around his neck and we were dodging through a press of angry-faced strangers. I felt the hot bursts of Father's breath against my cheek.

The railroad station's roof loomed above the heads of the mob like an unattainable mountain peak, now standing out clearly, now vanishing in a cloud of engine steam. I turned my head away, not believing we would ever reach the building. Alongside us ran Chang Ma, carrying Victoria and Joan, and somehow keeping pace with Father. I saw Mother far behind, pulling Alice by the hand, and my hobbled grandmother, moving through the rabble in the arms of Lao Chang.

On the train platform itself the crush of humanity was even

more overwhelming. I was aware of nothing but jabbing fists and sweat-soaked clothes and darting, ratlike eyes. Then there was a change I cannot account for. One moment I was surrounded by ugly, twisted faces, and a strident whistle was blaring so loud that I could not hear myself cry. The next, I was sitting in the crowded aisle of a third-class car with Alice, Joan, and Chang Ma. Only when I listened hard could I separate the murmurs of the passengers from the din seeping inward through the windowpanes and doors. We jolted into motion. I looked through the nearest window and saw, one after another, the backs of fifteen to twenty policemen who had positioned themselves at the platform's edge and were fending off those desperate enough to make a lunge toward the moving train.

The Yang children on the campus of Yenching University (Clockwise from bottom left: Joan, Victoria, Katherine, Alice)

Cato Yang in the living room of his house in Peking

Alice and Katherine in their western-style dining room

Entrance gate to the Forbidden City

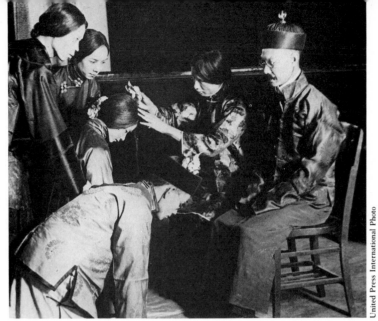

A Chinese wedding scene: the newly married couple kneeling before the parents of the bride

Two coolies carrying a woman in a sedan chair; the servant walks alongside

While the author has no photographs of her own from Hunan, this three-generation portrait of another family is typical of that place and time

The four sisters in front of their Chungking bungalow, wearing outfits knitted for them in Hunan by their mother

The Yangs in their South Bank neighborhood (Front row: Joan, Katherine, Victoria, Father; Back row: Alice, Mother)

Shanghai's Bund

Katherine in a ch'i-p'ao *at the age of fifteen*

At Shanghai Airport, seeing Albert Wong off to America (Left to right: Joan, Alice, Victoria, Albert, Katherine, and her parents)

Katherine at sixteen in a Shanghai photo studio

(BELOW): Katherine's mother and father in Hankow, 1978

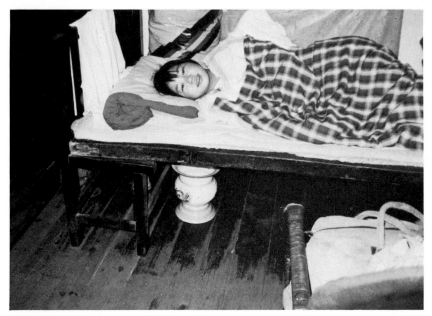

The one-room apartment of Katherine's parents: a visiting relative rests on one of the room's makeshift beds

Three Yang sisters reunited in Canton, 1983 (Joan, Katherine, and Alice)

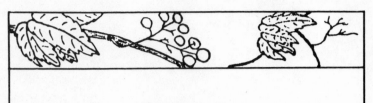

PART III

Hunan

5

IT was almost dawn before we reached Tientsin, a city only seventy miles southeast of Peking. There were unexplained delays all along the way, and I could read on the strangers' faces in the car the same fear I felt: that perhaps we had not quite gotten away in time. But we arrived without incident, and Father found us a small hotel where we slept until the next afternoon.

Tientsin, because of its size and importance as an industrial center, was sure to be the invaders' second objective, and so we stayed there for only one day. I was glad to leave that smoke-shrouded metropolis, with its dingy canals and gray sprawl of warehouses and food-processing plants. The following morning we moved southward again to a small town that lay between Tientsin and Jinghai. There we settled into a three-room bungalow on a small plot between a farm and a wool mill, and waited for the message from Hunan that would decide the family's fate. That suburb was no more inspiring than Tientsin. It was flat, quiet, boring. What few homes I saw looked exactly the same as ours. They were all too small and too tidy.

We shrank from mixing with anyone in that town. My sisters and I did not even attend school. "Who could think about such a thing," Mother asked the walls, "with certain death staring one in the face?" Once Grandmother had continued on to Shanghai, Mother began spending the better part of her days pacing the length of the kitchen and occasionally snapping at Chang Ma, the one servant left her. The rest of the day she spent lying or sitting on the coal-heated *k'ang* — the raised platform that served both as sleeping area and living room in the traditional northern Chinese home. The shoddiness of our quarters and the provincial quality of the surroundings depressed her. That and the curious spate of activity that consumed Father from the moment we settled in that place.

There was, in fact, something perverse about the way my peace-loving father became enlivened, almost impassioned, by the war. If his life had been busy before, it could only be described now as harried. In Peking he had maintained an air of serenity in the midst of his numerous professional responsibilities. Now he behaved as if possessed. Once he had informed Lao Chang of our whereabouts, he did not write or read all the time we were there, activities as natural to him as eating and sleeping. The morning after we settled in, he launched with relish into the design and construction of an underground air-raid shelter. This Mother immediately pronounced a folly, "a rodent hole" into which she, for one, would never crawl. Each morning and afternoon, for weeks on end, Father worked alongside a team of six coolies he had hired to help him with the digging and the laying in of beams and planks. At night, every night, he attended war-preparedness meetings of the local Kuomintang. During our Peking days he had admitted to being far less inspired by Chiang K'ai-shek than by the Generalissimo's mentor, Sun Yat-sen, and had barely kept up his membership. Now, however, he embraced total involvement as his and his countrymen's sacred duty.

There was a third project Father took on, one in which he involved me from the start and that, though it did not occupy as much of his time and energy as the other two, was the most resented by Mother. In that bleak, war-threatened district where we expected to stay for a month or two at most, my father planted a tree garden. "He's insane," Mother muttered to the blank-faced Chang Ma. "A garden! It's the shock of the war. He fancies he's back in America tending his professor's beans and carrots."

I knew the story she alluded to: Father had worked for seven years as a gardener at the University of Michigan while earning doctorates in sociology and agriculture. It was one of the handful of anecdotes we children were told about his earlier life. I knew, too, why Father designed and tended our little grove of plum seedlings. All the while we turned the earth and planted, he talked to me quietly of the satisfaction he had always gotten out of the gardens of his youth, both in Hunan and America. He said that it had never been blossoming time that had pleased him most, but the time of waiting, before the seeds even sprouted. "The time," he said, "when you share a secret with the earth."

The Japanese bombed the Tientsin vicinity three times while we were there. Although no effective systems had yet been devised for warning the populace of an impending raid, Father seemed to sense when an attack was coming. He would sound the alarm well before I, at least, could hear the muffled drone of planes and the rumble of far-off explosions. At the sound of his shout, Chang Ma, Victoria, Joan, and I made ready to file into the shelter, but Mother and Alice refused each time to leave the house. To Father's dismay, Mother would sit stoically in her armchair near the center of our *k'ang*, ignoring his pleas. Alice, her eyes downcast, would sit beside Mother, saying nothing, shuddering at the very thought of such an entombment. It was understood that she fell under Mother's protection. Father would beg, first calmly, then desperately, but to no avail. In the end he would turn dejectedly and guide the rest of us to the narrow iron slab that lay flush with the ground between the rear wall of our house and the garden. He would climb down the five wooden steps, light the black cavity with a gas lamp he had set into a rough-hewn niche, then help each of us below and position us on the cold pine bench, where we would wait in silent fear. No one knew what to say. We sat there, endlessly, it seemed, and stared at the facing, empty bench, or at the play of shadow and ghostly light on the wall.

The first two times, the raid itself was a strangely peaceful experience, with sounds no more threatening than thunder heard at a great distance. When we finally crept out of the shelter, Mother and Alice were stirring about in the house, and everything looked, sounded, and smelled no different from an hour before. Father seemed a bit ridiculous, standing in the sunny yard with a gas lamp in his hand.

The third time was different. As usual, Father anticipated the raid and vainly pleaded with Mother to come with Alice to the shelter. And as usual, the rest of us filed into the retreat, took our places, and sank into silence. However, before we heard any warning sound at all — not even, it seemed, the whine of an engine overhead — I felt the air around my face and body push against me with the force of a blow. A second later came a deafening blast and an earth tremor, then the clatter of wood and stone on the ground above. At once, Father placed the baby in Chang Ma's hands and pushed open, then darted through, the iron hatch. I felt the beginning of panic, sitting beside Chang Ma, who was as still as she had been in the carriage the night of our flight from Peking. I climbed the five steps, not intending to leave the safety of the shelter, but simply to escape that sense of confinement with her. Halfway up I felt the tug of a small hand pulling at my coat and turned to find three-year-old Victoria one step behind me. I could see only her hair and her outstretched arm, for she kept her head bent down out of fear. When I stopped, so did she; when I climbed again, she followed, still clutching my coat hem. Fifty yards away, in a neighbor's field, the smoldering remains of a toolshed sent a thin column of smoke skyward. Charred, jagged hunks of wood and mortar were strewn about our property and gave off an acrid odor that stung the inside of my nostrils. All was still and quiet. It was like standing in the middle of a landscape where there were no people, birds, insects, or even wind.

A moment later Father rushed out of the front door and

into the yard. He was carrying Alice, struggling and screaming, under one arm. I turned and hurried down the steps with
Victoria, regaining my place on the bench just as Father pulled
the iron lid shut with his free hand and clambered down the
stairs. I watched in alarm as Alice flailed her limbs like a
snared animal and twisted against Father's grip in a paroxysm
of terror, her face contorted. She kicked the light from its shelf
before Father could wrestle her to the bench across from us.
The lamp crashed to the floor and spread flames in one corner,
which Father, still carrying my sister, quickly stamped out. He
sat down again. Alice fell silent for a second or two in the
nightlike darkness, afraid even to breathe, before redoubling
her moans and shrieks. Joan began wailing too, though her
cries could scarcely be heard. No one else spoke or moved for
the eternity we remained there listening to Alice's cries, the
scraping of her feet against the packed soil of the shelter floor,
and a horrible thudding and clawing sound. At last Father told
Chang Ma to open the iron door and to take Joan, Victoria,
and me back to the house.

The air and light above came as the most precious gifts
imaginable. Once inside, I saw Mother sitting at the table
where we dined. Her armchair, not in its normal position, had
been purposely turned so that she faced the threshold. Beside
her, like a piece of damning evidence, stood the empty chair
from which Alice had been snatched.

After Chang Ma and my younger sisters entered the house,
I went back into the yard. The screaming had ceased. I walked
to the hatch and peered in. Both benches were empty. Then I
spotted Father, seated on a solitary wooden chair at the northern
border of our garden. Alice lay curled inside his jacket, asleep
in his lap, her long, loose hair hanging almost to the ground.
He was watching her intently and stroking her shoulder. I could
not hear, but it looked as if he were humming to her, the way
he used to hum western lullabies over Joan's crib in Peking. I
went back into the house, confused and angry.

Hour after hour passed, yet Mother did not budge from her
place, nor did Father come in from the garden. All through the

late afternoon, Mother held to her vigil without moving or saying anything at all, simply eyeing the door with patient fury. At one point I brought her a cup of tea, but she brushed me away without so much as a glance. From then on my sisters and I cowered in the kitchen, not daring to say a thing, even to one another. At dusk Chang Ma at last plucked up her courage and asked Mother whether she would not take something to eat. When she received no answer, she asked permission to prepare food for the children and herself. Again there was silence, after which Chang Ma stalked into the kitchen and set about serving us a meal of broth and wheat cakes. Once we finished, she put the baby in her crib and gestured to Victoria and me to go quietly to our beds, which were in a corner of the *k'ang*. Mother sat unmoving in her chair, Chang Ma stood at her post in the kitchen, and I lay awake, feigning sleep.

The wait was a long one — as it turned out, too long for Mother. Whether it was a question of vanquished resolve or of concern for Alice, she called out suddenly, in a voice made creaky by hours of disuse, "We're made to bide our time in this mud-caked village, just waiting to be slaughtered, while the head of the Yang clan decides whether we're worthy of being saved." There was a pause, during which Chang Ma dutifully padded from the kitchen to the dining area. I could not see from where I lay, yet every word and movement sounded clearly. Chang Ma knew Mother's code implicitly. Had she failed to rush in and listen to the complaint, had she forced Mother to move to the kitchen and lose more face than she already had by breaking her silence, she would have exposed herself to a reprimand. The tacit understanding was that she stood in attendance not as the confidante she was, but as mere furniture; as a mute, faceless menial in whose presence one might mull over private matters with impunity.

"Look into the garden," Mother commanded in a louder, more energetic tone, as if only those words had been meant for her maid's ears. I could see Chang Ma open the door and cover her throat against the chilly night air.

"They're still there," she said.

"Bring in my daughter," Mother rasped. Once alone, she drew a deep breath, steeling herself for the long-awaited confrontation. Chang Ma returned carrying Alice, asleep and still swaddled in Father's coat.

"Where is he?" Mother asked when Father did not arrive at the same time. Chang Ma kept moving across the room in the direction of the kitchen. "Chang Ma!"

"I must waken the child and bathe her," the woman said, her voice for once betraying strong emotion.

"Where is he?"

"Imagine, Mistress. I found the Master asleep in the garden chair, with only a shirt to protect him from the cold. The moment I woke him, before he even handed me First Young Mistress, he asked anxiously after your health. He's closing up the shelter now. He'll be here in a moment."

Chang Ma hurried into the kitchen when no word of dismissal seemed forthcoming. I strained to listen. There were the sounds of the servant stoking the fire in the stove and of Mother moving stealthily from the chair to her bed. Father must not realize that she had waited there for hours, believing she was engaged in a test of wills.

When Father walked in, he was shivering violently. The light in the hallway revealed the wounds Alice's nails had left in the flesh of his neck and face. *"T'ai-t'ai?"* he called from the doorway, then repeated his greeting in a soft, affectionate tone once inside the main room. Mother did not so much as stir. *"T'ai-t'ai,"* he said once more, "let me tell you how awful it was during the raid. How poor Hsiao-hue was . . ."

"I don't want to hear of it," Mother interrupted with such conviction that Father knew to make no further explanation. Following a short silence he walked toward the heat of the kitchen, while Mother remained as motionless in her bed as she had, for so long before that, in her armchair.

Early the next morning a government messenger delivered two parcels to our door. One contained the news from Lao Chang that, as far as he could determine, the family was welcome at the ancestral estate — this scrawled on a sheet of rice paper in Cook's barely legible hand. The second was a formal invitation executed in a calligraphic style whose power and delicacy were breathtaking. That scroll bore my grandfather's seals. Mother appeared satisfied with the gist of her father-in-law's message, many of whose characters were so arcane that only Father was able to read the document in its entirety. "It pleases me greatly that the Firstborn Son thinks to return to his people, to the place of his birth," Grandfather wrote. "The praises of your scholarship have flown from the East, as on falcon wings, and have reached even Sinhwa and this humble valley. Your coming brings honor upon a head turned white with age." Father wept as he read us those words.

The thousand-mile journey to Sinhwa took more than two months. We traveled south by train through Hopei, Shantung, and Anhua Provinces to Nanking, then to Wuhu and the Yangtze. We next sailed west to the Hunan border and across Lake Tunting to the Tze Shui River. A sampan conveyed us to the small port of Sikwangshan, which we reached in late November of 1937. From there the seven of us and our baggage were borne overland, in bamboo carriages, by three-man teams of coolies. Each night we slept in primitive inns whose earthen aromas Mother pronounced disgusting, and whose food she never touched, contenting herself with a meal of white rice cooked from a supply purchased before the journey.

Sinhwa came as scant relief to any of us. There were no paved ways, and the dirt paths that meandered through that tangle of markets and glorified huts (some of which, we learned, were provincial government buildings) were covered with a permanent layer of animal manure. Oxen, water buffalo, and burro-drawn carts cluttered the roads. Toothless vegetable hawkers hollered at us from open-air stalls. Beggars knelt at the roadside and made a loud, insistent display of their misery.

Everywhere we walked, even in the town's official guesthouse, where we awaited an escort from the valley, the squat, flat-featured Hunanese gawked at us in wonder. How strange it was to watch Father deal with these people who seemed to belong to another race entirely, and to hear him speak fluidly a singsong dialect undecipherable to us. Moment by moment our status improved as Father's identity and the news of his arrival swept through the surrounding neighborhoods. Once we had bathed and rested for an hour, a delegation of elders greeted us in a reception room facing the inn's courtyard. This group included several men whom my father clearly recognized. He was at his ease, while Mother and we children were reduced to looking on alertly and guessing at the nuances of the improvised ceremony.

Soon that select ring of well-wishers grew into a horde of dignitaries, tradesmen, and barefoot peasants, all vying to shout the loudest their words of welcome, and plying us with food and beverages. We settled for the one refreshment we could recognize — black tea. After every sip our cups were whisked away and replaced with new ones, steaming and full to the brim. There was not a single woman in that crowd, so that Mother, my sisters, and I felt all the more uncomfortable. Though the room seemed filled to capacity, people kept barging in and either fighting their way toward Father, or staring, from no more than a foot away, at Mother's dress and earrings.

Just when the situation threatened to move from the awkward to the dangerous, we heard sounds of a great commotion outside. Shouts, mingled with hollow clopping noises, caused a sudden evacuation of the reception chamber. For us there was no choice involved. We were swept out into the courtyard with the rest.

At first I saw nothing. Separated from my family, I wandered aimlessly through a forest of strangers' legs. I felt, as much as heard, the drumming of horse hooves, a sound that seemed to rise from the stones through my feet and to make my breastbone vibrate. When I had despaired of ever seeing what was happening, I was hoisted up bodily by a brown-faced Hunanese farmer whose thick, oily hair was musty with tobacco fumes. I peered out over the sea of heads spread beneath

me, some uncovered, others topped with wide-brimmed, coni-
cal straw hats. At the center of that motley ring, the heads of
five gray stallions tossed and reared, their bloodred mouths
spouting clouds of steam into the chilly air. Higher still appeared the dour faces of five riders arrayed side by side. They
wore short quilted coats on which were emblazoned the character that stood for the name Yang.

Father stepped forward to a position facing the mounted
party. At once the central rider swung from his saddle to the
ground. He stopped at a distance of ten feet from the spot
where my father waited, then fell to both knees, placing his
hands open-palmed on the cobblestones and touching his forehead to the ground. I had once seen Lao Chang kowtow to
illustrate a story episode, but this was different. The gesture
had an almost frightening power. The man's subordination was
complete.

A few phrases were exchanged in Hunanese dialect. Then,
when Father turned toward the doors of the room where the
boisterous reception had taken place, the man followed him.
The spectators in their path scattered like birds, and no one
tried to reenter the inn. Though no discouragement was
needed, the four remaining riders dismounted and took up
positions at the tiled entranceway, where they eyed the sub-
dued onlookers with scornful indifference.

The crowd revived gradually, as if it were shaking off sleep.
Town elders nodded with satisfaction. Peasants whispered excitedly to one another, then began shouting their impressions
of the ritual welcome. The man who had held me up by the
armpits now lowered me to the ground and toddled off, lighting a crude pipe as he went. I found Mother and my sisters,
who looked as dazed as I was by all the hubbub. When the
innkeeper sought us out, we were huddled like rabbits in a
corner of the yard. He led us to our quarters.

An hour later Father returned and told Chang Ma to take
us children into the second room so that he might speak privately with Mother. Bits of their conversation filtered through
the bamboo wall. We heard clearly enough Mother's heated

objections to drinking wine, to "bowing to the dead," and, for reasons I failed to overhear, to remaining behind in Sinhwa for one day while we went ahead. It surprised me that she eventually agreed to such an arrangement; yet here, it was already becoming apparent, my grandfather ruled. Mother was not to wait alone, however. Outside the inn's gate stood a group of ornate carriages and an assembly of servants scarcely less impressive in their dress and bearing than the mounted vanguard that led us, that very afternoon, into the valley inhabited by my father's clan.

6

"THEY'RE going to receive your mother as a bride!"
Those were the first words I heard Lao Chang speak
after a separation of four months. It was just the sort of
morsel he loved to share with me. Our party had come through
the outer gate only moments before; we had just descended from
the carriages and were stretching our legs in the courtyard. I was
too tired to focus on the particulars of the surroundings, but
from the start I was aware of an understated beauty. Everything seemed perfectly proportioned: the lofty evergreens and
neat rows of one-story buildings; the terra-cotta walls and the
careful configurations of earth, stone, and water they encompassed. "The food here is vile," Lao Chang continued, before I
could say a word. One of his favorite gambits was to dangle
some tantalizing revelation before his listener, then pretend to
withdraw it, covering it over with a thick mat of banalities.
He chattered away in a low, excited voice. "Their customs and
manners aren't offensive so much as, well, 'primitive' is, I suppose, the word. (Let's not even mention their ludicrous way of
speaking.) But the food . . . no, the food I can only call
vile."

I remarked that to look at him, one would never guess that
the Hunanese cuisine was anything but the most delectable in
all of China. He had, in fact, grown positively plump. What I

said displeased him not only because I seemed to disbelieve his tale of a season of deprivation, but also because I had refused to lunge at his bait. "Tell me what you mean about Mother," I added, and his face immediately brightened.

"Ah, Second Young Mistress, put yourself in my place. You're exiled in a land where no one's ever heard of any but the most rudimentary civilities, and you're made to eat and sleep with a pack of garlic-breathed servants. I've scarcely laid eyes on your grandfather. Until the day before yesterday, I wasn't given a shred of news as to whether you were actually coming here to live or not. And I'll admit, I was hoping your father had changed his mind. War or no war, let's take our chances in the North, I say. All right, so they don't let me associate with anyone above the level of their shaggy-haired, buck-toothed excuse of a kitchen steward—a scrawny son of a turtle who had the crust to tell me that the food I cooked wasn't spicy enough for the clan's refined tastes, and that I'd best stick to preparing nobody's meals but my own!" He paused for a moment and rubbed the little knob on his forehead. "Well, I detected a glimmer of consciousness in the face of a scullery laborer they'd hired just a few days ago. He was born in the South, like the rest of them, but he'd served for a year in the household of some second-rate Hopei warlord. After a few hours of mangled Mandarin and sign language, I finally worked out what all the to-do in the kitchen was about. Oh, did I fail to mention? Every cook in the compound's been slaving away for a week now on fancy dishes and pastries."

Here I was made to wait again as Lao Chang pulled from the depths of his long woolen coat a flat, handworked cedar box whose corners, hinges, and hasp were all of polished brass. "A gift of greeting," he let drop, unfastening the tiny latch, pulling back the lid, and drawing out a cream-colored paper and a generous pinch of black tobacco. The cigarette he rolled —it was the first I had ever seen him smoke—looked lumpy and, for a startling moment, burned as brightly as a torch.

"And your friend said?" I prompted him.

"My what? Oh yes. And so he told me, in his fashion, that

there was to be a series of banquets to celebrate the heir's return to his father and home, and to welcome his bride into 'the big family.'"

"But don't they know that Mother . . ."

"Nobody here cares much about the way things *are*, Second Young Mistress. What matters is the way your grandfather wishes things to appear. And so, if the Old Master proclaims your mother to be a maiden, she *is* a maiden. As far as I can make out, your relatives won't even recognize her existence until she arrives tomorrow for the purpose of being seen — for the first time, mind you — by her betrothed."

"And where do my sisters and I fit in?"

He shrugged. "First things first, I suppose."

And it was clear, there in the courtyard, that for the time being our relatives intended to pay Alice, Victoria, Joan, and me no heed. Father gathered up the four of us and explained that we were to stay with Lao Chang and Chang Ma while he went to greet his father. Then he was off on his mission, trailing behind him the six eager servants who had flocked to his side the moment he had stepped from his sedan chair. How diminished the rest of our little group then felt. And how quiet, dusty and unimportant a place the outer court seemed to be. Even the carriage bearers had abandoned us and were busy gambling at dominoes beside their poles and canvas slings.

"Off we go!" Cook announced. He led the four of us and Chang Ma toward what he told us was the Southern Gate. "There begins the compound proper," he said with a magisterial air, pointing out that the bungalows on our left and right were occupied by the clan's dozens of servants. I saw several figures in drab blue cotton jackets appear and disappear at the doors and windows. "The men are cooks, stable attendants, craftsmen, carriage bearers, gardeners. The women see to the care of the young and sew all the clothes worn here — everything from the Old Master's fur-trimmed satin cap with the jade piece stitched onto the crown, to the quilted shoes the lot of you will be wearing by tomorrow morning."

We passed through the stone gate and entered a large paved courtyard surrounded by low buildings. Though autumn was almost ending, the colors of summer were everywhere. Chrysanthemums bloomed in painted porcelain tubs. Flowering trees, their blossoms protected by the compound's high walls, shone red and violet in the sunlight. And orange-spotted carp darted about in a pond on whose surface floated delicate white lotuses. "The Great Courtyard," Cook informed us. "And except for the one we just left, the least preferred."

"But why?" I asked, awed by its size and beauty, and by the height of the four cypresses grouped at its center.

"The further one's dwelling lies from the main garden and the Old Master's quarters, the less impressive it's bound to be." Cook indicated with a sweeping gesture, first to the left of us, then to the right, two rows of earth-colored structures built on mahogany frames and ornamented with glazed lintels and roofs of burnished tiles. "These are the pavilions of your most distant relatives," he said. Two girls Victoria's age were playing nearby with a shuttlecock made of an old-style coin in whose square hole a chicken feather had been fixed. They kicked the weight back and forth with the quilted sides of their shoes, keeping it in the air as long as possible. I had been good at that game in Peking, and started walking over to make friends, but Lao Chang checked me with a stern look. "Those are the calligraphy tutor's daughters, Second Young Mistress. You don't play with them."

"You seem to have learned all about life in this province," I observed.

"I've had time enough to see what goes on," he replied, "and the answer is: practically nothing. Outside the walls, the Old Master's farmhands raise their rice, barley, tea, and sweet potatoes. Inside the walls, the men play Mah-jongg and the women embroider all day long. The only breaks in the boredom come at mealtimes, when you run the risk of permanently damaging your stomach lining."

I put little stock by his cynicism. So far everything I could see or smell intrigued me. And when we walked through the round Moon Gate at the northern end of the Great Courtyard, the sight of the main garden made me catch my breath. It was a classic scholar's garden, with artificial hillocks and a variety of trees, all arranged around a miniature lake in such a way as to suggest seclusion in some boundless natural haven. It was a child's dream. I could hardly wait to explore the shaded network of walkways and wooden bridges, the crusty *taihu* rocks and the fragrant pine copse filled with hideaways, the two unwalled teahouses that overhung the water's edge.

"Come along, come along," Cook chided, still strutting about like a landlord.

By walking one quarter of the distance around a covered walkway whose latticed railing ringed the pond's bank, we reached a paved path that guided us to a limestone arch. "Here," said Cook, "is the Pavilion of the Second Garden." There were four houses surrounding a courtyard. Ours was situated in the most favorable position, at the north end facing south. The house had the same earthen walls and glazed roof as all the others in the compound, but it was a full story taller and had a balcony that ran the width of the facade. At the center of the courtyard lay a small garden dotted with plum and cherry trees and bordered by a carp moat, which one crossed by means of an arched marble bridge.

"Who's that?" Victoria asked, pointing to a woman sitting in the garden. She held an umbrella and wore a hat with a brim, to protect her face from the sun, but one could see even from a distance that she was beautiful. Four female servants busied themselves around her, each one holding a shallow tray in her lap.

"That's Yang K'ai-ying, your father's sister. You're all to call her First Aunt," he said. "That is, if you ever have the pleasure of speaking with her."

"Why do you say that?" I asked.

"No reason," Cook replied when a frown from Chang Ma warned him that he was overstepping his bounds. "Your aunt raises silkworms as a hobby, just as her mother did. Those trays have screened bottoms. They hold the silkworms. Your aunt chooses the prize worms she wants her servants to cultivate, then the women feed them mulberry leaves and take the silk from their cocoons."

I wanted to see for myself. I was eager, too, to meet my aunt, the first of my relatives I had ever seen other than Grandmother. Yet I knew Lao Chang would stop me, as before. First Aunt might at least have taken some notice of us by then, I thought, yet she just stared at her milk-white hands, folded on her purple robe, or examined the trays the servants held before her.

"Until several weeks ago," Lao Chang whispered to me, "your First Aunt lived in the quarters you'll be occupying. She had to move, of course, to one of the other three houses in order to make room for the family of the Firstborn Son. This way," he said aloud, and led us over a crisscross pattern of bricks.

Our house was furnished in a restrained style that emphasized the rich varnished wood of the floors and support pillars, the severe play of verticals and horizontals, the balance achieved through subtle contrasting of light with shadow, textured surfaces with smooth, the colorful with the bland. I had never seen so graceful and calming a dwelling. Our home in Peking had been exciting, filled as it was with books, art objects, and western-style knickknacks. Here no one feature of the environment demanded one's attention. It was a spare, artistic whole that at once instilled, even in a child of seven, a feeling of composure.

No one seemed as weary as I was. While my sisters explored the house, I had Lao Chang show me the bedroom I was to share with Alice. Again, its most inviting feature was its simplicity: a pearwood bench with a basin and chamber pot beneath it; a view of the garden from the south window. I stretched out on the hemp bed with its firm, oversized pillow and wondered why I could not fall asleep at once. I walked to the window and saw First Aunt ignoring the trays and the servants, and instead staring directly at our house.

From the moment I awoke the next morning I felt that nothing would ever be the same for me again. That whatever I had learned and become comfortable with in Peking would from now on be useless to me. I had never before slept in a bed made almost entirely of intertwined rope. A broad-nosed, beige-skinned girl opened the shutters on a radiant sky, then greeted me with a head bow and a burst of mysterious sounds. She dressed me in festive, newly made clothes that included a jacket and trousers of brilliant red silk and a pair of the thick, quilted shoes I had seen on the young girls the day before. (The soles were soft and bouncy, consisting of eight to ten layers of cotton.) Even the breakfast my sisters and I were served that morning was so different from what we were used to, in taste, smell, and appearance, that Alice pushed it aside.

While Joan and Victoria remained at home under the supervision of the amahs who had been assigned to our quarters, Alice and I set forth to explore the grounds. Clan members and servants alike kept their distance. We nosed about as we pleased, even venturing to stand next to a party of our uncles and male cousins who were watching the arrival of the wedding procession from a point just beyond the outer gate. It was wonderful to see the many-colored caravan of monks, musicians, servants, and dowry carriages wind its majestic way along the floor of the Yangs' own valley. The train seemed all the more vivid for the iron-hued hills that engulfed it on every side — dull, brooding slopes whose harvested terraces showed no vegetation but an occasional stand of firs. At the end of the cortege, like a garish caboose, came the red-lacquer bride's carriage.

Alice was in one of her dreamy moods that morning. We had hardly spoken to each other. I doubted that Lao Chang had told her what he had confided to me, and I could hardly wait for her to ask me, or wonder aloud, what all the fuss was about. Yet when the red carriage came into view, she said, as much to herself as to me, "It seems impossible that Mother should be confined in that little box."

"Then you know about the wedding?"

"Of course. Father explained everything to me."

"When?" I wanted to ask her, but restrained myself in time. Surely it was the previous night, when I had gone to bed early. Had I been awake he would have told us both.

The sight of the train at close range served as an antidote for my jealousy. The ranks of servants and bearers might have testified sufficiently to my grandfather's status, but there were six Buddhist monks in saffron robes, pipers, and string players, and a chorus of chanters who raised an ineffable din as the ceremonial chairs moved through the compound and spilled into the Courtyard of Earthly Accord at the north end of the main garden.

Alice and I joined the party that brought up the rear of the procession, skipping along behind Mother's sealed carriage with its feathered adornments and painted panels. Since great numbers of government officials and members of the gentry had been invited from as far away as Changsha, the provincial capital, the courtyard was filled to overflowing. Though it was difficult for me to distinguish the members of my clan from the guests, a handful of people dressed in the most resplendent robes stood in a semicircle in front of the doors to the ancestral hall, where the ceremony was to take place. At their center, Father smiled at the children's antics and at the gay turns of the mandolin and moon-guitar music. First Aunt, his sister, stood beside him. She looked slender to the point of frailty, and her face had a gauntness that undermined its lovely shape and complexion. She did not resemble Father at all either in physical appearance or, I could already tell, in temperament. Her lips curved downward slightly at the corners of her mouth, and her piercing eyes, so at variance with all the revelry around her, seemed scornful.

"She's three years older than Father," Alice said to me, guessing that I was staring at First Aunt. "Her husband, Wen-k'uan, is in Lingchi, the region of the tin mines."

Just then the door of the wedding carriage opened. Mother, dressed in a red silk skirt and a gold-embroidered jacket, her face hidden behind the traditional red veil, stepped down onto the courtyard bricks, thereby becoming a member of the Yang clan. Fireworks exploded and cymbals and gongs resounded. The noise was deafening. The leader of the ritual kept crying out, "The bride has arrived! The bride has arrived!" Next everyone proceeded into the ancestral hall, which was situated between my grandfather's stately quarters and the now vacant rooms where his late wife had lived. Surrounded by her new relatives, her face still hidden from view, Mother walked the length of the immense room, at the head of which was a Buddhist altar.

There Grandfather waited. I had not seen him before this moment, yet the tall, straight-backed figure standing alongside the ancestral shrines could have been no one else. The folds of his blue robe were stiff with gold-thread patterns that glittered in the altar's candlelight. At that time he was nearly seventy years old. I saw a likeness to First Aunt in the forbidding bleakness of his facial expression. But instead of disdain, his gaze showed a lively curiosity. I could look at nothing but his eyes as they followed Mother's deliberate progress toward the altar. The whites were blood-streaked, as if he had not slept for several days. Still, the brown-black irises focused unfailingly on their object. It seemed to me that he never once blinked.

I wondered what the pressure of that stare, benign though it appeared to be, felt like to Mother. I recalled her altercation with Father at the mountain inn as I now watched her kowtow before my ancestors' memorial tablets. Joss sticks burned, the Buddhist monk intoned invocations, and everyone in the crowded shrine room, but above all Grandfather, looked on. It was a blessing that her face was covered, I thought. I could not imagine her participating in this ceremony without the protection of that veil.

Mother turned and made a full kowtow on both knees to Grandfather, who directed her, in a strong but gentle voice, to rise. Then he handed her a red envelope full of money and jewels. At that point Father took a place next to Mother, and a servant brought them each a red brocade cushion. They inclined on one knee to First Aunt's generation, who stood at Grandfather's right and left, according to rank. Each of the clan members greeted Mother, as she bowed with folded hands, and gave her a red envelope smaller than the first one she had received. Then the younger generation began parading toward her, one by one, and each made a full kowtow to her. It became clear right away that there was some confusion, and Alice said with a start, "There should have been envelopes for Mother to give to her nephews and nieces. Father should have seen to that."

There was a second embarrassment as well. Just before the wedding feast in the ancestral hall, when the first dishes were being laid on the altar as symbolic food for the spirits of the Yang dead, Mother had no paper effigies of money and carriages to burn in the ceremonial fire. All the rest of the evening, she did as she was expected to do: dutifully drinking the endless prescribed toasts, though she despised liquor and wine; abstaining from all food with maidenlike bashfulness; and even submitting in silence to *nao-dung-fang*, the customary series of pranks (ducks hidden under the bed, firecrackers tossed through the doors and windows of the bridal chamber) designed to disturb the newlyweds' first hour of intimacy. I would guess, however, that she discussed in full with my father, later that night, the mishaps that had made her lose face.

Once the marriage was recognized, our relatives accepted Alice, Victoria, Joan, and me into the clan at a gift-giving ceremony on the following day. As Grandfather smiled and handed us our "first-time-I-see-you" presents, I came to a foolish decision. I had made a determined effort to learn a few words of Hunanese by talking with my amah, and ventured now to thank Grandfather in his own dialect. Not only did I draw stern looks from Father and most of the adults in the reception room for presuming to speak, but I butchered the pronunciation of the simple phrase. Mother lowered her head as Father apologized. Grandfather nodded once, but said nothing.

To add to the shame I felt, First Aunt smiled derisively when it came her turn to hand me an envelope. She was seated in a blackwood chair, a pair of dull-faced porters waiting in attendance behind her. I kowtowed, hot-faced. When I looked up to accept my envelope, her attention was focused on the floor, several yards behind and to the side of where I waited. The same ironical smile played on her thin red lips.

"She was staring at my feet," Mother insisted to Father as we walked through the garden after the ceremony. "I can understand your sister's loathing me for being a Christian. For dressing differently from her. For being educated and able to read and write, though I'm a mere female. But am I to be mocked at as well because my feet are not bound, like hers?" Father pursed his lips and kept his eyes trained on the wooden walkway. "She'd have me pay for things I had nothing to do with," Mother added in a bitter whisper. "Things from the distant past."

"Let's take this path," Father suddenly said, leading us into an area of the compound where we had not yet been. This was not the first time I had seen him neutralize a charged situation; postpone a crisis in the hope that it would fade away. As Mother vented her frustration, he just nodded or grunted a "Yes" or an "Ah," all the time interjecting remarks on the scenery. He showed us the four buildings and the Courtyard of Celestial Peace, which balanced our own court on the opposite side of the garden. We walked by the Pavilion of Clear-Night Seeing, the Bridge of Serenity, the kitchen yard with its chickens and pigs and its bloodstained slaughtering block, and the gardeners' sheds where saplings were cultivated and fragile plants sheltered from the winter. At one point he stopped and raised his hand.

"A lute!" Alice exclaimed. She and Father shared a quick smile. I could not hear what they had both heard until we moved ten yards closer to a house that lay in the shadow of the

Southern Gate. As we all stood and listened, a faint stream of tones filtered through the walls and windows.

"Those are the quarters of Tu Chao-ming, the lute master," Father said with a wistful smile. "As a child, I was a less than successful pupil of his. Even then he was old, and yet he plays as beautifully as he ever did."

"He won't take me as a pupil, will he, Father?" Alice asked. "At Yenching no one objected to my playing the *hu ch'in*. But here I doubt they'd permit it."

"I'll speak to Master Tu," Father answered her. "He'll consent to instruct you."

"It's time we returned for the noontime meal," Mother interrupted in a way that conveyed her impatience with such traditions as the one that decreed that the lute, far from being an instrument that a female might presume to play, was not even to be played in a room where women were present. It did not impress her that Father might succeed in bending the rules. Her First Daughter's music lessons were not a privilege but a right.

"Very well, we'll go back," Father said, turning an ear once more to the delicate strains. "What piece is that, Ming Princess?" he asked. Alice replied immediately that it was a Sung dynasty melody entitled "The Song of Cool Emptiness." Father smiled and nodded. As he led us homeward, he lapsed into a mood of almost total detachment, saying only, "Tu Chao-ming is a man of great learning. And he's blind." It sounded as though Father wished he were that man.

7

I n the beginning we were lost. A week after our arrival in the valley, Father left for Chungking to join the war effort. It was no different than if he had sailed with us to the coast of some foreign land, put us ashore, then drifted off again.

It was jarring to have to learn a new dialect and to get used to new foods, but I applied myself from the start. It took me weeks to sort out the elaborate set of kinship titles that were insisted on there. I could call no one by name who was older than I, and had to use the fourth-cousin, second-uncle, older-sister system that had been deemed unnecessary at Yenching. In addition, every relative, depending on his or her relationship to my father, called me by a different name, so that I had at least ten modes of address to respond to. There was an age-old code of restrained behavior, as well, that all my little cousins seemed to have been born with, while I had all I could do to stifle my natural brashness and at least make an effort to conform.

There was no nursery or school, as there had been on Yenching campus. We breakfasted in the dining room of our own pavilion, then were tutored at home by three stooped and wispy-bearded retainers in Chinese history and literature, mathematics, science, and calligraphy. Following a noon meal, Victoria, Joan, and I played in the main garden with our cousins, First Aunt's two sons, or, surreptitiously, with the children of the servants, who were far more lively companions. Alice seldom joined us, spending most afternoons in the quarters of the lute master. At night the entire clan converged on the ancestral hall for the evening repast.

No one broke the oppressive routine except Grandfather. We learned, early on, that his waking and sleeping hours were, for reasons not explained to us, the opposite of everyone else's. Yet there were rare exceptions. Perhaps once a month he would dismiss the calligraphy master and instruct us children himself. He did not speak to us individually, and he often winced at my brushwork, since I was by far the least artistic child in the class. Nonetheless I felt that he paid more attention to me than to any of my sisters or cousins.

Outside of holidays and those calligraphy lessons, Grandfather would leave the mystery-shrouded realm of his private living quarters for only two reasons: medical emergencies and an occasional evening meal. As a traditional poet-scholar, he was a master of herbal medicine, hydrotherapy, and even surgery. He treated members of the clan in the privacy of his quarters, but there was a small infirmary in a corner of the outer courtyard where he ministered to those of his tenant farmers who, his majordomo decided, were in serious need of medical attention. Sometimes my cousins and I were permitted to observe those sessions. Alice refused to go near the place, but I would always be there to watch. It was wonderful to see Grandfather work. I would lose myself in concentration and imagine I was the one setting a broken bone or applying a sharp-smelling poultice to a cut.

Once every two weeks at most, Grandfather appeared at the family dinner. It was his custom to invite two children to his big round table near the altar, and I was picked more often than any other grandchild. I would watch in awe as he devoured the delicacies his chef cooked especially for him. Ham the servants had cured by wrapping it in the flesh of a slaughtered dog, then burying it in the ground for two months. Duck's blood, congealed and cut into cubes to resemble bean curd. A dish of twenty chicken hearts. He would smile when he caught me staring, then offer me a heart or gizzard in jest.

Those experiences helped counteract the feeling of being cut off from the outside world. I missed the liveliness of Peking, the elegant beauty of the Mandarin dialect, and, above all, my father's company. Still, Hunan offered a new range of exotic possibilities.

It proved far more difficult for Mother to adapt to the seclusion of Sinhwa Valley. There were people who saw to it that that was so. Or at least Mother believed that there were.

"She hates me, I know that," I heard her say once to Lao Chang as she sat at a window watching my aunt at work with her silkworms in the garden. In the time of my father's absence, Cook became Mother's confidant. They both felt disenfranchised, I suppose, and gravitated to each other for support. Mother never tried to learn Hunanese. And she only picked at the fiery dishes, losing weight from one month to the next. Her life in Hunan was ruled by her obsession with her sister-in-law, whose status in the clan was surpassed only by Grandfather's, now that Father was gone. "No one will accept us here," Mother complained bitterly, "because *she* won't accept us. They won't dare risk her anger." Mother watched First Aunt for hours on end.

Whether it was because we were thought of as special guests or because of our standing in the clan as the family of the heir, Mother was given a permanent place at the head table in the ancestral hall, where we dined. She looked comfortable enough there when seated at the left hand of the Old Master, whose aura of priestlike power so filled the room that its outsized dimensions seemed bearable. But when Grandfather was not there, we were all — my family and the others as well — pitifully dwarfed by the chamber's great void. And no one looked more burdened by the lofty, beamed ceilings, the carved-wood walls, the polished stone floor with its four medallions of inlaid jade, than Mother as she sat picking at her meal in silence.

～　～　～

Later that first winter Grandfather became, for me at least, more than an occasional apparition. One morning shortly before dawn I was wakened with a touch I did not recognize. I was used to the feel of my amah's hand on my shoulder as she coaxed me gently from sleep. This time I was being shaken, almost violently. "Get up, Katherine, quickly. He's asked for you." Mother's face, when I could make it out in the unlighted room, was radiant with joy. She nearly yanked me from beneath my coverlet when I did not move quickly enough to suit her. Alice stirred in her sleep but did not awaken. Mother took me by both shoulders once I was kneeling upright, still in a stupor. Looking into my half-open eyes, she slowly repeated what she had said.

"Grandfather?" I asked. "Now?" She nodded and smiled excitedly. Within seconds she was washing my face and hands and dressing me in a new red jacket. She rouged my cheeks, then applied a touch of jasmine scent to the collar of the coat in which she bundled me. Her hands shook nervously. I could not understand why this meant so much to her, but it thrilled me that she was paying me this much attention.

"Be careful of what you say," she warned. "You mustn't spoil this chance. Speak only when necessary, only when he puts a question to you. Try to remember everything he says, then come to me as soon as you're dismissed." On and on she went, even as we hurried toward the door. The more advice she gave me, the more anxious we both became.

From the south end of the garden, Grandfather's upright form was visible in the Great Courtyard. He wore a ground-length coat and stood alone near the cypresses. When Mother spotted him, she rasped to the amah, "Go! Go quickly!" and turned back toward our house. "Remember, Katherine," she whispered after us as the girl and I stepped briskly over the textured stones, "don't say anything foolish."

At last there was only the sound of our foot scrapes and the chuffing noises we made as we inhaled the icy air. The sky was clear and, except above the compound's eastern wall, still purplish enough to allow the night's last stars to glimmer. In his dark blue coat and peaked hat, Grandfather looked like an obelisk carved from a block of lapis. Even when we were close enough to him that he must have heard us coming, he did not turn to greet us, nor move at all. We walked in a wide circle, so that we ended up approaching him head-on.

I stood there looking downward, unsure of myself. No one said a thing. I could feel Grandfather's eyes upon me, but could not force myself to meet his gaze. I heard the sound of a great intake of breath. Braced for a rebuke of terrifying volume, I dared to look up and saw a contorted, white-whiskered face. In an instant the head came straight forward, mouth agape. In my fright I fell backward onto the stones, scarcely breaking my fall with outstretched hands, and from there watched Grandfather complete a soul-wrenching sneeze.

He recovered well before my amah and I did. Straightening up, he gazed at me for a moment, then erupted in a paroxysm of laughter. The confused nursemaid fidgeted at my side until Grandfather, who had not yet stopped laughing, dismissed her with a flip of his hand. He bent down and gazed into my eyes until I relaxed enough to smile. He began to laugh again, and I laughed along with him. At first it was nervous laughter, but in time the old man's beaming face dissipated my fear, and I laughed purely for joy. When I finally stopped I could feel the tears drying on my cheeks in the winter air.

"You're called 'Little Swallow,' aren't you?" he asked in Mandarin. I answered, in my primitive version of the Hunan dialect, that I was. To indulge me, he spoke from then on in Hunanese, only lapsing into Mandarin when he felt I might not understand him. "Come, Winter Swallow," he said, giving me my first nickname as he crossed the courtyard with a stately pace. "I'll show you the sun rising over the land that will one day belong to your father." There was great warmth in his voice. If I had ever taken Mother's admonitions to heart, I forgot them then. I walked alongside him to the Southern Gate, across the entrance court and through the wooden portals, which two servants opened long before we reached them. From time to time I snatched glimpses of Grandfather's pallid face. It seemed to me that the gaiety he had just shown did not come naturally to him.

We climbed a dirt path and stopped at a point on the rock-hard soil perhaps two hundred yards from the compound. The stars had vanished by then and the violet in the sky had turned a definite blue. We were standing on a rise that exposed us to a knifing wind. As we watched in silence, the sun bobbed up, suffusing with muted gold a delta defined by diverging mountain slopes.

"These are the things K'ai-tao has forgotten," he sighed. "The things beyond learning that elude all but the poet, and even the poet in the end."

"Who is K'ai-tao?" I asked.

He smiled, somehow keeping his unblinking eyes focused on the sun. "Here your father is called K'ai-tao. That, at least, is something he cannot change." There was no bitterness in Grandfather's voice. "When he returns from this business he finds so pressing, perhaps I'll bring him here, too, and show him this sight." It shocked me to hear my father's behavior questioned by anyone.

"Father's helping to fight the war," I said.

"The war. What do border disputes far to the North have to do with us, Winter Swallow? What army of foreigners could ever again succeed in piercing China's defenses? You may be too young to understand this, but your father should have known." He seemed now not to be focusing on the sun or mountains but to be looking beyond them. Eager to change the subject, I pointed to the vast stretches of farmland and evergreen forest that separated our lookout from the mountain pass, and asked how far the Yang estate reached. He laughed and hoisted me onto his shoulders, then slowly pivoted about. "All that you can see in every direction is land of mine. Nor is that the extent of it. There are the mines, beyond the western mountains. It's from there that Wen-k'uan, my daughter's husband, will soon return." His voice faded as he repeated his son-in-law's name with tenderness. "I haven't slept yet," he said, setting me down and smiling. "We'll go back now."

Later that day I learned that I had passed the morning's test, if that was what it was. Grandfather's majordomo, a man named Liu, paid Mother a visit in our quarters after breakfast; and although she did not share the news with me directly, her manner of strolling about the inner courtyards in the late morning was sign enough. After the noontime meal Alice confirmed what I suspected, and what all of my relatives no doubt knew by then, so swiftly did such gossip penetrate the layers of the clan's social strata. "I'm happy for you, Hsiao-yen," Alice said without a trace of the envy I would have felt had our positions been reversed. "Grandfather has chosen you as his favorite." I smiled and looked grateful, yet I was thinking that I did not know what the honor meant, or what I would be called upon to do.

Elsewhere, I learned, Grandfather's decision gave rise to resentment. Lao Chang grinned and chattered like a mischievous monkey the whole day. "Your status as the preferred grandchild, Second Young Mistress, confers even greater face on your father," he gloated.

"And on my mother as well?"

"Without question, on your mother as well."

"Is that what excites you so, Lao Chang?"

"Well, as you may or may not know, you're not the first of your generation to attend the Old Master. No, no, there were others before you. Most recently, as I'm given to understand, your cousin, Shu-jen. Yes, the one you'll replace is your First Aunt's eldest son." I asked Cook to explain to me why Mother and First Aunt did not get along. "In good time," he replied with a coy smile.

"Good time" turned out to be more than a month later. In mid-February, 1938, on the morning of Wen-k'uan's return from the Lingchi mines, a feast day atmosphere prevailed on a hilltop to the west of the compound, where most of the Yang clan was gathered. All but Grandfather, Mother, and First Aunt herself were present. It was sunny and the first smells of spring were in the air, but winter had not ended. We all wore coats and carried muffs. Servants hauled great hampers of hot food and caldrons of tea to the site as the morning hours passed and expectations rose. The adults traded stories while warming their hands at charcoal braziers. The children played chasing games around their amahs. And everyone kept turning his or her eyes westward toward a pass, twelve miles distant, in the hope of being the first to spot the popular Wen-k'uan and his armed bodyguard. I was eager to see this man whose character had earned him the stewardship of the principal source of the clan's wealth, though he was not a Yang by birth. (Grandfather's standing had earned him a rare *chiao nu-hsu*, or called-in son-in-law, who had changed his name and left his own family's household in order to live among his bride's kinsmen.) For the first time in weeks, I was in high spirits. The promised invitation to Grandfather's pavilion had not yet been extended, nor any explanation of the delay given to Mother. She was furious, and blamed me for what she feared presaged a reversal of our family's fortunes. "Tell me again what you said that morning," she kept insisting. And when my account did not satisfy her, she would accuse me of knowingly concealing some damning detail. The excitement surrounding my uncle's homecoming distracted me from that pressure.

I was playing with Victoria and Shu-jen when I heard a faint hissing noise, a signal Lao Chang and I had often used in Peking. I found him in the area of the tea urns, standing a few paces apart from the other servants. His face bore a pleasantly complicated look. "You'll be summoned soon, Second Young Mistress," he began without preliminaries. "Clearly the Old Master wanted to avoid slighting your uncle on the eve of his return." He pulled from his jacket pocket a cold, boiled sweet potato and took a bite. "I predict you'll replace your cousin before the month is out."

Though he said this to console me, his assurances had the effect of rousing dormant fears. "I won't know what to do," I said.

"Ah, but you will. You'll be trained in your duties beforehand by one of the concubines, just as your First Aunt's son was." He shrugged, as if to make light of my worrying.

"How do you know that Shu-jen was taught what to do?"

"Why, from the servants. Your cousin was instructed by the youngest of the three concubines, Fragrant Lotus by name. He was trained in the care of musical instruments, the grinding of ink, everything."

"Do your new informants speak Mandarin?" I asked.

"Not a word. But once I realized we were to be marooned here for an indefinite period, I determined to do what I had to in order to remain . . . aware of things."

"Then you speak Hunanese?" I asked in that dialect.

"Well enough to make myself understood," he answered in like manner, but with a superior grasp of the proper inflection. He smiled, entirely self-satisfied.

"What have you found out?" I pressed him.

"Plenty."

"Then tell me."

"What, my little noseybody, would you know?"

And the sluice gates opened. Lao Chang sat down on the ground and recounted everything he had learned, through weeks of dogged research, about my father's true connection to the people in whose care he had left us. By birth, Father was neither First Aunt's brother nor the Old Master's child. Grandfather had sired four sons, but all by a procession of concubines whom "the big wife," now deceased, had selected for him after succeeding in bearing only a girl, First Aunt. "Apparently, none of the sons of the lowborn concubines found favor in the Old Master's eyes," Cook reported. "And so, anxious to provide for a worthy heir, he availed himself of a traditional prerogative and formally adopted the eldest son of his younger brother, who lived at that time on the estate. Your father was sixteen then, and was recalled from his studies in Nanking to receive the honor."

I asked what my real grandfather's name was, but Cook did not know. All the same he tantalized me by saying there had been a scandal involving that man, and that no one was permitted even to discuss him. "Whatever the nature of the later falling out, the Old Master had already officially established your father as his legal heir. Of course, due to your father's absence of twenty-odd years, the issue has become a bit . . . murky. The Old Master, reluctant, I suppose, to contemplate the subject of his own death, has avoided any sort of decision on the matter, so that neither side knows exactly where it . . ."

"Neither *side?*"

"Well, yes, your First Aunt has been busily lining up supporters of late."

"First Aunt? But does she think the clan will be ruled by a woman?"

"To hear it told, she thinks the clan will be ruled by her husband, who bears the Yang name and who, so the tales go, virtually runs things when he's here, as it is." Cook paused for a sip of tea and smiled complacently. "There're lots of things your First Aunt and the concubine sons are grumbling about, Second Young Mistress. No one but the Old Master believes your father will want to stay here after the war. And your father, unlike Wen-k'uan, has no son. Then there's the matter I referred to earlier."

"The scandal? Did that involve Father?"

"I'm not at liberty to discuss that, I'm afraid."

A single shout rang out, then a chorus of voices rose on all sides. The children stopped their games. Everyone looked toward the sunlit pass, where a dust cloud could be distinguished against the backdrop of the slopes. It was my uncle and his escort. The cheers my relatives sent up were more than joyful; they seemed to blend into a communal sigh, a concerted release of tension.

What happened next perplexed me. No sooner had the party of horsemen been sighted than the adults in our party began calling together their children and walking back toward the compound.

"Where are they going?" I asked Cook. But he too seemed taken by surprise and kept looking about for a clue to explain what was going on. This was one of hundreds of times during our days in Hunan when I sensed a barrier far more formidable than that of language. Reluctantly Lao Chang and I joined the retreating column. He stomped down the stony path, exaggeratedly heaving his misshapen shoulder at every second step and creating his own little dust storm as he went. Suddenly he pulled up short. Turning to eye me conspiratorially, he directed my attention to a site a quarter mile north of the lookout we had abandoned. There at the top of a barren foothill one could make out a party of servants and a solitary female form. It was difficult to tell whether First Aunt's stare was directed toward the pass or toward our sheepish procession, yet I was convinced that the mere awareness of her brooding presence had caused the welcoming party to break up.

Before entering the outer gate, I turned to catch a final glimpse of my aunt and her retinue. I was surprised to see that they, too, were returning. They had already left the hilltop and were descending the treeless slope. Two men bore a carriage in which my aunt was seated. It may well have been proper that she should travel back to the compound then, before her husband even saw that she had watched for him. Protocol required, after all, that Wen-k'uan greet Grandfather before being reunited with his wife. Nevertheless, I was left with the impression that K'ai-ying had occupied that crest with no other purpose than to drive back the members of the clan. And so, when my uncle rode into Sinhwa Valley after an absence of many months, none but the voices of the servants at the gate cried out to him in welcome.

Three days later I was summoned. It was early evening, just after a dinner at which Grandfather had not appeared. Mother had my amah dress me in satin trousers and a short, persimmon-hued jacket. Once again she cautioned me at length not to displease through word or action.

My amah and I were admitted into an ornate reception room by a man who, though he was almost blind with age, opened the doors at the sound of our approach and guided us through the slate-floored halls with their narrow pillars of dense nanwood, then into an antechamber where the Old Master's majordomo patiently waited. Liu was of medium height yet alarmingly slender, with long, sunken cheeks, tiny wrists, and browless eyes. He had the partly male, partly female look of the Imperial Eunuchs Lao Chang had described in his tales of the Ming and Manchu courts, and the same aura of authority. Liu was no coolie-class menial. He supervised the compound's entire service staff and arranged for Sinhwa's merchants to come to the estate with their tea and fabrics, from which he made a selection. He screened the candidates for Grandfather's practice of medicine, kept the estate's accounts, and let only those enter Grandfather's inner sanctum who had been invited. Visibly cowed, my nursemaid stammered through a long-rehearsed speech about having brought the Second Daughter of the Firstborn Son, as she had been instructed, then bowed and quickly padded away.

Without so much as a word to me, the majordomo proceeded toward a door at the rear of the room. I assumed I was to follow.

"Are we going to my grandfather's study?" I made bold to ask, falling prey to anxiety now that I thought the long-awaited moment was at hand.

Liu stopped and faced me, folding his hands before him. "You're not expected in the inner chambers for some time, Second Young Mistress," was all he would say.

With that, we entered a corridor whose length was lighted by small candles set in wall niches. We passed two formal archways before entering a room on the outer perimeter of the passage where a beautiful, white-faced woman stood waiting. She was swathed in a loose-fitting robe of apricot silk. Scarlet booties, only a few inches in length, peeked out from beneath the hem. Her hair, fragrant and glistening with oil, was pulled away from her face and set at the top of her head in a compact bun from which the shafts of two silver pins protruded. Her mouth and nose were as delicate as the finest white porcelain. Her fingers looked like frail birch twigs.

As Liu announced me, the concubine briefly surveyed me and smiled in a way that hardly softened the ivory planes of her face. "You'll come here each of the next ten evenings, Second Young Mistress," the majordomo said, "and Third Concubine will teach you the tasks to be mastered."

When I looked behind me, he was gone.

"Come in, Hsiao-yen," the concubine said in a thin, glass-like voice that made me realize she could not be more than sixteen years of age. "My name is Fragrant Lotus. Would you like something to eat?" she asked, gesturing toward some silver sweetmeat dishes filled with candied walnuts, dried lichees, and watermelon seeds.

"Thank you," I said, taking a handful of the nuts. I followed as she slowly walked, in the "swaying willow" manner of a woman with bound feet, toward a table on which lay an assortment of stone, wood, silver, and pottery objects, most of them unfamiliar to me. She sat on a stool and told me to sit beside her. In my haste to comply, I almost knocked over the second stool. "I'm sorry," I quickly said, forgetting for the moment what Mother had told me as part of my preparation. Concubines, she had said, were beneath me and were not to be accorded those signs of respect reserved for legitimate members of the clan. Fragrant Lotus giggled at my frightened apology. That eased the tension between us, and we exchanged a quick smile. "Shall we begin?" she said. She dipped an ornate inkstick into a little round reservoir before transferring it to the inkstone's surface. "You have to use a lot of water," she murmured. Then she began the circular grinding motion that would make the ink.

"You must grind it in, Hsiao-yen. The Old Master likes his ink very thick."

"Please let me try," I begged, after what seemed to me an interminable wait.

"Not yet," she said. "But tomorrow evening, perhaps, if you pay close attention and learn."

For two full hours that first night, I watched impatiently as my tutor ground ink precisely to the thickness, graininess, and sheen favored by my grandfather. As she poured tea and offered dishes of real food to an imaginary master. As she demonstrated the proper way to carry and present a jade flute. There were dozens of procedures, each of them reiterated with numbing exactitude. At the very end of the lesson, she brought to the table a candle, a small dish of dark brown paste, a silver implement that resembled a thin chopstick, and a long-stemmed pipe. I asked her what the paste was, but she just giggled as she had at the start of the evening. She lit the candle, twirled the stick in the dish until a dark globule adhered to the tip, then heated the paste to the bubbling point, at which stage she swiftly conveyed the sweet-smelling mass from the flame to the pipe's shallow bowl. Then she held out the pipe, tilted her head and smiled, as if someone were beside her, about to take it. The odor was overpowering, and I was relieved when the servant girl arrived to fetch me after only one demonstration.

"Good night, Hsiao-yen," Fragrant Lotus said. "And don't fret so. I know you'll do well."

When I returned to my family's pavilion, Mother was awake and ready with questions. She was disappointed that my tenure would not begin at least for another week and a half. Little else in my report interested her until I mentioned the smelly paste. Then she threw her head back and laughed. "Opium!" she cried, as though to herself. "I suspected it might be so! The odor stays trapped in the clothes and hair. Hah! It explains everything. The hours he keeps, the faraway look in his eyes, the way he relies on others to manage his business and his household." She turned to me and laughed. "Your father refused to discuss this matter. Still, I knew, I knew."

8

"KATHERINE," Mother said, "you must go to bed now." It was still very early in the evening — by Hunan reckoning, the hour of the cock. We had just returned from the family meal and Mother had called me into her bedroom. She sat facing a mirror, pulling two twirled strands of thread over the top of her forehead to remove the small hairs that marred her brow.

"But it's long before I usually go to sleep, Mother."

She turned about in her chair. I saw at once that she was not going to scold me. I wondered if she sensed the change between us. The longer I stood there in mild defiance of her order, the more I became aware of a power I held over her. I could not exactly account for the source of that power. It seemed to be an accumulation of advantages growing out of my beginning knowledge of a dialect she could not speak, my comfort with customs and foods she still abhorred, my relationship with Grandfather, which had already gone beyond the civility he showed Mother during his infrequent appearances in the dining hall. She softened her expression until her mouth and eyes composed themselves in a smile. "You'll be summoned tonight in earnest, Katherine. You must be rested if you're to acquit yourself properly of your duties." This was welcome news. My period of instruction had ended more than

94

a week before that night, and once more a tense silence had ensued. It seemed now that our waiting (it was hers as much as mine) was truly over. "This first night, I'm to accompany you to your grandfather's study. We'll be joined by the lute master, Tu Chao-ming, and by your uncle, who has consented to escort us."

"Wen-k'uan?" I asked, excited by the news.

"Do you think I would seek the company of the concubine sons?" Her smirk made it clear that she was inviting me to share in this barb at our relatives' expense. She turned toward the mirror again and resumed her task. Her whole manner was so carefree that it distracted me for a moment, as it may have been calculated to do, from the illusion she was advancing. Surely Wen-k'uan had not "consented" to join our party. He must have made the offer, which Mother would have readily accepted. And it had probably been Wen-k'uan who had secured permission for her to accompany me that night in the first place. Her trifling lie was a betrayal of deep feeling. She was thrilled to have been invited to participate that night.

For the first time ever, I realized, Mother had judged me worthy of a self-serving fabrication. I was both gratified and saddened, for I sensed that her choice was, more than anything else, a measure of her loneliness.

"Good night, Mother," I said.

"Good night, Katherine."

Mother had never looked more beautiful than she did several hours later. She was wearing a formal *ch'i-p'ao* of green silk, a jade necklace and earrings, and her imperial jade ring. Alice woke up while the amah was dressing me, and the two of us just stared at Mother when she came to the door of our room to see if I was ready. It was not merely the clothes or the jewelry. There was a look of regained confidence in her eyes, a look that inspired excitement bordering on danger. Alice moaned softly, the sound she always made when her headache attacks began. This time Mother did not seem to hear. "Come, Katherine," she said, and walked away. I left, not knowing what I could say to comfort Alice, but aware, from my own experience, of what she was feeling.

Shortly before midnight Wen-k'uan, Tu Chao-ming, Mother, my amah, and I all converged on the monarch birch at the center of the small garden outside our house — the pre-arranged meeting place. It surprised me to see how simply my uncle was dressed, in a blue robe and plain black tunic. I had seen Wen-k'uan more often than he, or anyone else, knew. Once at the banquet held to celebrate his return home, and four times at the hour of dawn in the Great Courtyard, where he and a number of the clan's eldest males daily practiced *t'ai chi*. Four times I had stood behind the trunk of a wide-girthed cypress and watched in wonder as my uncle's lithe body assumed the postures of beasts and birds in motion.

Wen-k'uan's face was an exotic blend of contrasts. The skin was darkened and roughened by the sun, the lips, earlobes, and nostrils as thick-fleshed as a peasant's. Still, his high forehead and gentle eyes gave him a noble, strangely vulnerable air. That mixture held true in his movements, as well, which were swift, fierce, and menacing, yet softened by a grace and muscular control I had seen only dancers display. I was infatuated.

Wen-k'uan gave a polite bow and voiced a greeting in his dialect, Mother responding in hers — remarks so obvious in their meaning that the lute master, who was there to serve as interpreter, left them untranslated. A moment or two of casual talk should have followed. Tu Chao-ming, with his blindman's random stare, looked eager to be of service. Yet the few phrases exchanged seemed forced. I wondered if my uncle felt shy in Mother's presence, or if he was angry for some reason, and exercising restraint. He held his broad shoulders stiffly, and a cool reserve made his gaze opaque. We set out toward the central garden and its walkway leading to Grandfather's quarters. I could tell that Mother was anxious to break the uncomfortable silence. In Peking, on her own terrain, she would have done so without a moment's delay.

We traveled the western leg of the covered walkway and approached the Pavilion of Clear-Night Seeing before a phrase

was spoken. And that phrase, to the interpreter's consterna-
tion, was spoken by Mother. "I had hoped my husband's sister
might have joined our pleasure walk," she said with a cutting
smile. "As ill health must surely have prevented her from coming, I would have my sincerest sympathies conveyed to her,
and my hope that she recover most speedily."

There was a delay in translation. The placid lute master
did not have the stomach for his office. Still, at Wen-k'uan's
pointed insistence, he persevered. "The Wife of the Firstborn
Son inquires after the health of the Old Master's daughter."

My uncle halted, causing the entire party to do likewise. For
the space of a heartbeat, he looked startled at my mother's
boldness in addressing the rift between herself and his wife.
But then he raised his thick eyebrows and smiled. Mother
smiled in return. And to everyone's relief, the last leg of the
walk was devoted to harmless comments and scrupulously
faithful translations. Mother and Wen-k'uan had reached an
understanding.

Once we were admitted to Grandfather's quarters, my uncle
led the way toward the majordomo's room and the entrance to
the inner corridor. Striding through the halls with a spirited
air, he bid the lute master to tell Mother of the difficulty he had
had preparing the tradition-minded Liu for her visit. "Apart
from the concubines and your daughter," he said, "no female
has been received here since the passing of the Old Master's
wife." Mother only nodded.

Liu received our company with dignified ease. He spoke first
in one dialect, then in the other, and was mindful even of me.
"Behold the Second Daughter of the Firstborn Son," he proclaimed, favoring me with a glance. "Was scholar ever served
by fairer apprentice?" I lowered my head, pleased but embar-
rassed by the attention. "By the standards of the Northern
Capital," Liu now said to Mother, "I've exhibited poor breed-
ing indeed and have covered myself with shame for having
neglected this long to offer refreshment to such esteemed
guests."

"You're too harsh on yourself," Mother replied. "When the

conversation is sufficiently refreshing, one's thoughts seldom turn to food and drink."

Liu reacted with a smile and a courtly motion. "All the same, let us proceed to the reception hall, where a service of regrettably inferior tea awaits us." He nodded to a servant girl, who led me at once toward the door that gave onto the inner hallway. It surprised me that I was to be separated from the company, but I followed the girl, until Mother's voice stopped me.

"Please, one moment," she said, "I don't understand. Where is my daughter being taken?"

Liu maintained his composure, but as he drew himself up to speak, he had the look of one poking gingerly into a dark and unknown place. "It's the appointed hour, Mistress. The Old Master awaits her."

"Yes, but . . ."

Liu stood there, visibly straining to make sense of Mother's words. "What is it?" my uncle asked him.

"I'm not quite sure," the majordomo replied in their dialect.

"I believe," the lute master interjected, also in Hunanese, "the Wife of the Firstborn Son assumed she was to accompany her daughter even to the Old Master's study." Upon hearing this, Liu and Wen-k'uan looked at my mother in disbelief.

"What are you saying?" she exclaimed. She took a step backward. Her eyes leapt over the tongue-tied figures before her. "Katherine!"

I was terrified. "Yes, Mother?" I said, hardly able to hear my own voice. Though I was staring at the floor, I could feel Mother's eyes on me. When I looked up, the others were gazing at me too, as if I might dare to tell Mother what had been said. I knew now why Wen-k'uan had looked at her quizzically earlier that evening.

It was the lute master who finally stepped forward and broke the spell. "Mistress," he pleaded, "forgive, if you can, my incompetence as a messenger. It's a long-standing preference of the Old Master's that the privacy of his study be preserved. When I conveyed the message from the First Daughter's husband that he had obtained permission for you to . . ."

"I see," Mother interrupted stiffly. "Yes, I see," she said again in a weaker voice.

Now even in my eyes and surely in her own, Mother looked foolish. Her fur-lined, brocaded coat, her robe with its gorgeous sheen, the jade piece hanging at the level of her breastbone, the mother-of-pearl hair combs, all looked garish and pathetically out of place. In her dull eyes one could read what she was thinking. She had dressed this way for nothing. For the chance to drink a cup of tea with three men in whom she had no great interest. It was clear to everyone how high a value she had placed on her presumed access to Grandfather's chambers. It was clear, too, that the denial of that privilege sickened her to the heart. "Thank you for your offer of refreshment," she said in a low, hoarse voice to the majordomo, "but the lateness of the hour . . ." A lightning glance drew my amah to her side. Without another word, Mother swept from the room and down the hall that led to the outer doors.

I felt an urge to run after her, to flee with her to the safety of our house. Yet I could see, in Liu's resolute face, that from his point of view nothing was changed. He signaled the servant girl again. I glanced at my uncle, who nodded to me reassuringly. Then I walked through the door and into the corridor, trying to push the incident out of my mind.

At the far end of the dark passage there were rooms I had not seen before, including a suite of chambers apparently shared by the concubines, and a large bedroom. I stopped and peeked into the latter. Its main features were a canopied bed covered with a quilt, curious wall panels made of rice paper, and an ancient apothecary chest fitted out with dozens of little camphorwood drawers, each one bearing a tiny brass label on which a character signifying a medicinal herb was engraved. I would have loved to linger there and search through the fussy compartments of that chest, but when I saw how nervous the servant girl looked, I followed her the rest of the way.

Once we stepped into the warm light of the study, I saw, first with relief, then with a twinge of resentment, that no one took notice of my arrival. Not Fragrant Lotus, who sat at a small table alongside a giant mahogany desk, grinding an inkstick on an oblong inkstone. Not the two older concubines, who were quietly embroidering swatches of silk. And least of all Grandfather, who stood before his desk and contemplated a bone-white sheet of paper that lay on its surface.

The servant girl disappeared behind a screened alcove, and I felt abandoned in a world of intimidating art. I had the same feeling of being dwarfed as I had experienced in the great dining hall, but this was even more humbling. Carved paneling rose on all sides from the hardwood floor to the ceiling, and accommodated poetry scrolls, paintings, and silk tapestries dating from before the time of the Ming. Everything was exquisite, an ideal specimen of its kind, whether it was an art object or some functional fixture; whether it was one of the dozens of antique stringed instruments or one of the four braziers whose brass seemed to glow like fire in the light of the painted-silk lanterns. The room was too perfect. I wondered if I could last an hour there, or in the presence of Grandfather, who stood unperturbed in the midst of all that splendor. Before, I had thought of our talk at dawn as a promise of companionship. Now I laughed inwardly at that hope, and wondered what I could possibly say to him, or what he would care to say to me.

Grandfather murmured a phrase I could not make out. Fragrant Lotus's circling hand halted. She rose from her stool and beckoned to me to take her place at the little table situated no more than three feet from Grandfather's elbow. Her smile did little to soothe my anxiety. Seeing that the ink had not yet been brought to the desired texture, I ground the stick as I had been taught. An excruciating interval of several moments elapsed between the time when I judged the ink to be ready and the time when Grandfather broke eye contact with the paper and selected a brush from the thicket of bamboo shafts that stood in brass containers on his desk top. Fearful that the ink might thicken, I moistened and ground the tablet again. He tested the liquid on the tips of the bristles. His hand froze for an instant above the well, and I was afraid I had failed. Fragrant Lotus delicately cleared her throat; I turned to see her signal me to withdraw. No sooner had I stepped down from the stool and moved back three steps than Grandfather's hovering arm swooped to the upper left-hand corner of the sheet, then began a swift yet controlled descent. From where I stood, well behind him and out of his vision, I could follow the pressing, twisting motions of the wrist, the curling and dotting flourishes, the sudden slashing strokes. But I could not see the bamboo stalk magically materialize, with its joints, scars, and play of light and shade. Nor the emergence of the foliage. The sprouting of fainter, smaller plants in the background to give the illusion of distance and depth. The balancing of two rocks. Nor did I get to view the finished product until two hours later, when I walked past the desk with a pot of tea.

It was that way the whole night. There had been little cause for me to worry about my ability to perform my duties, or to think I would learn from, or even be entertained by, the activities in Grandfather's study. I was a mere child, and of interest to no one there. I was a mascot, a touch of color and motion to help enliven the staid atmosphere. When Tu Chao-ming was invited to play music, the concubines and I were obliged to retreat to the bedroom further down the corridor, where the lute's ethereal melodies did not penetrate. And later, when Grandfather was joined by a fellow poet-scholar and they played *go* for an interminable time, I had to sit quietly next to the Second Concubine and watch from afar a game whose rules and strategy no one would bother to explain to me. The high point of the night came when Grandfather interrupted a poem he was composing (a poem whose meaning I could not begin to decipher) to commend Fragrant Lotus on the thoroughness of my training.

At three in the morning, after his guest had retired, Grandfather took his opium. At the far end of the study, a carved screen concealed a broad bed, divided along its length by a pearwood shelf. Grandfather lay on the left side of the bed, his head resting on a white porcelain pillow. Fragrant Lotus placed on the shelf the dish of paste, the brass and wood pipe, the candle and the silver stick, then retreated to a corner. As she sat there, warming her hands on a cloth-covered coalbox, I cooked the paste and prepared the first three of Grandfather's pipes before I was dismissed. By then my eyes were heavy with exhaustion and irritated by the smoke. The servant girl walked me to the corridor, and my amah was sent for. I wept with relief when I felt the cold air of the garden on my face, and saw the stars, growing pale in the light of a false dawn. I did not let the servant see that I was crying. I did not want to talk, or do anything but sleep. Sleep the whole next day, and forget that I had ever been chosen as Grandfather's favorite.

9

WE were to live in Hunan for more than five years, but on my grandfather's estate time slipped away with an imperceptible regularity. The planting and harvesting cycles gave a tidal rhythm to our life, a rhythm accentuated only by the feasts and rituals that marked each season. News from beyond our valley seldom worked its way down the road from Sinhwa. The war itself was transformed into a fable, though Father's letters talked of nothing but the invasion, and of our army's humiliating retreat westward. In time Father's reasons for not returning seemed so irreconcilable with our peaceful setting that his words began to sound almost false.

Following the incident at Grandfather's pavilion, Mother retreated farther and farther from the rest of the clan, virtually holing up in our quarters and even claiming illness on some of the major feast days. To give vent to her store of nervous energy, she involved my sisters and me in language and etiquette classes—elaborate simulated tea parties conducted in the main room of our house and entirely in English. She began knitting obsessively as well, sometimes busying herself for ten hours a day. At the same time, she designed closetfuls of western-style outfits for Chang Ma to sew. She made us wear those clothes, so foreign to that staid environment, with the result that her four daughters became living advertisements for her spirit of defiance.

It was worse for me than for Alice, Victoria, or Joan. I hardly needed western skirts and jackets to make me feel out of step with my relatives' lives. As one whom First Aunt regarded with special disfavor, I was held at arm's length by nearly everyone. And my service in Grandfather's quarters caused such a drastic shift in my schedule that I sometimes went for days without spending time with anyone my age. I slept later than the rest of my family and ate by myself. I seldom got to play with my sisters and cousins, and we were tutored at different times. My image of myself then is as an observer who witnessed every nuance of an unchanging regimen. I lived like a watchful bird of the night, spending longer and longer periods in attendance on Grandfather, then sleeping until the early afternoon. And in the hours before nightfall, I walked about with the bleary-eyed look of an opium smoker.

I think back to the period between my eighth and eleventh years, and nothing distinctive stands out. But in 1941 an incident occurred that destroyed the Yang clan's sheltered ambience beyond recall.

On the stillest of summer nights, at an hour when all but Grandfather and his concubines were long asleep, a man's scream billowed out over the roofs of the compound like a breeze-blown shroud, then fell in haunting echoes among the gardens and courts. Servants spilled into the courtyards, and hand-held lamps were soon visible on every side. I had not been summoned to the study that night. From where I listened with my family on the second-floor balcony of our pavilion, the servants' chatter below sounded like the rustling of birds in dead leaves. There came a burst of shouting from the region of the outer gate, followed by the sharp, measured clicking of a horse's hooves on dew-slicked stones. No one spoke for a time as we listened to the animal slowly make its way through the Great Courtyard toward the northern end of the main garden.

"Lao Chang!" Mother called down into the court. When he answered she ordered him to find out what was happening. We could see nothing, but five minutes later we heard Cook bound back with his peculiar loping gait.

"It's the war, Mistress!" he cried out breathlessly. "The rider was wounded badly, but they say he's still alive."

"Who is he?"

"A messenger. He galloped all the way from Sikwangshan to warn the Old Master that Changsha has fallen and the Eastern War is upon us. The Japanese are expected to reach Sinhwa in a day, at most two, then swarm down into the valley!"

Joan began to whimper. Mother, lost in thought, said nothing. "Will we flee again?" Alice asked her, but she did not answer. We heard a din of wooden clappers, a call for the men of the clan to assemble in the shrine room.

"Go back," Mother called to Cook, "and find out more details."

It was at least a quarter hour later before Lao Chang returned. "Mistress," he said in a mortified tone, "it appears now that the first report I was given may have been inaccurate."

"Do you know yet at least whether the war has reached this province?" Mother asked testily.

"They claim now that the man was wounded in a skirmish between the government forces stationed in Sinhwa and a band of Communist guerrillas."

Four times Lao Chang was sent out to gather information, and each time he returned with a different story. At five in the morning, the eldest of the concubine sons left the council and made the rounds of the courtyards. He confirmed the third version Cook had brought back, namely that the rider was a member of the bodyguard assigned to Wen-k'uan, who had left for the tin mines only two weeks before. Nothing else was known. The man had died that night.

Four days later a search party came back with a third of the number who had earlier set out for Lingshi. Fifteen of the bodyguards had been slaughtered by brigands. The food supplies and payroll had been stolen. And Wen-k'uan had been so grievously wounded by gunshots to the head and right leg that when his body was brought to the gate in a horse-drawn litter, it was nearly impossible to recognize him. First Aunt met the sight with tight-lipped composure. She calmly ordered four servants to carry the litter to her quarters.

Three nights later, Grandfather let me accompany him to First Aunt's house, which was as spare and beautiful and unyieldingly cold as I had always imagined it must be. Though it was the middle of the night, it struck me as strange that she was not sitting up with her gravely wounded husband. Grandfather and I were shown into a large, airy, wood-paneled chamber where my uncle lay on a bed, so still that I thought he might be dead. His leg was heavily bandaged, but the wound on the left side of his face was not. All the skin and flesh was black, and a glistening salve made the cheek, the twisted eye, the shaved, sunken temple, look like something inanimate. Wen-k'uan's head turned toward me once as Grandfather treated him. Though he was conscious, he did not seem to see me or to be aware of his surroundings. One side of his dark blue lips moved slightly. The sound he made was unintelligible. This was not my uncle.

During Wen-k'uan's long recuperation, I saw rage fester beneath my grandfather's serene exterior like a boil beneath the smoothest of satin collars. In his study at night all was different. He abstained from smoking opium and banished music from his rooms. The meals he took were lighter, and he drank no wine. He painted for hours on end, yet his body turned stiff as he worked, and his strokes lost their suppleness of line. Often he would halt in midpainting to pace about for a quarter hour or more before returning to his composition, as to a cell.

I told Alice about these changes and asked her what she made of it all. "Once the murderers are found and punished," she said, "Grandfather will return to the comfort of his drug."

Lao Chang seconded that opinion, and added some observations of his own. "Not only have none of the criminals responsible for the deed been brought to justice," he pointed out nearly a month after the ambush, "but the law officers in Sinhwa haven't even bestirred themselves to pillory a local thief or two for the sake of appearances. Word has it, Second Young Mistress, that your grandfather looks in vain for favors that would have been rendered instantaneously by the public authorities of old."

One week later Grandfather invited the mayor and elders of Sinhwa to grace his Mah-jongg tables. No one declined. I knew something was afoot, but there was no chance I would be allowed to attend. The three concubines and a pair of hired singsong girls were the only females permitted in the gaming chamber that night, as the host and his twenty-odd guests gambled for seven hours and drank great quantities of rice wine, special-grade tea, and the fiery liquor called *mao-t'ai*.

Early the next evening I approached the servant of the Second Concubine.

"I'm not sure what Second Young Mistress wants to know," the girl simpered, her eyes fixed on a jade pendant that I held before her. The stone was chipped and murky, but more valuable than anything she could ever have dreamed of owning.

"Ah," I replied, catching the swinging bauble in my fist and making as if to leave the bench where we sat, "if you don't know what I'm after . . ."

"No, wait. I wasn't there, myself, at the gaming tables."

"Still, from time to time one overhears idle talk." The jade piece was dangling again at the end of its thin silk cord.

"Well, it's rumored that the Old Master had the bad luck to lose a very large sum to one of his guests," she whispered. Then, mistaking my silence for a lack of comprehension, she made a straightforward play for her prize. "I believe that the man on whom the gods of fortune smiled happens, by coincidence, to be . . ."

"You're dismissed." I laid the pendant on a nearby tabouret. She scooped it up and hurried off. I was ashamed enough of the crassness of my offer and of the brusque manner I had assumed with the girl. The prospect of being told outright that my grandfather had publicly bribed the mayor of Sinhwa was

too much to bear. I had found what I was searching for, yet
did not like the look or smell of the dirt left by the digging.

Several more weeks passed before the matter came to an
end. It was during that period that I damaged my own and my
family's status in the clan's social order. Alice was in no way to
blame for my disgrace, but a conversation I had with her acted
as a catalyst.

In Hunan I often sought out the company of my older sister.
On the evenings when I was not called to Grandfather's pavilion, we would lie awake in our bedroom at night and talk
about whatever came into our heads. Alice usually listened
more than she spoke. She did not seem to need those sessions
as much as I did, though she never grudged me the time. I had
begun to feel deprived of human warmth. Mother virtually
lived in her room. I missed Father. It pained me to blot his
voice and playful smile from my consciousness, as I did whenever I remembered him, but I began to think him callous and
unmindful of me, of all of us, whenever I dwelled too long
on his memory. And I found no solace in Victoria and Joan.
We were four and five years apart, and not of an age when our
interests overlapped. In Hunan, as had been true in Peking,
my younger sisters were more a responsibility than a comfort
to me. And so I clutched at my tenuous bond with Alice.

I had told her of my disenchantment with serving Grandfather, and of the sadness I had felt upon seeing Wen-k'uan's
wounds, as well as many far less troubling things. Yet it was
Grandfather's antique possessions — his flutes, inkstones, and
tapestries — that interested her most. Those and anything having to do with the concubines.

On the night in question, Alice had asked me to describe to
her, item by item, the clothes Fragrant Lotus had worn the
previous evening. Her curiosity in such matters was insatiable,
and it was not enough that I detail the colors, shape, and
texture of the woman's robe. When I got to the bright, figured
swirls embroidered on the sides of the bindings that showed
beneath the hem of the outer garment, Alice said, "Ah, a

phoenix pattern. Probably a connection with the sexual origins of foot-binding."

I was dumbfounded. No one had so much as mentioned the word "sex" to me before, and I had been afraid to ask Mother or anyone else about it. I could scarcely believe that my sister, too, had thought about so suspect a matter. Her comment electrified the air between us.

"Older Sister," I stammered, "please tell me what you know about it. About . . . about the origins of foot-binding."

"Certainly," she replied, and for the next ten minutes she reported on the things she had read in the library of her lute master, who had not, I supposed, always been blind. She spoke at length of Li Yu, a love poet of the Sung dynasty, and his passion for Yao-niang, the consort he induced to undergo a physical alteration that became an upper-class fashion for the next ten centuries. In a voice whose calm could not have run more counter to the feverish coursing of my blood, she expounded the theory that the bound woman's halting step increased the development of the muscles used during sexual activity.

"I see," I interrupted. "But what do you know about . . . what have you read about . . ."

"About what?"

My mouth was so dry I could hardly pronounce the words. "About sexual activity itself."

"It's such a broad topic," she replied, genuinely dismayed.

"I don't care how long it takes you. It doesn't matter to me in the least. I just want to know."

"You've seen nothing in Grandfather's quarters? Overheard none of the concubines' banter?"

"I've seen nothing, heard nothing, and know nothing."

Alice laughed, amused at the urgency of my appeal. Then she began to share with me what she had gleaned from her tutor's dense harvest of ancient love odes. She described ointments and herbs used centuries ago in the preparation for sex, then spoke of jade stalks and ivory portals, mortars and pestles, and a host of other metaphors of which the poets had availed themselves. "Alice," I wanted to cry, "what goes where?" But in my bewilderment and shame, I put the question more modestly. And for my pains, I was buried ever deeper under a mound of impenetrable erudition.

"Oh, you want to know about the love positions: Close Union, Firm Attachment, Exposed Gills, and the Unicorn's Horn. Those and what the Sui dynasty scholar Tung-hsuan called the Twenty-six Playful Variations." The more involved her lecture became, the more I began to suspect that at the most fundamental level, she too was in the dark.

Alice's lesson had not totally been in vain. Her words, for all their vagueness, spurred me to imagine and to speculate. And a few nights later, a great deal of her instruction became clearer.

Since Grandfather was not taking opium, I was being dismissed much earlier than usual. One night he sent me off after only a half hour of brush painting, and as I left the study with the servant girl, I heard the concubines titter at my back. When we reached the majordomo's room, we found it empty. I told the girl to return to the study, assuring her that Liu was certain to come back presently and send for my amah to take me home. At that point, as I waited alone, I was innocent of any devious design. But the unaccustomed freedom of my position suddenly came over me in the form of a tingling rush of blood through my stomach and abdomen. I sat still for several seconds, as if restrained in my chair, then bolted toward the corridor with no other purpose in mind than to spy on my grandfather.

In the first, almost unbearable, moment, I considered how dreadful an act this was and how, if I were surprised at the turning, at the archway leading inward, at my hiding place outside the bedroom, I would offer this or that explanation for how I had come to wander there. Yet the nearer I got to the snug little post I had envisioned from the start, the less I bothered with transparent excuses. I was exhilarated. For the first time in my memory, no one knew or cared where I was.

They were there, as I had guessed. I could hear soft noises beyond the wall's translucent panels, and could see two silhouettes moving about in the brightly lit chamber. As a T'ang spy had done in one of Lao Chang's history lessons, I licked my right thumb and applied it to the surface of a panel. This produced only a disappointing light gray smudge. After a second lick and a more forceful push, the light from within began glowing more clearly through the tiny wet oval. One last bit of pressure and the fibers gave, leaving a peephole large enough to reveal the bed with its sapphire quilt, and the reclining figures of two of the concubines.

Grandfather was just out of sight. I could see only the sleeve of his black and silver lounging robe as he foraged among the crannies of his apothecary chest. I heard the scrape of a drawer opening, the tinkling of glass, the hollow rattle of bamboo implements. The women — Fragrant Lotus and the Second Concubine, an older, darker, yet equally beautiful woman named Summer Jasmine — lay side by side, almost naked. Besides their foot-bindings and slippers, they wore only the flimsiest of undergarments: the one, a loose-fitting pair of cerise pantaloons, belted at the navel; the other, nothing but a camisole, unbuttoned in front. I was startled by what I saw, for they were languidly caressing each other's thighs, and in Summer Jasmine's case, the tips of the younger woman's nipples.

Soon the First Concubine entered the bedroom, fully dressed and holding a long, thin ivory flute. She seated herself on a rattan stool, lit a fragment of sandalwood incense, and waited. A moment later Grandfather approached the bed, carrying a shallow porcelain dish in one hand. The sight of his face in profile, his lack of expression as he glanced at the half-robed women, made me shiver with fear. I told myself to leave then, but I stayed — less, I think, because of prurient feelings, though I was certainly aroused, than because of a rapacious hunger just to know.

As Grandfather leaned down to place the salver on a table at the foot of the bed, his garment fell open. His erect penis looked more like an instrument of pain than of pleasure to me, and I gasped in surprise, banging a section of the wall's bamboo frame as I raised one hand to cover my mouth.

At once Grandfather and the women snapped their heads in my direction. My knees buckled as their eyes seemed to burn through the paper panel, widening the little hole until I stood exposed before them. "Who is it?" Grandfather bellowed. He repeated the challenge, but I could not answer him. Soon I heard the shuffling of the servant girl's feet in the corridor and turned to see her face. When she recognized me she dropped the candle she had been carrying and dissolved into tears, convinced, no doubt, that she would be dismissed from the household for her unwitting part in this scandal. A moment later Liu pushed past her and quickly traversed the distance between us until he was standing toe to toe with me and glaring into my eyes. He glanced at the peephole. "Do you consider this worthy behavior?" he hissed. I bowed my head and awaited whatever punishment was to be meted out. I wished it would come at once. Already I sought release from the burden of shame.

An ominous silence reigned on both sides of the wall. "Please wait here, Second Young Mistress," Liu finally said, leaving me in the company of the abashed servant girl. It was torture to have to remain in the very place where the offense had occurred. From beyond the wall I heard one protestation, then another. A moment later a scowling Liu appeared again in the passage and petulantly told me to follow him, turning immediately on his heels and gliding down the corridor toward his station. I crept along as noiselessly as possible, but could not help casting a furtive look backward. There stood Grandfather in his robe. I fled, but heard at my heels loud, resounding laughter that swept down the hallway as I scampered away.

By the following noon no relative of mine, no amah or house servant, no black-knuckled stable boy, had failed to hear an account of my fall from honor. Enraged and chagrined, Mother took to her bed for an entire week. What I had done was so inconceivable to her that she never found a way of so much as acknowledging it in my presence. For three nights running, Cook, my sisters, and I listened to her berate Chang Ma, with whom she closeted herself.

Lao Chang, his public face expressive of severe reproach, bolstered my spirits during that time of ostracism by lavishing me with surreptitious winks and smiles and giving me pep talks when he was certain of not being overheard. Alice at first seemed shocked at what I had done, yet she recovered sufficiently within two days' time to extract from me all the delicate shading effects not included in the gossipers' blurry renderings. From Grandfather himself there were no remonstrations. He called me to his study three evenings later and could not have appeared more oblivious of the episode if it had only been a dream of mine. The rest of my relatives and the concubines, on the other hand, shunned me for a time. It hurt me that Fragrant Lotus would not talk to me.

Within a week I had trained myself to disregard the lingering signs of censure. I became inured especially to the hostile silence of those whose good will I could not have regained had I prostrated myself in the Great Courtyard and, like some felon in the marketplace square, stooped for three days over a written account of my crime.

"I feel different now, stronger," I whispered to Cook in the course of one of our secret chats.

"Ah, like a proper grown-up, answerable only to yourself?"

I could not tell if he was jesting, nor did I care. Something in what he said was true. I did not deny to myself or to anyone else that I had done wrong. And yet I did not crack, either, under the clan's severe social pressure, nor hide away until the offense was forgotten. I felt, for the first time, that I did not need everyone to like me. I took pride in that.

"It's over now," Lao Chang said solemnly on a fair October morning. He was sitting between Alice and me at the edge of a mountain lake where we were watching the servants drag bamboo crab traps from the sun-flecked water. "Hunan justice has been done."

"They caught the brigands?" I asked.

"Well, let's just say that the Sinhwa authorities tried and punished a likely enough gang of scoundrels. It worked out fairly neatly, too: one man sentenced for every member of the bodyguard killed, and an even ten for the wounding of your uncle. Beggars, alley thieves, suspected Communist spies, a bona fide murderer or two. Still, it took them a good deal longer than the Old Master might have liked, so I'm told, to throw that party together."

"Is all of that true, Lao Chang?" I was dying to know every detail.

"It certainly is," Cook replied absently. He was gazing far down the lake's scalloped shore, where the loinclothed servants were knocking live crabs from the traps into barrels. Some had already begun lugging the catch back to the estate's kitchens. There the preparation of the autumn's *Chung Ch'iu*, or Moon Festival, banquet awaited only that traditional delicacy.

"Who knows when to believe his tales anymore?" Alice sighed, sounding more bored than annoyed. Her comment left a wake of poignant silence. It seemed to mark a break — a shockingly clean and sudden break — with the days when my sister and I had hung on Cook's every opinion. Even if we all knew that that time had passed, no one had ever hinted at the fact.

Lao Chang smiled ironically and arched his eyebrows. "All the same," he said with a burst of energy that made it look as though his feelings had not been hurt, "I'm prepared to back up what I've told you. Come with me," he cried, springing to his feet. "Should it please you to follow, that is." And before we could answer he was hurrying across the apron of soft green grassland toward the path that led to the valley.

We caught up with him at a clearing a third of the way down. Though there was barely room for the three of us to stand abreast, that patch of ground was free of the summer foliage that hooded most of the path, and so offered a wide prospect. Lao Chang extended one arm, in the manner of a master orator. "From here you can see, can you not, most of the twelve foothills that ring your grandfather's estate?" I nodded, chafing a bit at his condescending tone. "Very well. Choose any hill and hike with me to its crest. There, I wager, we'll encounter ample evidence of revenge as it was practiced centuries before the Old Master was born, and as it may never, upon his passing, be practiced again."

"And *what* do you wager?" Alice asked.

"A half-year's salary, for the pair of you to share," came the instant reply. "Should I win, I demand nothing but your company there and back."

"This hill will do," I said and turned to start the climb.

"Wait," Alice protested. "I choose that one over there, the bare-topped one they call 'Goat's Head.'" The hill she pointed to was higher than all the others and lay half a mile away. To scale it and return would take the entire afternoon and possibly make us late for the start of the Moon Festival activities. I was prepared to accept anyone's choice, but Lao Chang eyed Alice's far-off goal in a way that made me wonder if he had not been bluffing all along.

"Very well," he conceded with a sigh and a heave of his lumpy shoulder. "'Goat's Head' it is." We had not taken two steps before my sister, who, I suppose, had only been gauging the strength of Lao Chang's resolve, said that the hill we were on would serve the purpose after all. Insulted by her ploy, Cook continued downhill and would not be dissuaded from marching on the more distant objective. "'Goat's Head' it is," he repeated, and on that peevish note we embarked on our daylong trek.

At first, hours later, no one would acknowledge the horrid smell. But soon the stench and guttural snarling, carried downward on a breeze, brought us to a halt. Lao Chang insisted at once that we retrace our steps, but Alice's face had already turned pale. She began gasping for breath, almost choking, then crying hysterically.

"Come, First Young Mistress," Lao Chang said to her in a consoling, repentant voice as he led her downslope toward a pine copse. Covering her nose with one hand, Alice submitted.

Quickly, stealthily, I continued to climb. Lao Chang called after me once he realized what was happening, but I did not turn back. I would not.

Soon Cook's yells came from so far below that they were drowned out by the furious barking. I reached the edge of a shallow ravine and saw on the opposite side two human heads fixed on upright stakes. The eye sockets were black, the hair clumped and matted. Through gouges in the bluish skin, pieces of bone gleamed white in the sunlight. At the base of both poles were propped rectangular placards whose characters no doubt told of the crime these men were supposed to have committed. A short distance from there, a quarrelsome pack of wild dogs tore at what was left of one corpse, while huge grayish-brown birds fed on the other. Giant wings fluttered, beaks and talons poked and slashed in all directions, as the birds kept maneuvering clumsily for position.

The mysteries of death and cruelty were laid so bare there that I could not look away. I ignored the cries, which seemed to come from miles away, until I felt a rough hand on my wrist.

"Second Young Mistress!" Cook's voice exploded, jolting me back to full consciousness. His face was flushed red with panic and the effort of the climb. He and I said nothing to each other then, nor for hours thereafter. In fact, none of us spoke for the duration of the descent. Alice was so sick with migraine that Lao Chang had to tend to her the whole time, even carrying her in his arms for the last hour of the trek. That suited me. I wanted nothing more than to savor in private the troubling elation that lingered for a time. I felt no remorse; but I was not ready, either, to admit to anyone the satisfaction I felt at knowing the look and the odor of death.

10

GRANDFATHER failed to preside at the New Year celebration in 1942. The year before, when that had
happened, Wen-k'uan had directed the week-long festivities. But First Aunt was hiding him away now. The responsibility fell to the oldest of the loutish, ox-eyed sons of the
First Concubine. It was a dreary affair, marked by second-rate
musicians, acrobats, and fireworks, and by less than inspired
dishes at the banquets. Lao Chang said that the problem was
one of money. The mine was faltering in the absence of
Wen-k'uan's management; and the cost of running the huge
household, and of luxuries such as Grandfather's opium, was
beginning to be felt.

It was then that Mother started to talk of leaving Hunan,
and not only because of the downward turn the clan's fortunes
had taken. Father's letters were becoming more optimistic.
The American presence in Chungking, he wrote, was having an
encouraging effect, and there was at last a letup in the enemy's
bombing attacks. He said we should remain in the valley until
further notice from him, but that he was seeking permission to
have a new house built for us, at the government's expense, in
what he called the safest suburb of the war capital.

The final impetus for our departure came in June of that
year, on the feast of *Ch'ing Ming.*

The central *Ch'ing Ming* ritual involved the sweeping of the ancestral graves. In past years, Mother had fulfilled that sacred duty along with representatives of every other family in the compound. This year, however, she designated me to take her place.

"I advised her not to participate," Lao Chang told me, as though he were responsible for her decision. "Your grandfather isn't expected to go with the others to the graveyard this year, and it's his presence alone that restrains your First Aunt."

"What do you mean? Restrains her from what?"

"From striking back at the Mistress in some way, of course. Your First Aunt has been defeated, don't you see?"

"No, I don't," I said, already not liking the sound of what he was saying.

"Your uncle's unfortunate accident has weighed the scales against her, Second Young Mistress. It has settled the issue your grandfather was so unwilling to decide himself. Now there's no doubt in anyone's mind as to who the heir must be."

It sickened me to take that view of Wen-k'uan's tragedy, and yet on the morning of *Ch'ing Ming*, when I saw my aunt at the assembly of the clan in the Great Courtyard, I could tell that Cook's estimation had been correct. I was intent on calling no attention to myself that day. But it was as if First Aunt meant to seek me out and challenge me in some way. Even in the courtyard she made a path through our relatives to stand within five feet of me. When I looked at her, prepared to return her greeting, she said nothing and looked away.

We set out on a road that ran through the rice paddies and sweet potato fields toward the fir-bordered meadow where generations of Yangs were buried. It was only then that I realized Wen-k'uan was among our number. In the past, as was the custom there, he had walked several paces in front of his wife. Now he limped behind the chair in which she was being carried, struggling to keep pace with those around him. A third of his face was blotched dark red and ribbed with scars. He met my eyes once, but did not recognize me. It made me want to cry to see how he was being treated. No one paid him any attention, least of all First Aunt. His undamaged eye shone as carefree and innocent as a child's. He could not have known how lost and forgotten he looked.

"Come with me," First Aunt said to me in a quavering voice shortly after we had arrived at the sacred field, and the ritual sweeping had begun. With her bound feet, she could not walk steadily on the uneven terrain. She used the arm of a servant for support, then dismissed her once we had reached a grave site whose stone was almost completely covered by gorse. It looked as though it had gone untended for decades.

"Clear the underbrush away, Second Niece," she commanded me. When I did, I read on the face of the grave the name Yang Mei-cheng and characters signifying the date 1913.

"Do you know who she was?"

"I don't, First Aunt," I answered, not daring to look up.

"She was the first wife of your father, who was responsible for her death."

If I had been of First Aunt's generation, I would have walked away then. I knew everyone was watching us and that she had planned it that way. I knew, too, from her words and from the tremor in her voice that she was about to disgorge the bile she had kept inside her for so long. In trying to shame me — and, indirectly, my mother — she was about to bring shame on herself by making a public show of her innermost feelings, and by treating an eleven-year-old girl as a worthy opponent. Yet I did not have the right to leave. I stared at the untended grave and listened.

"You didn't know that your father had been married before, did you, Hsiao-yen?" First Aunt said hoarsely. "His bride wasn't like your mother, the daughter of a mere merchant. No, she was the jewel of the respected Nieh clan, betrothed to K'ai-tao from the day of her birth by the sacred agreement of her father and mine. And the dowry. Ah, the dowry made an impressive show." She spoke more hastily now, slurring her words. "The train of donkeys carrying it went on for miles. And the fifteen-year-old maiden, seated like a princess in her lacquer carriage as they carried her to one who did not await her. Tso-lin, my father's brother and your true grandfather, gave K'ai-tao money to flee the girl he was never even to see. And for that, Father banished Tso-lin from the valley."

A warped smile played on First Aunt's face. I looked about me. All my relatives, even the servants, were frozen in mid-gesture.

"And Mei-cheng's life, too, was ruined. Ruined by your father, who thought it more important that he should travel to the West and pursue his beloved studies. But Mei-cheng became his spouse once she passed through our gates. She was doomed to remain here and while away her years among strangers who could only see her as a reminder of their disgrace. It was I," she suddenly shouted, turning away from me, "I who found her lifeless body in the lotus pond one dawn. And even that was forgiven him." She laughed bitterly. "Even that the Firstborn Son was forgiven."

By the night of *Ch'ing Ming*, it was clear to everyone that my mother and First Aunt could not live in the same compound. Now I was as anxious to leave as Mother was. It was not that my aunt's revelation itself had left me distraught. Her passionate words about what she saw as my father's transgressions, decades in the past, had sounded somehow unrelated to me. It was as though she had been talking about a stranger. But the scandal that had brought such shame on First Aunt had the effect as well of isolating my family and me more than ever. I could hardly stand the coldness and silence any longer. I was glad that we were soon to escape.

Still, nothing ever happened quickly in Hunan, and our departure was delayed for months. Grandfather did not press the issue. In fact, he never gave any sign that he knew what my aunt had done. While Mother wrote several times to Chung-king that summer and fall, it was not until October that Father said it would be safe enough to travel there. But starting in December, the Yangtze gorges were impassable, and so we had to wait until early spring.

Those months were an easier period for Mother. Now it was she who walked the garden in our courtyard each morning, while First Aunt confined herself indoors. And it was she who presumed to tell Grandfather that we would be leaving in March, when Father's letter to him produced no effect.

Grandfather had Liu prepare lavish farewell presents for us. There was a chest filled with silver coins, another with bolts of silk, brocades, and embroideries, and a third with delicacies for our trip — smoked ham, candied turnips and plums, bird's nests, dragon-eye fruits. At the departure ceremony, Mother kowtowed to the ancestral tablets and to Grandfather, as she had her first day there. No marriage veil hid her features now, and one could read the irony on her face as she bowed to her relatives in turn — even to First Aunt, who kept gazing, horrified, at the three laden chests on display.

On March 13, 1943, my family and I passed through the outer gate for the final time. At a place not far removed from the rocky spur where I had first talked privately with Grandfather, I now bid him farewell. None of my uncles, aunts, or cousins had accompanied us from the shrine room. He stood alone, among a ring of his servants, watching from a distance as Mother directed the loading of the chests and assigned my sisters, Lao Chang, and Chang Ma to their carriages.

"Your mother looks well, doesn't she, Winter Swallow?" Grandfather said. And it was true. There was a sharpness in her voice and eyes, a freedom and purposefulness in her movements that I had seen before, if he had not. He smiled as he watched her, in obvious admiration of her strength of will. It was as if he were seeing someone he had never met.

"Good-bye, Grandfather," I said. "I wish . . ." I wanted to tell him of the regrets I had, but I could not speak. I was too saddened by the stoop of his shoulders and the vacant look in his eyes.

"You won't ever live according to the Old Way," he said, "nor should you, I suppose. Still, try not to dismiss what you cannot understand. Once, in other times, one had only to follow that Way to reach contentment."

"Good-bye," I said again, then walked toward the train of sedan chairs.

As the last preparations were being made, I waited with Alice in the shade of the dun-colored walls. "Will it be Father's responsibility to come back here when Grandfather dies?" I asked her.

"Of course," she answered, smiling at my naivete. "But should Grandfather die tomorrow, neither Father nor anyone in our family would return. And should he live another seventy-five years, the same would be true. We don't belong here, Hsiao-yen."

It was now undeniable that that had been so throughout those years. Whether it reflected well or poorly on us as a family, we had no place in my father's clan. As Alice had said, we simply did not belong.

PART IV

Chungking

11

"I only have one clear memory of him."

"Oh, I've got a lot. But you go first."

The sudden clarity of my younger sisters' voices took me by surprise. It was late May, 1943, during the third month of our journey west. We had been traveling by boat for weeks, and as arduous as the upriver voyage was, I was happy to have left the mountain paths of Hunan behind. Our slow-moving party had been an easy target for the bandits who roamed the area, consisting as it did of an unescorted woman, four children, two servants, and the huge nanwood chests Grandfather had given us. At the stagehouse where we stopped to eat and sleep, Lao Chang had brought back from the servants' quarters tales of robbery, rape, and murder by Communist guerrillas and bands of renegade Kuomintang soldiers. Alice and I had shivered with fear as we had made our way toward the Yangtze. And whether it was actually any safer to be on the river or not, I at least felt less exposed to the threat of immediate violence.

"I guess I was about four then. Anyway, in my memory, he's handing me a plum."

All of us but Mother had left the thirty-foot-long sampan and were splashing through the silty shallows of the river's northern bank. We walked in the wake of the boat people, who were towing their craft through a narrow channel. The owner of the sampan, his wife, and their four muscular sons all chanted as they strained against the current, climbing the rocks on the riverbank to get better traction. I walked in silence alongside Alice, who shuddered each time her foot sank into the pale green slime of the riverbed. Behind us were Lao Chang and Chang Ma; ahead, the look-alikes, Joan and Victoria. Seconds earlier I had heard our servants grumbling, while no sound other than the boat family's cries was audible from ahead. Now, due to a trick of the wind in the gorge through which we were passing, Joan's placid, deliberate voice and Victoria's husky alto rang out clearly.

When I realized they were talking about Father, I felt a sharp stab of jealousy. I had worked hard at forgetting Father when the pain of his absence had become too acute. I had made a part of myself numb. But it seemed safe, now that we were nearing Chungking, to let myself feel that aching again. Just hearing my sisters' words stripped away the last of my reserve. I admitted to myself that I longed to see Father; that I craved to be with him.

I suppose Father was on everyone's mind during those months of travel, yet we did not acknowledge our need for him as a family. In fact, we scarcely were a family any longer. In the bleak seclusion of Hunan, we had all — Mother, Lao Chang, Chang Ma, my sisters, and I — been thrown upon one another. Alice and I had become close, Mother had gravitated toward Cook and Chang Ma, and Joan and Victoria had taken solace in each other's company, virtually to the exclusion of the rest of us. No one had the wisdom or generosity of spirit to bind us together the way Father had done in Peking.

"He's holding the plum out and inviting me with his eyes to take it."

"Sometimes," Victoria interjected, "his eyes would open so wide that if it weren't for his smile, he'd seem to be afraid."

"It was just that kind of look."

Joan was seven then and Victoria was eight. Both were of heavier build than Alice and me and wore their obsidian-black hair as short as Mother would allow them to, insisting that the length be identical. Joan was prettier than Victoria, whose upper lip curled back in a way that gave her a slightly surly mien and whose nose seemed too small for her otherwise broad and strong-featured face. Neither of them had ever once incurred Mother's wrath, but it was less that she judged them well behaved than that she took no special interest in them.

"He looked so kind."

"That's just the way he was. Isn't that the way I said he was?"

"Oh yes. I even wonder whether the memory's real or just something I've made up after hearing you."

"No, it's real," Victoria pronounced. "I'm sure of that."

"And you'd know, I guess," Joan said with gentle finality. "You were his favorite."

Victoria chose not to reply, and her silence gave Joan's statement the ring of accepted truth. It was that silence that infuriated me. I could not fathom Victoria's presumption. I wanted to stamp through the stretch of water between us and scold her for deceiving her younger sister; prove to her with any number of examples that it was I whom Father preferred. Yet even as a scathing speech raced through my head, I saw my own image of Father's face, and in it I glimpsed the mistiness that had always come over his soft brown eyes when he called Alice his "Ming Princess." I swallowed my rage and listened intently, but either my sisters had stopped talking or the winds had shifted once more. Now the only sounds that came from that quarter were the rush of turbulent water over stone, the boatmen's cries, and the creaking of the ratty lines that stretched from the sampan's gunwales to the peasants' waists and thick hands. I stole a glance at Alice, who still seemed preoccupied with the river bottom and the crude sucking noises our feet made. Then I looked to Mother, floating regally in the stern of the boat, no more than twenty feet away. She returned my glance with a nod that made me suspect she may have heard what I had.

Within a quarter hour we were all back in the sampan with a long, wide reach in prospect and a meal of trout on the boatwoman's stove. The four sons pushed against their oars. The father smiled toothlessly from his position at the tiller. And our little group huddled in the two-two-three alignment that had emerged, with no one's having noticed it, during our lengthy sojourn in Hunan.

We moored that evening within sight of a military outpost. There the boatman led Lao Chang and me to a large stone bunker manned by six Nationalist soldiers whose function it was to scan the skies all day with American-supplied binoculars and to radio Chungking when they spotted enemy aircraft. Cook and I composed a message, which a technician transmitted to army headquarters in the capital. The soldiers assured us that it would be relayed to the Nationalist Trade Commission, where Father was second in authority.

That cumbersome means of communication hardly inspired confidence. Yet when we completed the final leg of our journey the next morning and rounded the last of the ten thousand bends in that interminable river, we spotted a gathering of carriages and coolies on the shore and, at the end of a broken-down pier, a solitary figure who kept waving one hand. At first no one but Victoria believed it was Father. "Look, it's him!" she exclaimed when we were still three hundred yards from the landing. She laughed for joy and capered about the deck of the bow. The rest of us followed Mother's lead and kept our emotions in check for several moments, lest we be caught waving wildly to some servant.

Yet one by one we realized Victoria was right. "His clothes!" Mother lamented under her breath. And it was true. I had never seen Father in anything resembling the creaseless pants and frogged blue jacket that the man on the pier was wearing. They were the garments of a peddler. This man's hair, too — what little there was of it — was not black, like Father's, or even gray. It was white. And the features of his face, as they became visible, looked more like Grandfather's than his. "It *is* Father," Alice murmured with a bemused smile, as if she were leafing leisurely through an album of faded photographs. I ran to the front of the boat to stand beside Joan and Victoria, and the three of us shouted toward the shore with abandon.

The instant the sampan nudged against the rotting wood of the landing, my sisters and I scrambled onto the pier and ran to where Father was standing. He hugged Joan and Victoria and whispered something to each of them in turn. They squealed with delight at his little jokes. I was third in line, and when my time came, he did not hug me but took my face in both his hands and looked into my eyes with such love that I forgot for a moment the changes I saw in him. I wanted to tell him how badly I had missed him, but I could not talk. And even when he spoke in his familiar low voice, his words seemed less precious a thing than the pleasure that shone in his eyes. "You look quite the little woman, Hsiao-yen," he said. "I wonder if you've outgrown your taste for mischief." In that simple way he let me know he had been informed of the incident with Grandfather and the concubines, and that the matter would be forgotten.

"It was terrible to be apart from you," I finally blurted out. And his smile promised that all of that, too, would be made to disappear.

I purposely did not look at Father's eyes when he greeted Alice. I let myself be distracted instead by the depth of the lines at the corners of his mouth, the skin folds beneath his chin, the way the knuckles of his hand looked almost as gnarled as Lao Chang's, the startling white of his hair — all of which saddened and frightened me.

After a moment everyone stood aside so that my parents might conduct their reunion in as much privacy as that setting would allow. As they faced each other they did not touch, yet there was the feel of an embrace, of mutual joy and relief, in the way they looked at each other during that first happy moment.

"I won't ask why your hair has grown white, Cato," Mother said, "but you must tell me why it's so short."

"Months ago a number of other Kuomintang officials and I shaved our heads completely, *t'ai-t'ai*, as a pledge of loyalty to the Generalissimo."

"If you dressed as well as Chiang Kai-shek," she said sternly, "perhaps the style would become you." When she smiled, Father broke into unrestrained laughter. And everyone on the pier — family and servants, those who had heard and those who had not — laughed as well.

All during the overland trek, Mother's face had been dark and lined with tension; and during the river journey, she had quietly suffered the discomfort of living in such inescapable proximity to the servants and the coolie-class boat family. I watched her now with admiration as she briskly settled accounts with the helmsman and oversaw the loading of the three chests onto the sedan chairs. (Mother's parents were originally from Szechuan, and she knew enough of that province's dialect to make herself understood.) She looked free of the indignity and hardship of the journey, and free of the lingering effects of whatever restraints the Yang clan had imposed on her. By the time Father finished greeting Lao Chang and Chang Ma, Mother had assigned each of us girls to a carriage. At the noon hour, we set out in caravan style for Chungking.

The skies looked threatening when we descended from the passes toward the fertile valleys that led upward again to the hilly city. From an elevation of several hundred feet, it was pleasant to catch glimpses of Chungking through the scudding fog. I was alone in one carriage and spent the first hour of our slow descent idealizing the far-off cluster of houses nestled so prettily between the Yangtze and Kialing rivers. Yet once we left the terraced hills and crossed the rich rice paddies and sweet potato fields that girdled the capital, my illusions began to vanish.

Chungking looked ugly to me. A palpable despair seemed to hang like a mist over the buildings and people alike. Five- and six-story office buildings were visible in the distant central-city area, but on both sides of the primitive thoroughfare that rose out of the valley there were hundreds of mean little shacks. A good number of these were abandoned shells. Others, though still inhabited, showed large holes in their roofs and facades.

Those jagged apertures revealed the simple structure of the huts, whose walls were composed of stacks of bamboo wattles woven with straw and fixed with mud, then smeared with whitewash. There were few glass windows, and most of those were shattered. It seemed as though no one repaired anything. Damaged houses were lived in until they fell. Burned buildings were simply deserted. Bomb craters in the roadway itself were left unfilled. Father had explained in his letters that no one expected to have to stay very long in Chungking; that the city's half-million refugees saw living there as a temporary ordeal. Still, I did not understand how anyone could tolerate this squalor or persist in thinking that it would soon be left behind.

Closer to the city proper the houses were sturdier, but many of them were painted black so they would be less visible to Japanese bombers. The people looked mournful and drained of all spirit. Bony rickshaw coolies trudged past my carriage window in one direction or the other. Three soldiers in ragtag green uniforms stood in front of a fruit vendor's stand. A pair of farmers walked through the mire carrying baskets of vegetables suspended from springy balancing poles. Twenty or so tight-packed refugees sat on their luggage in the rear of a flatbed truck. Rows of speechless riders stared from the dusty windowpanes of a wooden-bodied bus. And an odor of decay pervaded the whole place — a stench so similar to the one that had wafted down from the corpses on the hilltop in Hunan, that I shivered when I first smelled it. The strangest thing of all, however, was that no one on that road seemed the least curious. My family's train of carriages attracted so little notice that in time I started to feel we must be invisible to these people. Anywhere else we had been, such a sight would have drawn open stares. Yet of the hundreds of adults and children I saw that afternoon, only one man looked at me.

We were halted when that happened. A convoy of American jeeps and supply trucks was slowly passing by on a road that intersected our own, and so we waited among those who, like us, intended to cross the paved way once it was clear. The coolies set my carriage down and I felt the chair squish into six inches of mud. The last jeep in the convoy stopped. There were four American soldiers in the vehicle, and one stepped out to toss a handful of candy to the children. Tall, ruddy, and fair-haired, he looked like a being from another world as he towered over the onlookers. He glanced at our caravan, and when his shockingly blue eyes met mine, he grinned. Then he jumped into the jeep and he and his friends drove off, shouting boisterously to one another over the din of the motor. As my chair swooped into the air in preparation for our moving again, I felt strangely unsettled at having seen, for the first time in almost six years, someone who was not Chinese.

"But this is preposterous," Mother said when she saw the cavernous dormitory where Father had been living, and where he now hoped we might stay until our new quarters were ready.

"Ten more days is all they say they need, *t'ai-t'ai*. If it hadn't been for the harsh winter and the unexpected raids in the early spring, the house would have been ready by now."

"It's just not thinkable." Her tone suggested at first that we would move on just as soon as she had quenched her curiosity as to the extent of that building's horrors. I did not know where we would go from there, but I was certainly in favor of leaving. The whole place consisted of one enormous room with a very high ceiling and dozens of bamboo partitions forming cubicles in which unmarried male government workers, or men whose wives and children were not located in Chungking, lived. Father pointed out several times that he had succeeded only with difficulty in getting the housing officials to make an exception on our account.

"It might as well be a warehouse," Mother sighed to Alice, her words cutting cleanly through the chatter of strangers all around us. Then she turned to Father and said in a determined voice, "We'll stay here two nights, at most three. Then we'll go to the new house, whether it's finished or not."

Father secured a week-long leave from his work at the Commission. He spent most of his days at the construction site, hurrying the workers along, or at consignment stores, where he bought bedding and secondhand furniture with the silver that Grandfather had given Mother. The rest of us hardly stirred from the dormitory, leaving only for an evening meal when Father returned at nightfall. We ate at the home of one of Father's colleagues — a man named Chow Hsueh-fu, who lived with his wife and two sons in a small one-story house near the decrepit wall of the old city. A constant tension hung over the hours we spent with that family because Mother kept hinting that they should give us temporary housing, even though they were already overcrowded. Our host would laugh nervously and instruct the servant to pour more tea whenever Mother made an insinuating remark, while his wife merely stared at the floor.

Early the third morning, Father woke everyone and said to us, each in turn, "The house is ready! We'll move there today." He took us to a restaurant in the central district where the five-story banks, a hospital, and an American Friends Mission gave the fleeting impression of a great metropolis. Yet even there, where blocks of retail stores flourished and where the merchants had repaired most of the damage caused by past bombing raids, I smelled the stench of open sewers and saw two shelter camps with lines of bedraggled refugees waiting for soup and rice. Father was jubilant. He ordered a dozen different dishes in celebration of our move — as if we were still rich, and as if it were dinner we were eating instead of a morning meal. There were noodles, pork dumplings, chicken giblets, thin slices of braised beef that one dipped in hot pepper sauce, and apricots with lichee nuts.

"It's not quite finished yet, *t'ai-t'ai*, you understand," he said several times to Mother, "but we can move in." She nodded, her tense mouth and eyes making it clear, however, that she would withhold final judgment until she had seen for herself. Still, she ate heartily, and that was a promising sign.

Father arranged for our luggage to be hauled to the South Bank, the suburb just across the Yangtze that was to be our new neighborhood. Meanwhile, all eight of us traveled ahead, unburdened and in high spirits. We first took rickshaws to the crest of the city's southern cliff. From that height one had a sweeping prospect of the harbor and all its varied traffic — from small passenger craft whose oars were propelled by a single boatman's feet, to an enormous motor launch that bore bright American flags on its prow and stern.

"There's where our house is," Father said, pointing across the river toward a range of hills that were layered with fog. There were no visible features in that landscape; it was as though we were about to follow him into a shapeless cloud.

Next we switched to teams of coolies who carried us down the cliff in sedan chairs, by way of a set of more than one hundred wide stone steps, to a ferry slip at the river's edge. We put out only when the ferry's wooden deck had filled with passengers. The Yangtze was like a separate country, with its own peculiar sounds and smells and sights. The water was brownish-yellow in hue, and when we neared the deepest part of the channel, it bubbled and frothed beneath our hull. We passed within twenty feet of the American launch, and Victoria yelled and waved to the six American officers on board until they all turned in our direction and laughed and waved back. They lifted the glasses they held, as if they were toasting Victoria, who clapped her hands wildly and shouted into the widening gap all the English phrases she knew.

Halfway across the river, Alice smelled something that none of us did until minutes later, when a crusty black scow came in view about one hundred yards upwind of us. "Hold your noses," Father said. "That's one of the night-soil boats." The nearer it drew to us, the more pungent was the odor. Alice and Joan nearly vomited over the railing as the tin-sided boat passed behind us, but Victoria and Lao Chang screamed greetings to the two burly Szechuanese who stood waist-deep in their cargo of human excrement and, never letting themselves be distracted, rowed steadily toward the farmlands east of the city.

"Look there!" Father cried. In the western skies, where he pointed, we saw a grumbling, deep-bellied airplane fall slowly toward us, then, when it seemed it would crash into the

Chungking side of the river, land right in the Yangtze itself on a cement-covered sandbar that I had not even noticed. "When the river's low," Father said, "there's an airport. When it's swollen there isn't. Now watch." Before the plane's propellers had stopped whirring, two trucks drove over a causeway onto the landing strip and pulled up to the side of the aircraft. A crew of American troops in green fatigues pushed a wide ramp in place. A set of doors opened and two more soldiers emerged from the plane, herding three steers and a pair of pigs down the ramp and into the first waiting truck. Minutes later, they carried out dozens of wood-and-wire coops filled with squawking poultry, and loaded them on the second truck. "They breed their own livestock in Burma and fly it here, *t'ai-t'ai*," Father said, "choosing the bad-weather days, when the Japanese aren't likely to attack."

"I suppose we should be thankful," Mother replied, "but are there ever anything but bad-weather days here?" And it was true. We had not once seen the sun since our arrival.

"Soon," Father said, "when summer comes, you'll pray for the clouds and the fog you see now."

Once we had docked on the South Bank and climbed for nearly half an hour up a steep dirt road, we spotted four identical, newly built houses on a shallow ridge of the hillside. The topmost, Father said, was ours. The closer we got, the more the house resembled the crude bungalows I had seen as a child in the shabbiest sections of Peking. The roof was single-pitched and covered with a thin mat of twisted bamboo. The whitewashed facade had only one little window and a door of unvarnished wood. Two elderly laborers, dressed in the pale gray uniforms of the government engineering corps, were gathering up tools and brushes and brickmaking forms and heaping the lot in the barren yard that bordered on the unpaved road.

No one said a thing. We were all stunned by the primitiveness of this hovel — at least all of us but Father. I drifted apart from the others and circled the house before entering it. From the front yard one could see the Yangtze, hundreds of feet below, and the sheer ocher cliffs of the Old City. Downslope from us, and halfway to our nearest neighbor, stood an outhouse, which, I assumed, our servants were to share with those of other families. A single bamboo tree stood beside our house, its bright green leaves serving only to point up the bleakness of all that surrounded it. Behind our building site was a thirty-foot-wide scar that the workmen's black blasting powder had left in the hillside, and scores of stacked boulders — intended, so Father had said, to guard against mud slides.

When I walked inside and passed through a small, unroofed court, I saw Father and Mother standing in the center of a fair-sized room. That main living space was flanked by two sleeping alcoves with sliding doors and was sparsely furnished with the chairs, tables, kerosene lamps, and the one wardrobe Father had purchased at the consignment stores. A pitiful-looking rug of faded blue wool covered no more than twenty square feet of the earthen floor. Alice sat quietly in a pinewood chair. The others were further inside.

"There's no electricity, then," Mother observed in a neutral tone, as if she had not been warned of this ahead of time. "And no running water."

"No," Father replied, "but they say that within a year's time the city's power lines will reach this far. As for water, Lao Chang will have to fetch it daily from the municipal well system."

"Ah." Mother pursed her lips and nodded. She appeared to restrain herself from saying anything more.

I walked through the remaining rooms. There was a small kitchen, equipped with a squat clay charcoal-burning stove. Chang Ma was already scrubbing the iron grill set into its top, while Cook eyed it with unqualified disgust. Behind the kitchen lay the servants' quarters, then a closet-sized room with a gently pitched floor, a chipped porcelain spittoon, a single drain, and a tin basin filled with water. A set of enamel chamber pots lay heaped in one corner beside an old portable toilet seat. That room was similar only in purpose to the bathroom we had in Hunan. There had not been any modern

plumbing in Grandfather's compound either, but each family
had been provided with a clean, airy enclosure outfitted with
polished brass spittoons for urine, and chamber pots concealed
beneath a porcelain *ma t'ung,* or toilet chair. There was a
servant available whose sole duty was to see to the disposal of
wastes. Now our family would use the ugly pots in this dingy,
close space, and Lao Chang and Chang Ma not only would
have to do all the cooking, marketing, laundering, and water
carrying, but also would be expected to take the soiled pots to
the outhouse after each use and clean them.

Finally, there were two bedrooms in the rear of the house
— one for Victoria and Joan, I supposed, and the other for
Alice and me, since my parents planned to use the sleeping
areas in the front of the house. I found my younger sisters
gazing in fascination at the beds, which were composed of a
slab of wood, flimsy cotton padding, and quilted covers. Each
one was enclosed by a white veil of netting, the top of which
hung from a bamboo hoop near the ceiling, and the bottom of
which was tucked under the wooden base.

"That's for the mosquitoes," Joan said. "Cook told me we'll
be chewed to the bone if we don't keep our nets drawn and
fastened at night."

"Yes," Victoria added with irony in her voice, "and that
we'll die of malaria if we don't take our quinine pills. And that
no matter what we do or don't do, the bedbugs are sure to
leave long rows of bites on our arms and legs by morning."

"Didn't First Sister go pale when she heard him say that?"
They giggled and left the room.

When I returned to the living area, everyone was gathered
around Father, at a loss again for what to say or do. And in
that stillness it became evident to us all that the house was not
properly insulated. Since it was only early June, the tempera-
ture was no higher than eighty degrees, and there was a constant breeze at that elevation. Yet the draft we could feel
promised that the house would admit too much heat in the
summer and too much cold in the winter.

"Of course," Father hastened to repeat as we all looked in

vain for the place where the air was seeping through, "the workers haven't finished yet." Joan walked up to the western wall and scratched at its rough surface, causing a cloud of brownish powder to fall to the floor. "It's dirt," she said faintly. Then she cried to Victoria, "The walls of our house are made of dirt!" and the two of them laughed in amazement. Lao Chang, too, joined in their helpless glee until he saw the dour cast of Mother's face.

"No," Father quickly said to Mother, as though she had been the one to make the discovery. "No, there's a good deal of cement in the walls. But cement is scarce. It's rationed, like everything else." He spoke more and more hurriedly as Mother only stared at the scratch on the wall, and Joan and Victoria laughed uproariously. A single tear slipped down Alice's cheek. I myself could neither laugh nor cry. What I felt, more than anything else, was pain on Father's behalf. "These walls, all the walls in this district, *t'ai-t'ai,* are composed of earth-and-cement bricks that the engineers set in wooden forms, then dry in the sun."

"The house will do," Mother said so abruptly that Father was at first taken aback. But when he realized what she had said, he smiled. I wondered at Mother's decision. She may have been too weary to consider moving elsewhere. She may have reasoned, too, that it hardly mattered where one lived in that desolate region, fourteen hundred miles upriver from what she regarded as the habitable world. Although the city and its suburbs were a rank, blackened pit of infestation, there was nowhere else to go. For six years we had escaped entrapment in the cities, ports, and rural areas of the East that the Japanese occupied and administered with brutal efficiency. We had reached the last refuge. Mother could not have liked what she saw. She must have forced herself to settle for that barbarous cliff dwelling with its stingy measure of privacy and its illusion of distance from Chungking. She must have told herself that it was as acceptable a place as any to wait for the war to end.

12

M Y parents wanted Alice and me to attend a Baptist missionary school located a full day's journey from Chungking, in the mountains north of the Kialing River. They were intent on our becoming fluent in English and benefiting from the boarding school's reputation for high scholastic standards. The fall semester was the first we could attend, if we were accepted. To prepare for the entrance exams, we stayed in Chungking during the torrid summer months and studied math, English, and music at a small government-run school near Father's office building at the foot of the South Bank.

On the first day when the clouds finally cleared, which was in late June, Father instructed Lao Chang not to walk us to the school, because he feared there might be an air raid. On the first clear day of summer for three years running, he said, the Japanese had bombed Chungking. No planes came that day, but at night Father gathered Alice, Victoria, and me in the big front room and talked to us of things few Chinese fathers would have thought to share with their children. He told Chang Ma to put Joan to bed. Mother stayed in her alcove.

"You must know," he began, "that this city isn't a safe place to live. There are things everyone has to learn to survive here." And then he explained in a calm, measured voice about the sirens, and about the colored balls that floated over certain government buildings before a Japanese attack. We had been in the temporary shelter beneath our school; our teachers had twice taken us there during drills. But Father told us of the mountain cave, upslope from our house, where Mother, Lao Chang, and Chang Ma were to take us, should the enemy ever strike while we were at home.

He might have left it at that, but I could see there was much more on his mind, as there was on mine. "Father," I said, "will you tell us what it was like here during the worst of the bombing?"

He hesitated for a moment, then continued. "In the very beginning, the bombers came infrequently, but when they did, they came in great numbers. And in the shelters you could feel the constant shock of the explosions. There were so many — hundreds in the course of an hour. Still, the all-clear siren would sound after a while, and we were free to go out into the open air again. That was in the first years. Then, during the 'fatigue bombing' . . ." He paused for a moment before going on. His face showed no outward sign of stress. In fact, he smiled, as if he were telling us a children's tale. Still, he closed his eyes for a time.

During that moment of hesitation, I sensed the pain that lay behind Father's deceptive expression, a pain so great that I knew he could not help but talk of it. I wondered then if Mother had allowed him to relieve himself of the accumulated anxiety and strain of his years spent alone. I wondered if she had listened. I realized then that he was saying these things to Alice, Victoria, and me for his own benefit, so that he might feel closer to us. He told us of twelve- and fourteen-hour periods he had spent inside the mountain caves, or in the ground-floor shelter of his office building, as shifts of no more than three or four enemy bombers at a time kept the city under daylong siege. He did not speak of death or wounding, but it was clear that he had seen enough violence to change his outlook on everything. In the end, his voice just trailed off into silence. I begged him to let me stay in Chungking instead of leaving for school. I said, without shame and in front of Alice and Victoria, that I did not ever want to be separated from him again. "That's the cruelest part of war," he replied, looking first at me and then at my sisters. "That it separates people."

Though I tried to keep my spirits up, that first month in Chungking disappointed me. Nothing happened. The cloudy weather resumed after that one sunny day, and persisted until the end of June, but a sweltering heat wave made it difficult to summon the energy even to hike to and from school. And the classes themselves were nowhere near as challenging as the lessons of my tradition-minded tutors in Hunan. On my free days, I tagged along with Lao Chang when he went to the well to get the day's supply of water, or when he did the marketing. We would walk all the way downslope to the South Bank ferry landing, where there were perhaps a dozen food and merchandise stalls, surrounded by the makeshift huts of squatters who camped on the stony river sand. There we bargained for vegetables we could scarcely identify, using a dialect and currency that were still strange to us, then drank a cup of tea in a clean but rickety bamboo shack before climbing back up the road. We said less and less to each other each time. Though I was only thirteen, my breasts had developed; I had begun to attract men's glances. Lao Chang's gossip and jests and complaints about all the work he was being made to do no longer held my interest. The distancing process that had started in Hunan was now almost complete. I felt I had outgrown him. And so, the two of us would sip our lukewarm tea in the tenth hour of morning and, barely aware of each other, stare at the curtain of fine, soundless rain as it fell on the surface of the Yangtze.

In the evening, our family would eat a dinner of steamed rice and vegetables cooked in oil and chili peppers, while Father told us stories about fiascos at the Commission — such as American cargo planes arriving full of luxury car parts instead of the sulfa powder and quinine pills that were in such demand. And in the hour before bed, I would read *Little Women* or a story in Father's collection of Sherlock Holmes mysteries. I felt restless and bored until early July when, of all people, my mother shook me out of my lethargy. "I'd like to talk alone with Katherine," she said to Alice late one afternoon when my sister and I returned from school. She chased Joan and Victoria away as well and sat me down across from her at the tea table in the front room. I was certain that a reprimand was coming and only wondered what I had done to displease her.

"You know, we're alike, you and I," she began, speaking in a more confidential tone than I had ever heard her use with anyone but Father. "Much more alike than you think." Her words left me thunderstruck. All I could do was stare at the tabletop in confusion. "I've received a report from your teachers, who think highly of your abilities. So highly that they suggest you apply for admittance to the third year of studies at the Baptist school this fall, instead of the second — the same class as your sister." Mother smiled as she delivered this news, and when I saw what pride she took in my achievement, I felt like crying out that the Chungking teachers knew nothing of my real ability. That I had hardly been trying. Her smile was like an unexpected gift. I lunged at it as a first sign of her acceptance of me, and swore to apply myself to my lessons as I never had before. I was dizzy with plans and resolutions when she spoke again. "They mention, too, that they don't believe you've shown your best efforts yet. Is that true?"

". . . I guess so, Mother."

"This is a time when none of us can afford that kind of attitude," she exclaimed so harshly that once again I thought she was angry with me. But her frown quickly vanished and she added in her earlier, confidential manner, "There are things to be done now. Difficult things, and ones that not everyone in this household can do. I'll want your help, Katherine." Then she dismissed me.

That five-minute talk was the beginning of a new phase in my relationship with Mother. Day by day after that, she kept

admitting me further into her energetic schemes to see to it
that our fortunes did not founder. In the mornings, before I
went to school, and at night after dinner, she drilled me in
English, even though her own grasp of that language was not
as good as my teachers' or Father's. On holidays she had Lao
Chang instruct me in cooking techniques. She entrusted me
with precious lengths of silk with which to barter at the consignment stores for carpets, wall hangings, flower vases, and
dozens of other furnishings meant to improve the dreary appearance of our house. Mother trained me in the rudiments of
household economy (for which she, and not Father, had always been responsible). I learned the intricacies of the ration-
ing system and the use of the black market as a necessary
means of dealing with the daily rising inflation rate. I saw for
myself how fast our store of silver was dwindling, and understood why my parents no longer entertained, and why Mother
instructed Cook to buy meat for only one meal per week.
Mother smoked cigarettes in Chungking, as she had not done
since our days in Peking. But rather than spend money on such
a luxury item, she encouraged Father to accept from his American contacts at work the packs of Old Golds that he was
constantly being offered. By midsummer, Mother began giving
me pieces of her jewelry with instructions to take them to a
broker in the business sector of Chungking, but to tell no one
what I was doing. The fierceness of her expression let me know
that the secret was to be kept even from Father.

No detail escaped her attention. "In the market," she said to
me once, "always sift through the rice once it's on the scales. If
you find pebbles, move on to the next stall." And soon she had
me assist her in a practice of which I would never have thought
her capable. Late at night, in the big room, she, Chang Ma,
and I would painstakingly unravel the wool of old-fashioned
sweaters and skirts, and steam out the wrinkles over a cauldron
of boiling water. Chang Ma would dye the strands in fresh,
bright colors. Then Mother, whose hands were once expert in
the art of gold-thread embroidery, would reknit entire gar-

ments for my sisters and me to wear, lest our neighbors or schoolmates think we could not afford to dress in the styles of the day.

I hardly troubled to ask myself why all this was happening. It was enough for me that for the first time in my life, I was virtually monopolizing Mother's attention. I reasoned only that my parents could not afford to hire all the servants we needed, and that I — rather than my less practical-minded sister — had been chosen to take up the slack. Alice and I did not discuss the fact that I had seemed to displace her as Mother's favorite. It would probably have been better if we had. As it was, I kept outshining her at school in every subject but music, and she often watched in open envy as Mother brushed my hair, something she used to do only for Alice, or gave me detailed instructions about an errand in the city. The result was that Alice refused to concentrate on anything but her music, in which she became so accomplished that she continually astonished our piano instructor with her expertise. When we were children in Peking, it had infuriated me that she could learn inside a quarter of an hour a piece that might cost me days of slavish practice; and that in the end, my rendition was certain to sound stilted next to the delicacy and freedom of hers. Now I was glad of that difference. I was relieved that there was one sphere at least in which she was more accomplished than I. For, as much as my newfound status in Mother's eyes elated me, I did not want it to be at the price of the understanding Alice and I had begun to achieve in Hunan.

On the evening of the August full moon, there was a painful celebration in our house. Mother sent Cook to market to buy two pounds of pork, and she had Chang Ma fetch Father at the Kuomintang meeting he had gone to after work, all because I had passed my exams with exceptional honors and had been accepted into the third-year class at the Baptist school. On Mother's prompting, Chang Ma had taken that news straight to Father, who did not learn, until he arrived at the door with a gleaming, prideful smile, that Alice's application had been rejected, and that she must now attend an inferior school in Kiangtsing, a city two days further upriver. The special food was wasted on our family that night. Mother had me sit next to her and talked for an hour about three influential colleagues of my father's who, she claimed, would certainly now offer me their patronage as godfathers. Then she showed me the silver coins she had set aside so that I might go to the one orthodontist in all of Chungking for corrective work on two slightly protruding incisors. Meanwhile, Father consoled Alice with whispered words, and, as usual, Joan and Victoria were ignored. The only ones who seemed to enjoy that feast were Cook and Chang Ma, whom I later saw in the kitchen, gnawing with relish at the leftover pork bones.

There had been talk all summer that Chungking was now safe; that the Americans would see to it that the city was never bombed again. But one sunny afternoon in late August, less than a week before Alice and I were to leave for our schools, a low, metallic sound reverberated in the valley and made my insides churn. Though I had never heard it before, I knew this was the air raid siren. Everyone but Mother stood as if paralyzed. Victoria called out Father's name, though she must have known he was at the Commission and would not be able to travel with us to the cave. Mother dashed about the house, doing all the tasks the servants, my sisters, and I were supposed to share, and shouting futile commands at us. The siren rose higher in pitch. It sounded now like the almost human whine of a cat in pain. Mother opened the three small windows under the eaves, as Father had instructed, to decrease the chance of their breaking during the explosions. She piled on a table a tea thermos, a rice carrier with six stacked bowls, her two best jewelry boxes, and seven white cards with the national flag stamped in the corner — our means of admission to the shelter. By now Lao Chang and Chang Ma were helping her. Lao Chang went about the house shaking Alice, Victoria, Joan, and me into reality, while Chang Ma threw together a survival kit for each of us: a change of clothing, a covered bowl of cold rice, a flashlight, and five silver coins, all tied up in a square blue cloth.

In less than ten minutes we were standing in the yard, waiting for Mother to padlock the front door. The siren's peal was strident and agitated now, and it made my head throb with its pulsing vibrations. A grim-faced column of neighbors and strangers hastened up the hillside path. Further down in the valley I could see the massive red balloons that served as an early-warning system. "Come!" Mother cried, and our party of seven joined the march upslope.

"I can't, Mother," Alice pleaded when, at the end of a half-mile climb, we saw the gaping cave mouth — a twenty-foot-high arc of serrated granite. I, too, wondered if I could go any further. We could already hear the heavy drone of bomb-laden planes and the muffled thunder of antiaircraft guns far to the east of the city. Then, at intervals of several seconds, the road itself seemed to shake and resettle, producing a queasy feeling in the pit of my stomach. I turned back once toward the city's cliffs and saw bright yellow flashes igniting, for an instant each, at the heart of Chungking's tangle of streets. Trails of smoke spiraled upward from toy-sized buildings. The scream of falling bombs obliterated the siren, and the explosions resounded so deafeningly that an intolerable pressure built up in my ears. When I could not stand that pressure any longer, I ran into the cave, leaving Mother to deal with Alice and the others. I found Lao Chang crouching just inside the cool, dark entrance. Both his arms were raised as if to fend off the din behind us, and he had tucked his head beneath his humped left shoulder. I was in a trance. I have no idea how long it took Mother to drag my sisters along, but in time she showed our identification cards to the military guard, and we all passed inside.

Hundreds of civilians had already crowded into that rank and stifling place, where the darkness was relieved only by an occasional kerosene lamp set in niches in the bare rock wall. There was a fearful clamor on all sides. And in that closed space, every noise echoed in a nerve-fraying way. My nostrils soon filled with mixed odors of food and urine, and of the minerals in the water that seeped through the walls. It seemed to me that in a quarter hour's time, there would be no oxygen left in that fetid underground prison. I thought the fear of suffocation would make me claw a path to the outside air, even if the cave mouth itself were being bombarded.

Others kept pushing from behind as we forced our way through the hundreds of encamped bodies. Large groups had staked out all the flat, dry spaces, often spreading cold meals and cups of tea in their midst. Servants stood by impassively or sat atop the knotted bundles that held their masters' most valued possessions. Finally we reached a set of wooden stalls reserved for the families of high-ranking government officials. Mother presented our cards to another soldier, and we were admitted, quickly finding that that area was no less crowded than the first.

We all sat speechless in a tight little circle. After the first hour, Victoria and Joan actually slept. Chang Ma stared straight ahead, like a blind woman. But it was Lao Chang's expression that truly frightened me. His eyes were hard and fixed, his lips as rigid as death. I had seen that look often enough in Chungking. It was not at all characteristic of the newly arrived refugees, who tended at first to confront the war with a defiant cheerfulness. He showed the strain that marked the faces of the longtime residents, whose resilience had been worn down by all the death and disease they had seen.

Mother held Alice against her breast and moaned in a soothing, rhythmic way. But Alice did not sleep. She kept peering at stones and crumbs of food on the cave floor and alternately tensing and relaxing the fingers of both hands. I hated to see her that way. She looked more animal than human.

Before I heard the sustained, low-frequency blare of the all-clear siren in the distance, I became aware of a wave of commotion that started in the vicinity of the cave mouth and spread slowly inward. People all around us scooped food into napkins, stretched cramped limbs, and rounded up their children and servants with businesslike efficiency. I felt proud that I had not panicked, even though the raid had been a short one. The air had not turned unbearable, nor the mood mean-spirited, as Father had warned sometimes happened.

Within seconds I was separated from my family and pulled along by the multitude that flowed out into the sunlight. It seemed impossible to reunite anywhere near the shelter, and so I began descending the stony path, flanked by women clutching children to their sides and by men hurrying ahead to protect their houses from looters. A quarter mile down the road I reached a vantage point that offered a view both of the city and of the neighborhood where our house sat perched on its shelf of granite. I looked first toward Chungking and saw three fires raging. Then, once I got up my nerve, I glanced at our house and saw that it stood intact. I turned toward the nearest person on the road, a peasant woman with an infant strapped to her back, and told her in broken Szechuanese that my house had not been damaged. When she only nodded, I told her twice more until she answered, almost angrily, that she had understood. I searched for the words to wish her equal luck, but she did not wait to listen.

13

THE next morning Father told Cook he was to escort Alice to her school in Kiangtsing. It was raining, and there was no chance of an air attack. Alice had thrashed about in her bed all night. Her face looked pale and haggard. She would speak to no one but Father; and to him she said only that she must leave Chungking that very day. That to wait another week would make her insane. I was glad when he consented, even over Mother's objections. I knew Alice had more reasons for wanting to go away than the fear of another raid. If I did not yet understand why Mother had shifted her attentions to me, then Alice must have understood it even less. Mother's strange initiative had had the effect of leaving her almost isolated. All Alice wanted to do, I believe, was to escape. No one else had a better solution to offer. Father seemed oblivious to the tension. Mother was conscious of it, but it did not appear to bother her. And though it bothered me nearly as much as it did Alice, I did not have the insight or maturity, or the required standing in the family, to intervene. I felt awkward and somehow guilty as Alice and I bid each other good-bye, being careful not to let our eyes meet. But when the rains abated and she and Cook set out by sedan chair for the Yangtze, I breathed more easily.

Six days later, my turn came. It was painful, at the age of

thirteen, to leave everyone I knew, especially Father. Still, I felt inspired by the fresh challenge that lay before me. "Remember all the things I've said to you, Hsiao-yen," Mother said, out of hearing of the others, as Lao Chang and I were about to leave. She did not touch me, but she did not need to. Her bright black eyes fixed mine, and her use of my Chinese name shocked me into rapt attention. "You should do better than all your classmates. I expect it. Make me proud of you."

"Kiangtsing and First Mistress's school were awful," Lao Chang said. "A great disappointment. But *this*. This is worse!"

My fantasy had been of a lush, green-hilled campus with gardens, graceful stone buildings, and perhaps a stream. A place as lovely and peaceful and manicured as Yenching. Instead, Faith Baptist Mission School, as it was called, was a low, flat complex of barracks-like, western-style buildings set in the center of an arid mountain plain. A miserable little hamlet lay a half mile away, and that was all. There were no beggars or signs of bomb and fire damage; but otherwise, this setting was as drab and disappointing as Chungking. We saw a group of students and teachers in an enormous cement yard, doing western calisthenics. The pupils — all girls and all Chinese — wore clean uniforms of quilted blue pants and blue cotton shirts with high starched collars. Every head was cropped close, like my father's. Two American women dressed in gray blouses and skirts led the exercises, while a tall, stout, white-haired man in a spotless white robe watched the proceedings with calm satisfaction. He smiled the whole time and nodded once or twice. He held a large, leather-bound book, gripping it in both hands, as though he were afraid it might fall to the ground.

"Do you think they'll let me stay long enough, Second Mistress? I'm supposed to leave in time to return home by nightfall."

"Long enough for what?"

"Why, to see what you look like bald," Lao Chang said.

And when he grinned, the sunlight glinted on his solid-gold teeth.

If Cook had remained there until the next morning, he would have had his wish, for I was awakened by a Chinese servant at five in the morning, a half hour earlier than the other forty-nine girls in my dormitory, and led to a makeshift barbershop. There a stocky, jovial woman — far too jovial for the time of day, I thought — sat me in a wooden chair and scissored my long black hair almost to the scalp, laughing and jabbering effortless Mandarin the whole time. Her name was Miss Peterson, she said. She taught English, but also served as the school nurse, having been trained in that profession before leaving the States. She had seen me yesterday near the exercise yard in the company of "that curious servant with a lump on his forehead." Had he fallen recently, or was the lump a permanent fixture? Did I know any English? But of course I did if I was the daughter of Professor Yang K'ai-tao. Still, why was I so quiet, she wanted to know?

I liked that woman right from the start. Though she talked frantically, always running ahead of herself, there was a wonderful air of self-assurance about her (I had never heard a woman laugh so lustily as she did), and an appetite for discovery. She *did* want to know about Lao Chang and Father and the rest of my family and, most particularly, about me. Eventually she saw to it that all her questions were answered.

When I told Miss Peterson I knew English quite well, she shrieked with delight. "First, we'll never again speak Mandarin to each other, you and I," she said, switching immediately to English. "And second, *I'll* be the judge of whether you know English quite well, well, or not too well at all." The shorn strands of hair rained about my head and shoulders as she spoke. "For example, do you know what the word 'lice' means, Kathie?" she asked, giving me my first nickname since Grandfather had called me Winter Swallow. When I admitted I did not, she said, "You see? I thought as much!"

There was a small mirror on the wall of Miss Peterson's

parlor. I recoiled when I saw my image, but she said I should take heart, that this was the procedure only at the start of each school year. "In accordance with Generalissimo Chiang's edict, you'll be permitted to grow your hair to the length of your earlobes, but no longer." I thought at once of Alice and hoped, for everyone's sake, that the Kiangtsing school took a more liberal stance on the cutting of students' hair.

Next I was taken by the servant to the office of the principal, who, I was surprised to see, was also a woman. I knew by then that there were both male and female teachers at the mission school, some religious and some lay. I wondered whether it was common in America, or perhaps just among Baptists, for women to occupy positions of authority over men.

"Good morning, Katherine," she began in English, sitting erect in her chair and making a generous effort, I thought, not to stare at my butchered hair. "My name is Mrs. Faye. Now, I don't believe you've been to breakfast yet, so I'll be brief. I made your father's acquaintance years ago, when he was a doctoral student at Michigan State University. Our entire faculty, too, is familiar with his books on the Revolution and his illustrious teaching career. I must say that we're extremely proud to have here the daughter of Professor Cato Yang." My spirits drooped. I was beginning to get the feeling that I had been accepted not because of my scholastic achievement but because of my father's reputation. But Mrs. Faye quickly dispelled that fear, mentioning that Father had written her only after the approval of my application. "As you know, you're being moved ahead, Katherine," she went on, smiling with a certain stiffness of the lips. "You're younger, by at least a year, than any other girl at your grade level. If things become too difficult for you, I want you to let me know. I promised Professor Yang I'd see to it that you weren't swamped."

Far from being swamped, I excelled during my entire eighteen-month tenure at the mission school, and cherished every minute I spent there. I found almost the whole academic program exciting: the history, geography, art, and calligraphy classes our Chinese instructors taught; and the English, health, mathematics, music, and science lessons offered by Miss Peterson and the five other missionaries. Only Bible class, presided over by the Reverend Philip Paulson in his starched white soutane, failed to intrigue me. From the first testing period in late December onward, I earned the distinction of being the top student in my class of thirty-seven, despite my age disadvantage. I became intoxicated by the day-to-day prospect of new knowledge, even applying myself to Bible studies until Dr. Paulson considered me his best pupil. And it was not enough for me simply to participate in every extracurricular program available. My compulsion to learn all I could, to develop the full range of my abilities, and, I suppose, to compete, was so strong that I soon became editor of the school newspaper, president of the debating society, lead actress in the annual play, and captain of the swimming and diving team. Even at night, in the dormitory, I had my classmates teach me the Szechuanese dialect until I was fluent. No one there ever knew what drove me to accomplish so much. Not my closest friend among the girls, Chang La-mei, who talked to me in confidence about her boyfriend in Chungking, and who, when I had my first period, in January of 1944, showed me how to make a napkin out of scraps of cloth. Not Miss Peterson, who invited me to her quarters in the administration building on the first Saturday of every month for an hour-long chat and, the sole luxury she allowed herself, a platter of scrambled eggs. I never admitted to anyone how consciously I was striving to earn not only my mother's respect, but her affection. I did not worry about Father's estimation of me, having long ago learned to rely upon his unselfish acceptance. But I felt that I was at last within reach of being loved by Mother, if only I worked hard enough. I could not help but take the highest honors. None of the other girls had a chance.

In February of 1944, my parents had Alice and me travel home for three days of the New Year celebration. That visit began as a triumphant return. Mrs. Faye had given me a sealed letter, addressed to Father, which turned out to be a glowing litany of my varied successes. With the penchant for the dramatic that she had shown so often in her Peking days, Mother splurged on a New Year banquet, to which she invited three of Father's colleagues and their wives, as well as several of the neighbors she and Father had befriended. Then she read to them, and to Father and my sisters, every word that my principal had written. It was not long before my initial embarrassment turned into a thrilling rush of pride. Father smiled brightly, all the guests nodded in approval, and Joan and Victoria clapped their hands at the most impressive passages, as Mother's voice rang out with a kind of vindictive clarity. Alice smiled the whole time, but I could see that she was trying to conceal how deeply this hurt her. There was a time in Peking when Mother had chosen to show *both* of us off to her friends. And for years after that, it had been the First Daughter, the Dragon Child alone, on whom Mother's boasting had focused. At the end of the impassioned recital, Alice applauded with everyone else, and her gesture made me respect her more than I ever had.

On the last night of our stay, Alice and I whispered to each other in bed, the way we had done so often as children. She lay on her side, facing me. Her cheek pressed against the hard pillow and distorted her voice. I could see her quite clearly. The mosquito netting had been removed for the winter months, and Alice always slept now with a small candle burning on the table that separated our beds. For a long time we traded stories about our schools: how many times a week we were served cabbage, turnips, and rice for dinner; how seldom we ever saw fresh meat. At her school, a Methodist-sponsored establishment, the students were permitted to take baths once every two weeks, which was twice as often as at mine. And she was not required, as I was, to launder her own clothes with a block of strong-smelling brown soap and a splintery wooden washboard. Only in one respect were the schools exactly the same. Neither had heat in the dormitories, so when we were wakened on winter mornings in the freezing, predawn darkness, we put on our uniforms, shoes and all, before emerging from beneath the quilted blankets.

For each triviality we discussed, there was a far more telling issue we avoided. In spite of the discomfort of menstruation, I derived a deep satisfaction from the experience, a definite feeling of having begun to leave childhood behind. And yet I could not have shared that feeling with Alice, who, I suspected, had not yet had her first period, and who would almost surely react hysterically when it came. We said nothing, either, about my scholastic achievements or about the fact, as Mother had twice hinted, that Alice was having a difficult time in every subject but calligraphy and music. And as had been so the previous autumn, we never alluded to what was by far the main irritant between us: the volatile shifts of focus in Mother's affections.

"There's something I must tell you, Hsiao-yen," Alice said, following a lull in our chat. Her voice bristled with emotion, as it had not the whole hour before that. "But promise me you won't say anything to Mother."

"Of course I won't. What is it? Tell me."

"Because if she . . ."

"You met a boy you like!" I almost cried out, certain of her secret and only barely in control of the excitement it made me feel. "Who is he, and what did he say to you? How could you possibly have met him, anyway? There aren't boys at your school, are there?" The questions sprang from me so quickly that I hardly knew what I was asking. I felt foolish when she told me to lower my voice and to give her a chance to reply. "All right, then, what does he look like?" That, I decided, was what I most wanted to know.

"Oh, I doubt you'd find him handsome, Hsiao-yen. No, he isn't handsome, I suppose. There's too much sadness in his eyes. He's taller than I am but slight of build. When he looks at you, it's not as though a man or boy were looking at you but a woman, and one who knows your inner thoughts. It's a strange quality. I hear it in his singing, too, and in his playing. His hands—he's a wonderful pianist—are delicate, again not like a man's. Still, his fingers fly over the keys with incredible strength and confidence."

"Where is he from?"

"Shanghai. He's known as Han Liang-ming, but his real name is French."

"Then he's not Chinese at all?" I knew then that Alice had done well to warn me not to let Mother hear of this.

"No, he is. He's half Chinese. His father was a French diplomat who died during the bombing of Shanghai in the first month of the war. His mother is Chinese and refused to flee from occupied Shanghai. He studies music at the Methodist boys' academy in Kiangtsing, where my classmates and I go to Sunday services. He sings, and I accompany the chapel choir on piano. You should hear how out of tune that old thing is."

"What did he say to you the first time you spoke?"

"*Please,* Hsiao-yen, lower your voice."

"Sorry . . . but what did he say? Or was it you who spoke first?"

"Neither of us spoke, or hardly at all," she whispered, and I could hear in her voice how much pleasure it gave her just to recall that encounter. "He walked over to the piano when the service had ended, and we stayed in the chapel for ten minutes or so instead of going right away to the communion hall with the others. He asked me to play the last hymn again because he admired my playing, and . . ."

"No, tell me just what he said, Older Sister. Try to remember the exact words he used."

She did not hesitate an instant. "He said, 'You play beautifully. I only wish this instrument were good enough to let me hear *how* beautifully. Won't you play that last piece again?' I was afraid our absence from the breakfast would be noticed, but I played on. When I did, Liang-ming harmonized the melody in the upper register, and with such a graceful line that I was distracted. I wanted to stop and listen. But at the same time, I wanted to play perfectly, so that he'd think highly of me."

"He already 'thought highly of you,' as you put it."

"All right, so that he'd think more highly of me still."

"And did he?"

"I don't know."

"What do you mean?"

"Well, when we finished the hymn, he just smiled, then we hurried to the other room, where the boys and girls and faculty were all taking their seats at different tables. I don't think anyone noticed us."

"You mean you never said anything at *all* to him that first time?"

"No, nothing. I was scared, Hsiao-yen. And that's been the only time so far."

"What? The only time you've seen each other?" I felt almost as if she were treating me unfairly.

"Well, there've been three Sunday services since then, but we haven't actually talked. I guess I don't know how one . . . I don't know how to bring that about. I thought I'd ask you. Do you know how that's done?"

"Not really," I said in as consoling a way as I could, all the time thinking that if I had been in her position, I would somehow have known what to do.

"If you could only have seen his smile." She seemed lost for a moment in her private vision. "His face is, I don't know, exotic, because of his eyes. They're large and shaped like a westerner's. And the sadness shows there, even when he smiles. I hope we get the chance to be together again."

"I do, too," I said, "and I know you will." Then, before I thought about it, I added, "Older Sister, I wish I were you." If she had laughed outright, I might have said what I really meant, only that I envied her what had happened. But I took her silence as a sign that she understood, and I let my impulsive words hang in the darkness. "Will you tell me more next time?"

"Of course. I'll tell you everything. That is, if there's anything to tell."

When I left home again the next morning, I felt hopeful that

Alice and I would succeed in recapturing all that we had let slip away. It surprised me to realize how great a comfort that was, and how threatened I must have been all along, even in the blush of my academic glory, by the thought of becoming irreparably distant from my sister.

Punishment among the Baptists came in two forms only. A student was struck across the palms with a ruler if an instructor judged her negligent in her studies. And for each "dormitory infraction," as they were called — such as violating the nine o'clock lights-out curfew or pilfering the little rose-colored candles that the servants set near the foot of each double bunk at night — the guilty student would lose a full day of August vacation. I always had my lessons prepared, and so was never hit. And even though the dormitory mistress caught me four times reading *Gone with the Wind* under my blanket (Miss Peterson had given me both the book and a tiny flashlight), my disobedience cost me nothing. Nine other girls and I were selected by Mrs. Faye as candidates for an experimental advanced-studies program that was to begin in July of 1944 and end with early graduation the next spring. When my parents gave me permission to stay at school for the summer, my four days' detention became moot.

There were two occasions, however, when I was accused of public insolence, an offense so rare that Mrs. Faye in the one case, and Dr. Paulson in the other, were at a loss to devise an appropriate chastisement, and ended by mailing stern letters to Father.

In early October, two days after my fourteenth birthday, my friend Chang La-mei confided to me that one of her brothers had joined the Communists in Shensi Province, and that the news of his "treason" had been posted in the squares of Chungking. She was expelled the following morning, and I never saw her again. Every aspect of that episode smelled of injustice, I thought, and I said as much to thirty of my schoolmates and to my history instructor on the day of La-mei's departure. It was the first speech of my life, and I thought I would never finish half of it for want of breath and saliva. I began by objecting to the fact that our history teacher, and the texts we were given, never once explained the Communist cause. Who were these several million countrymen, I asked, and why were they considered our enemies? What did they believe in? What were their complaints with the Kuomintang regime? What had inspired them to survive both Chiang Kai-shek's extermination campaigns and their desperate march to Yenan? What truth was there in the rumors that their guerrilla cadres posed the only effective resistance to the Japanese? "You call them 'bandits,' 'outlaws,' and 'traitors,'" I accused my teacher, "but why is it that more and more of our friends and relatives are leaving all they have and going to the Communist side?" Then, without allowing him the chance to defend himself, I leveled a more specific protest. "It's a shameful thing," I cried, "that Chang La-mei should have been made to pay for a choice her brother made." At that point my voice broke. My sense of loss began to overshadow my outrage. I felt *I* had been wronged, not just La-mei. When my teacher commanded me to step forward so that he might take me at once to Mrs. Faye, I stayed at my place. Then I banged my fist on the desk top and stammered in a tear-filled voice that, good or bad, the Faith Baptist Mission School had probably made my fifteen-year-old friend a lifelong supporter of the Communists that day.

No one made a sound. Even the history teacher seemed cowed. And in that total stillness, I walked without escort to the principal's office.

Mrs. Faye was furious with me — not on the merits of the central issues, I believe, but on a point I had not even considered. "Your father is a well-known member of the Kuomintang," she chided, once I had repeated every word for her benefit. "That gives you a responsibility to watch what you say in public, Katherine."

The argument brought me up short. I did not know yet if I agreed with it or even understood its implications, and so I decided to say nothing. Mrs. Faye wrote to my father, and I assume he responded, though I was never shown either letter. The only aftermath was a comment she made to me in private, almost three weeks later. "Apparently Professor Yang and I are not of the same opinion regarding the matter I discussed with you earlier this month, Katherine. In any event, let's consider the Chang case closed and move on from there, shall we?" But I was never to consider La-mei's case closed. And while I began to doubt the mettle of my history instructor and even of Mrs. Faye, I reaffirmed my belief in Father's personal integrity.

The only other skirmish I was involved in was religious in nature. To Dr. Paulson's horror, I refused to be baptized.

My grandmother, when she lived with us in Peking, had often reproached Mother and Father for being "convenience Christians" — pro forma believers, more eager to benefit from the church's social reforms and educational advantages than to follow in what her confessor used to refer to as "the Savior's bloodstained footsteps." I am certain she never suspected, however (and Mother was careful not to disabuse her), that her grandchildren lived in an unbaptized state. Had I been as discreet as Mother, I might not have risked expulsion in my second winter at the mission school. But when Dr. Paulson once chanced to ask me in which particular church I had been christened, I answered, with naive matter-of-factness, that I did not believe I had ever been baptized.

If I had stolen his chalice, I would not have made a more disastrous impression. He reeled to hear that admission, actually staggering into a chair. Then I worsened matters immeasurably by declining his offer of an immediate baptismal ceremony — lest, as he put it, I continue to court everlasting damnation. I told him that I respected his religious beliefs and only hoped that he would in turn respect mine, not a single example of which I could have produced if he had happened to ask me.

"Then you're a hypocrite," he murmured in an unsteady voice. "You've been a hypocrite from the day you arrived."

The accusation hurt me, because I admired Dr. Paulson and the other Baptist missionaries for traveling half a world away to fight disease, poverty, and ignorance among a people not their own. I told him that I had recited my lessons in Bible class, knelt and prayed, sung hymns at services, and listened attentively to his sermons not because I wanted to pretend I was a believer but because I saw no reason not to do what was expected of every student there. And that was the truth. It had always seemed to me that it would be ungracious not to participate.

He gazed at me, incredulous. "You don't even believe, do you," he finally asked, "in the existence of God?" Striving not to look disrespectful, I demurely shook my head. "Nor in the Devil, or the whole idea of sin?"

"I don't believe in any of those things."

By now poor Father must have feared he was destined to account to everyone for me, and for the rest of his life. I wish I had had the opportunity to read the letter he sent in response to Dr. Paulson's immediate report. I only know that four days later, Dr. Paulson called me into the faculty library and said that he and I "had work to do on the matter of sacred doctrine and belief," but that we could at least rest easy on what he saw as the more pressing issue. "Your father has informed me that you are in error, Katherine. As it turns out, you were baptized in the chapel of Yenching University in November of 1930." That, I have always thought, was a blatant fabrication designed to allow a well-meaning man a respectable path of retreat.

I saw that intolerance lay at the base of both my unsettling experiences. I saw, as well, that Father had dealt with two somewhat similar dilemmas in strikingly different, yet equally effective, ways. For years I had been aware of the high professional regard in which he was held. Even so, it was a revelation to me to *see* how masterful he could be when operating outside the boundaries of Mother's direct influence. I understood, and appreciated, the strong stand he must have taken with Mrs.

Faye in my defense, even though I had publicly expressed an interest in political ideas at variance with his own. I was less capable, perhaps, of quickly assimilating the wisdom he had shown in settling the baptism issue. Yet even in that instance, I learned enough of a lesson to avoid asking Father himself if he had lied to a member of the clergy.

14

In March of 1945, one month before I was scheduled to graduate with the accelerated class, Father sent Lao Chang to my school with instructions to bring me home at once.

"It's the Mistress . . ." was the first thing Cook said when I met him in the exercise yard outside my dormitory, having already packed a *pao-fu* and dressed for the journey. He kept rubbing the knot on his forehead with the back of his hand. "She's ill, Second Young Mistress. Very ill."

As we quickly walked to the village, where we were to hire two sedan chairs, I had Cook tell me all he knew. At first I was afraid Mother had been wounded in a bombing attack. "No," he said, "there aren't any more raids. Everyone says the war is practically over. It's something else — some sickness no one seems able to give a name."

"Has Father taken her to a hospital?"

"A hospital!" Lao Chang exclaimed. "No, I've made inquiries on your mother's behalf. The Methodist Hospital, the Baptist clinic, Double-Ten Hospital, they're all out of the question. Nothing more than places where people go to die. A servant of your uncle was taken to one last month for burns she'd suffered in a fire. Three days later the doctors claimed that she'd died of her injuries. But I found out otherwise. The brother of another patient told me that the girl died of the rats."

I made him stop, and only hoped he had not filled Mother's head with such horror stories, whether the incident was true or not. "Has she at least seen a doctor?" I asked.

"She can't be moved. The Master has tried to arrange for someone to come, but that's a difficult thing. I've heard it takes a considerable bribe. And the Mistress is insisting that he bring an American military doctor. But the Americans won't come. They won't treat any patients but their own."

I hardly recognized Mother. She lay in her bed, her back and head propped up with two pillows. Her breathing was shallow. The flesh had fallen away from the bones of her face, so that the afternoon light left ghastly pockets of shadow on her cheeks. Her hair was unbound and matted, and her throat had grown so thin that I could see the slow pulsing of a vein in the side of her neck. No one else was in the house but Chang Ma, who looked very tired. Her face betrayed the same fear as Lao Chang's, that Mother might soon die.

"Is she asleep?" I asked Chang Ma, who shook her head. Then Mother's eyelids opened slightly and her breathing became even more labored. Her eyes, still as brilliant as small black gems, fixed me as she made the effort to speak.

"Will he come?" she asked in a scratchy voice.

"It's the fever," Chang Ma whispered to me. "She thinks you're the Master. She's asking about the American doctor."

"It's me, Mother. Hsiao-yen."

"Yes . . ." she said, but I still could not tell if she recognized me until she added, "I'm going to die, Katherine. If no one helps me, I'm going to die." Then she lapsed into a fitful slumber.

It was two hours before Father returned home from work. No matter where I went in the house, I could hear Mother's violent coughing and the sound her head made on the pillows as she rocked it from side to side to induce sleep. I called Lao Chang from the kitchen and asked him dozens of questions, hoping at least to block out those noises, which, if I had known what to do to relieve Mother's pain, might not have sounded so maddening. He told me that Father had sent Joan and Victoria to a school in Hochwan once Mother's condition had become serious. Father, he said, now stayed up late every night writing letters of petition to the American health authorities, and free-lance political articles for Chungking's main newspaper. "Your grandfather's silver coins have all but disappeared," he explained. "No one understands what's happening. Rice costs ten times what it did less than a year ago, Second Young Mistress. *Ten times!*"

Father and I ate a meal together when he came home — the first, it occurred to me, we had ever shared alone. He looked as weary and overwrought as Cook and Chang Ma, never once smiling after his initial words of greeting. He said that he regretted having interrupted my studies, but that my help was needed, and that Mother herself had suggested that he summon me. I asked if he did not think Mother should be taken at once to a hospital. He said only that she would not hear of it, and that, in any event, he had persuaded a Doctor Ting to come the next morning, a man who had treated him, two years earlier, for malaria. "Tomorrow we'll know," he said before sending me to bed so that he could begin his writing in solitude. He spoke as if he were alone in the room and thinking out loud. "At least we'll know what it is."

"I must go now."

"That's the all-clear siren, Doctor. They made a mistake."

"No, I don't trust them to know when the planes are coming and when they aren't, Miss Yang. Anyway, I've completed my diagnosis. Kindly have your servant bring me my coat."

Ting Chieh-chang was a travesty of a physician. I loathed even his look and manner. He was very short and frail-boned, with a narrow ferret's face. His eyes, unnaturally alert, never rested on one person or object for more than an instant; and he spoke too quickly and too often, feeling the need to fill every silence. "Yes, yes, yes," he had grunted all the time he was examining Mother. He would beseech her in an obsequious voice to inhale or exhale or cough or lift her head, and once she obeyed, he would revert to his pattern of quick, ambiguous yesses. Now he was cutting his visit short, even though the all-clear siren signified that the first alarm had been a false one.

"What can you tell us, Doctor?" I asked. He hurried out of Mother's sleeping alcove, not even pausing to bid her farewell. He might have dashed right outside to his waiting sedan chair if I had not repeated my question, this time without masking my annoyance.

"Your mother has a serious chest disease," he said brusquely, as if his chief intention were to rid himself of me.

"What is it?"

"Tuberculosis, I'm afraid. I'll send a full report to your father this afternoon. She must be taken as soon as possible to Double-Ten Hospital, where I can get her a bed in our best ward. In the meantime there are precautions you and everyone else in this house must take. I'll explain them to Professor Yang." And he was gone.

Without even waiting for Father to return from work, I wrote a lengthy letter to Miss Peterson at the school. I described Mother's symptoms: the chest pains, shortness of breath, violent coughing, expectoration of foul-smelling sputum, difficulty in speaking, her thinness and lack of appetite, and the fever that always worsened at night. I took money from the lacquer box in my parents' dresser, deciding not to waken Mother to ask her permission, then sent Lao Chang to the ferry landing, where a messenger could be hired. "Tell him he'll be paid this much again," I said to Cook, giving him a larger amount than would be expected for such a service, "if he brings the return message by tomorrow night."

Father was nervous and depressed all that evening. He seemed to have no plan for dealing with what we both knew was a crisis. He said nothing to me about whether we should take Mother into Chungking or seek the diagnosis of another physician. All he would talk about was Doctor Ting's list of precautions and dietary recommendations. That Chang Ma and I wear cloth masks when caring for Mother. That we boil her dishes, utensils, towels, sheets, and bedclothes. That we encourage her to eat chicken broth and eggs to build her strength, regardless of her expressed aversion to taking anything but tea.

Miss Peterson's return message arrived the next afternoon. It was Sunday, so Father was home. He had sat alone in the front room all morning, and he barely glanced at the letter when I showed it to him. "She's a trained nurse, Father," I pleaded. "She thinks some of Mother's symptoms don't fit Doctor Ting's diagnosis."

"You should have asked my permission before writing to this woman," he replied.

"I'm sorry, Father, but I was scared by what Doctor Ting said. And she may be right, Miss Peterson. He didn't even seem to be listening when I told him of Mother's . . ."

"He's a perfectly capable physician, Hsiao-yen. I sent for you because Lao Chang and Chang Ma needed help tending to your mother's needs while she's ill, not because I wanted you to advise me on medical matters."

Though I was stung by Father's rebuke, I felt there was too much at stake simply to submit. "But what about this man she thinks might be helpful, Father? Doctor Li Chen-yu?"

"Leave me alone," he snapped in as harsh a tone as I had ever heard him use. When he saw how he had startled me, he relented a bit. "These matters are beyond your comprehension, Hsiao-yen. Doctor Li, whom your teacher mentions, has a severe disability and has not once left his home on the summit of Mount Pehpei for the past five years. And in any case, your teacher should know better than to suggest a practice that may be acceptable in America but not here. I could not now ask Doctor Li for a diagnosis without making Doctor Ting lose face. Furthermore, I know what your mother will or won't permit, and I must make my decisions accordingly." He handed back the letter, and I left the room.

For hours I pored over Miss Peterson's words as I lay in bed that night. Doctor Li, she wrote, was a celebrated, German-trained diagnostician who had made his reputation as a chest disease specialist in Shanghai. Just before the war began, he had lost both legs in a train accident. He now lived in virtual seclusion on a mountaintop west of Chungking and refused all cases except those referred to him by a former colleague from his Shanghai days — an American missionary named Bernard Larsen, who had since become the chief administrator of a Baptist clinic in Chungking. She had met Doctor Larsen once, at a Baptist convocation the year before. She said that my father should feel free to show him her letter, should he decide to try to appeal to Doctor Li. "This is a long shot," she concluded in her idiomatic style. "But even if it's not possible to reach Doctor Li, Doctor Larsen may have other ways of helping. The Baptist clinic is located, as your father probably knows, in a poor district of Chungking called the 'Village of the Dying.' All of us here are praying for your mother's swift recovery. Good luck, Kathie."

I awoke at six in the morning and waited impatiently for Father to leave for work. I listened from my bedroom door, not wishing to face him. In the past, his tread had been light, almost as soundless as Alice's. Now it told of the burdens he carried. As soon as he was gone, I walked to the water basin in the small room next to the servants' quarters and washed from my face and hands the sour odor my mattress always left on my skin. Still in my nightclothes, I went to Mother's bedside and gently shook her awake. "Mother," I said softly when she opened her eyes, "I'm going to try to bring a different doctor today."

"Did he say I would die?" she asked in a raspy voice.

"There are things of yours I'll need today, Mother."

She looked at me narrowly and smiled in her strange, distant way, and I knew what she was thinking before she spoke. "You haven't told your father, Katherine. He doesn't know." I shook my head. "Do you recall the sea-green *ch'i-p'ao* I received from your grandfather as a marriage gift in Hunan?" She would spare nothing that day. She would not have me fail.

"The one you wore during the New Year celebrations?"
"Yes," she said. "That will fit you."

For a time I felt self-conscious as I walked down the road
toward the ferry. It seemed that everyone in the South Bank
district had gathered to watch me pass. I must have appeared
ridiculous. The decline was so steep and the *ch'i-p'ao* so con-
fining at the hips, knees, and ankles that I was forced to take
countless mincing steps through the deep-rutted path. I held
one hand out for balance, and in the other, gripped a canvas
bag containing the letter from Miss Peterson, a small amount
of money, and a pair of Mother's best high-heeled pumps,
which I would not put on until I reached my destination. I was
half lost in reverie. Before leaving the house I had looked for a
long time at my reflection in the mirror, and the experience
had not yet worn off. In memory, I was still peering in wonder
at the image not of a fourteen-year-old girl but of a woman. I
had reddened my lips and darkened my eyebrows, then rouged
my cheeks, three times wiping off and reapplying Mother's
makeup, which in the end had seemed to narrow my face and
to lend it an air of mystery.

When I thought I had left all the onlookers behind, I heard
the taunting voice of a twelve-year-old boy named Wu Ming-
shan. Less than a year before then, in my first Chungking
summer, I had accepted his dare and swum the width of a
tributary of the Yangtze. I had stripped in his presence and felt
no shame. Now the mere recollection made my cheeks burn.
"Hsiao-yen is a grown woman," he jeered, barely out of earshot of the others. "One need only see her face or her . . ."
Then he used a Szechuanese word that literally means "flower
buds," but also serves as a metaphor for female nipples. At
once I became aware of a slight but definite friction between
the milk-smooth material of the dress and my own nipples,
which the experience of being watched in this way, or Ming-
shan's crude words, had made hard. I found that I did not
care. That the friction even felt pleasing.

I took the ferry across the river and, once I had climbed to the top of the stone steps, sought directions to the Baptist clinic. A heavyset Nationalist soldier told me the way. He was from the far North — a Mongol, I assumed, given his broad, nut-brown face and splayed nostrils. He pointed to a dirt road that was flanked by rundown houses with fire-scarred roofs and walls. "It's at the end of that path," he said, "but you shouldn't go that way." When he showed me a different route, I thanked him but said I could not spare the time to take the long way around.

I tried hard to distract myself, rehearsing over and over what I would say to Doctor Larsen, as I picked my way through the ruts left by cartwheels in that all but impassable road. I tried in vain to keep my eyes trained straight ahead of me. In every side street and alleyway of that nightmarish district, I saw whole families living on bamboo mats, with no shelter from the scorching sun or from the rains; hundreds of forlorn beggars, or people too disabled or dispirited even to beg, squatting in silence among piles of damp clothes and scavenged food; children with stick-limbed bodies and bloated stomachs, drinking from pools of brackish rainwater in the street and chewing pieces of tree bark for nourishment. Feces and streamlets of urine lay on all sides and, though it was the middle of the day, huge rats stalked slowly through the mire, seemingly unnoticed. The area had always been forbidden to me. I remembered then what Lao Chang had told me one morning as we sipped our after-market tea and gazed at this neighborhood from the other side of the river: "It's the city's worst slum, Second Young Mistress. Only the poorest, most disease-ridden refugees live in those streets and alleys. Even during the raids, I'm told, they sit there, not seeking the caves but waiting, maybe even hoping, for death."

I was nearing the northern border of the district and could even see the two-story building that I knew must be the clinic, when I heard the creaking of wood against metal behind me. I turned and saw a four-wheeled cart, perhaps sixty feet away. It was being trundled through the muddy street by a team of two soldiers who wore bulky, padded gloves and gray masks that covered their mouths and noses. As I watched, the men walked to the mouth of one of the alleys and carried back what at first looked like a plank of rotting wood. Then I realized it was a human body. The soldiers strained at their poles, pushing their burden straight toward me, and soon I could distinguish through the slats in the death cart's walls, a tangle of heads and torsos and limbs — some limp, some stiffened in grotesque poses. Though the cart was bearing down on me, I was mesmerized by the sight of the corpses and unable to move. Then I saw the soldiers' furious eyes and heard their muffled curses. I turned and ran without stopping until I reached the clinic.

That maze of crowded, understaffed wards was hardly a haven. I could find no reception desk at all, and walked through three rooms full of patients before I encountered a Chinese male nurse dressed in a blue, sweat-stained uniform. He was leaning over a teenage girl who lay in a cot raised six inches at most from the unswept floor, and whose bedsores were so deep that I could see the white glint of bone near her elbow. The nurse sprinkled a dark brown powder on the worst of the girl's several abscesses and prepared to lance it. The instrument he held could not have been sterilized. I turned away as he made his incision, and when I looked back, he was already hurrying from the room. I called out to him, but was so struck by the pallid hue of his face and the blankness of his expression that I forgot for an instant what I wanted to ask. He was no older than twenty-five. It was as though the torment and death all around him had drained the blood from his cheeks and hands. "What is it?" he said.

"Excuse me. I'm sorry to . . ."

"What is it?" he repeated sharply.

"I want to see Doctor Larsen. I have to show him this," I added, completely flustered, as I searched in my canvas bag for Miss Peterson's letter. I came across Mother's pumps and realized only then that I had forgotten to remove my mud-caked shoes. Before I could produce the letter, the nurse said Doctor Larsen was either in the burn-victim ward or the surgery room on the second floor, but that he most likely would not have time to see me. He left without another word.

There were patients lying everywhere, not just in the crowded wards themselves, but in the hallways and even on the staircase landings. Except for a single male child whose face had been badly burned and whose screams seemed to fill the whole building, everyone was quiet and practically motionless, and so apparently accepting of their fate that the sight almost angered me. Throughout the whole upper story, there was a repellent, sweet odor of burnt skin. I recalled with a shudder Lao Chang's account of the death of my uncle's servant, which I had not let myself believe until then. I could smell the scent that would attract rats, and I could see the wire-mesh screens that were lashed to the patients' low-lying pallets as a protection against the rodents at night.

Doctor Larsen was not to be found in the burn ward either, but I came upon an American woman who informed me in polite and perfect Mandarin that he was in the next room. When I thanked her, addressing her with the title of nurse, she corrected me with a smile, saying she was a doctor. That startled me. Miss Peterson had once told me that women could practice medicine in America, but I did not think such a thing would be permitted in China.

"What is it you want?" Doctor Larsen asked in quick Chinese when I approached him. He did not look up from the withered, grayish-black fingers of the man he was examining. Judging from the boots the patient wore, I guessed that he was a soldier whose hand had been crushed and who had been sent back from the front for treatment. He was being fed intravenously from a bottle hooked to a portable bamboo stand. When I did not immediately answer, Doctor Larsen turned to the nurse who was attending him and said in English (though the patient seemed heavily sedated and unable to hear him) that it was no use operating; that the gangrene had spread too far. "Yes?" he asked, half turning to me as he moved toward another bed. When I swiftly stated my request, he said only, "Impossible," and would have continued about his work. I handed him Miss Peterson's letter, which he quickly scanned. "There's no one better than Doctor Li," he said, "but he hasn't accepted a case in almost two years now, even from me, and . . ."

"If you'll just write me a note of introduction," I suggested, anxious to cost him as little time as possible.

"Doctor Li won't see you," he said plainly. "But even if he agreed to, how would you get your mother to the top of Mount Pehpei, Miss Yang? Are your father's connections good enough that he can arrange for jeep transport from the Americans?" I was ashamed of myself for doing it, but I lied to Doctor Larsen, telling him that Father himself was too ill to see to this matter and that that was why I had come to the clinic in his place. Assuming already that he would give me the letter of referral, I asked if he might also intervene on my behalf with the American military authorities and have them provide me a jeep and driver. I omitted saying that Mother could not be moved; that I intended to try to persuade Doctor Li to come to our house.

He laughed outright at my brazenness, his gray eyes wrinkling with delight. Then the nurse laughed too, perhaps for the first time in days, I thought, given the hysterical intensity of the outburst. Soon all the patients in the ward were gazing curiously in our direction.

Thirty minutes later I sat on a stone bench in a park that bordered the eighteen-year-old road in the northern sector of the city, Chungking's main paved thoroughfare. When an olive-green jeep drove up with a young American corporal at the wheel (the name tag on his shirt pocket said Hokenson), I exchanged smiles with him and climbed uncertainly into the rear seat. He had been given directions, he assured me, by his commanding officer. He was shy and hardly spoke, which suited my mood. I clutched Doctor Larsen's note in my hand and steeled myself for what lay ahead.

15

THE walled retreat of Doctor Li was not the fortress I had imagined, but a ruin. It sat like a damaged capstone at the crest of Mount Pehpei. The surrounding land was barren, as forbidding to the eye as the surface of a cold, dead planet. Small patches of the firs that flourished downslope stood out as mocking signs of life. Their upper limbs were withered, the needles parched to a sickly brown.

"Do you think that's it?" the corporal asked in dismay as the jeep quietly idled on the stretch of road that lay between the final bend in the ascent and a wall of crumbling terra-cotta. A huge wooden gate stood partially open. The top hinge of one portal was so damaged that the lower left corner of its oaken bulk seemed to have rooted permanently in the soil. The opening was small, but it offered a glimpse of a once-grand structure marred beyond the possibility of restoration by what looked like intentional neglect. The whitewash of the facade was faded and streaked by decades of rain. Two dead trees dominated a weed-covered court. And like the gate that framed this lifeless scene, the building's main door stood ajar.

I asked Corporal Hokenson to drive nearer, though the house looked uninhabited. He turned off the motor when we reached the gate, and the only sound we heard was the eerie whistle of the mountain wind in the branches of the firs. He looked back and smiled sympathetically, inviting me to acknowledge with him what fools we had made of ourselves by toiling up a deserted mountain. And yet, a moment later, a man in servant's clothes materialized in the dark recesses of the door opening. A hand reached out into the harsh sunlight and waved, as if to ward us off, then receded again into the darkness where the eyes still watched. When I told Corporal Hokenson that I might be a long time, and that there was a good chance our trip would turn out to have been in vain, he only shrugged and smiled. "It's not like I'm missing out on anything back there," he said.

I crossed the courtyard and called out a greeting from the marble sill. Every window was shuttered with rough-hewn boards. I grabbed the iron Fu dog affixed to the splintered face of the door, but the rusted nose ring would not budge. Then the man I had seen before cried, "What is it? What do you want here?" He stepped forward, moving with a hitch in his gait. He was completely bald and his head was tapered and leathery-skinned, like a serpent's. "Go away!" he warned in Szechuanese.

I entered the hall. The windows, besides being shuttered, were draped on the inside with lengths of black burlap that hung haphazardly from ceiling to floor. My eyes adjusted slowly to the change, and I could tell little else about the room, except that it smelled of dust. I had mastered my initial fear of the servant by then, and had determined that he would not stop me. His voice became shriller as I ignored his commands, and he gave ground, stopping when I stopped and scuttling aside when I changed direction in search for a passageway inward. I found an opening from which two corridors branched. When I chose one at random, the man fell silent. Still, as I wandered through one empty room after another, I heard him shuffling behind me. I came upon a kitchen and an aged cook who was kneading dough on a slab of smooth wood. I asked him several times, and in different dialects, where I might find his master. When he only turned back glumly to his labor, I walked on toward the rearmost quarters. It was there, in a space no larger than ten feet square, that I found the man I knew was Doctor Li.

That room was only slightly less somber than the others. A single stream of sunlight fell at a glancing angle through a vertical slit set high in one wall, and illumined the pages of a book that lay in the doctor's lap. A heavy brown blanket covered his lower body and dropped severely to the empty pedals of the wheelchair in which he sat. He scrutinized me with an air of detachment, apparently not the least curious as to how I had gotten there. I had never seen anyone who had undergone an amputation, and I was awed by the sight. I had to make myself stop staring at the blanket. The doctor's shoulders were so bent forward that there seemed to be no ribs in his chest. His forehead was as mottled by light brown spots as a sheet of ancient parchment, and his cheeks lay in folds over the corners of his ashen lips, further emphasizing the turned-in contours of his upper body. Still, though he was very old, there glowed in his face the same signs of exhilarating, almost reckless vigor that I had seen in my uncle, Wen-k'uan, before the catastrophe that befell him. The darkness of the house, and the fear of life that seemed to pervade everything, obscured, but could not quite obliterate, that quality.

"Jih-ch'uan!" he cried. The servant came in and began speaking excitedly in Szechuanese I could not follow. At one point his hands described in pantomime what I took to be the jeep. The doctor dismissed him with a curt nod of the head.

"Who are you?" he said testily.

"My name is Yang Hsiao-yen, the second daughter of Yang K'ai-tao."

"Professor Yang of Yenching University?" When I nodded, his expression softened, though he still did not smile. "What is it you want?"

"My mother is terribly ill, Doctor. We've been told she has tuberculosis, but . . ."

"I'm very sorry. I don't practice medicine any longer." When I made to protest, he raised a hand and said, "I'm not

able, Miss Yang." Pointing toward the blanket on his lap, he
smiled at last, but it was a forced, bitter smile.

"Doctor Larsen told me you might help us." I handed him
the note. He sighed before reading it, and again afterward.

"I would have thought he'd know not to ask such a favor
of me again. Then it was he who arranged for the jeep?"

"Yes."

"Very well," he said with petulance. "You may bring your
mother in here," and he indicated a small bed in the corner of
the room. "My servant will help you if necessary. What is it?"
he asked, as I delayed and tried to gather up my nerve.

"She was too sick to be moved this morning," I stammered.
"I'd hoped you might come with me to Chungking."

"To Chungking?" At first he looked amused by the proposal, then insulted. "That's out of the question, I'm afraid."
The situation was slipping beyond my control, and it made me
feel desperate.

"Please, Doctor, you must come."

"There isn't anything I *must* do." He pushed at the wheels of
his chair, and as he moved toward the doorway, the forgotten
book slipped from his lap to the floor. He stopped and said
without turning, "You presume too much, Miss Yang. You're
too forward in your manner. I can't do what you ask. . . . It
isn't possible. Now leave me."

"It *is* possible," I protested as we passed into the corridor.
He stopped again. "The soldier outside will help you." He listened to this without reacting, except to rub the armrest of his
chair with a clenched hand. Then he shook his head and
wheeled himself creakily down the hallway. Uncertain of what
to do, I followed behind him, moving at the slow pace he set.
When he steered the bulky apparatus through a doorway, I sat
outside the room in one of the hall chairs, willing neither to
force my presence on him again nor to give up hope. I felt I
could count on the patience of Corporal Hokenson. I was prepared to wait there indefinitely.

For nearly two hours, as it seemed to me, I sat in the corridor of that wretched house, listening to the minute sounds

that issued from what looked like a study. A section of book-shelf was visible through the open door, and I stared for long periods at the faded leather covers embossed with timeworn characters. Just as I felt myself lapsing into sleep, I heard the servant approaching from the front of the house. When he appeared, he was carrying a teacup on a salver. He looked at me scornfully as he passed. Inside the room, he and his master exchanged quiet words. There was the click of porcelain against wood, the sound of the doctor shifting position in his iron chair, the crackle of a page of parchment, the familiar dragging gait.

Once I was abandoned again to the dark silence, depression overtook me. For the first time, I gave over thinking I would ever succeed. I might even have walked away from that house if I had not felt immobilized by failure. But then the servant returned once more. This time the cup he carried rattled noisily on its tray. He stopped before reaching me, placed the tea on a tabouret, and withdrew. I rushed to the threshold of the study, where Doctor Li sat at a desk beside an oil lamp. His eyes were fixed on the doorway, as though he had been expect-ing me. I did not wait for him to speak, but fell immediately to my knees and kowtowed. Then I begged him, in my father's name, to go back with me to the city.

"And if I don't," he asked, "will you ever leave my hall-way?" His eyes and rigid mouth relaxed, signaling a change of mood. Then, when I least expected tears to come, I wept, out of relief for Mother's sake and out of an overwhelming sense of self-pity, until my body was wrenched with sobbing. Doctor Li turned aside to spare me. Moments later, when I had re-gained my composure, stood up, and made my face and dress as presentable as possible, he smiled and said, "Don't think you've compelled me to do as you wish. It's something else altogether." Now his smile faded a bit, so that it appeared to be only partly meant for me. "I was once the way you are," he said.

∽　∽　∽

Within a quarter hour's time Doctor Li, Corporal Hokenson, and I were ready for the arduous drive down Mount
Pehpei. The servant never showed himself again. Acting on the
doctor's instructions, I searched out various cases of medical
instruments, from which he selected a small assortment. The
corporal hoisted, as much as pushed, the wheelchair across the
uneven stones of the courtyard and lifted the doctor into the
jeep's rear seat. Then he jerry-rigged a brace made of cushions
and rope to protect against shocks. When the chair would fit
neither in the back seat nor in the small storage area, Doctor
Li said reluctantly that we might leave it behind.

It took us more than an hour and a half to descend into the
plain, traverse the Yangtze by means of a military launch, then
struggle in low gear up the dirt road to my neighborhood. It
was almost dusk when we reached the house. A much larger
crowd than the one that morning had gathered to watch. Lao
Chang was standing on our doorsill. He cast an incredulous
glance at the jeep, at the onlookers, at the jeep again, then
scurried inside.

I felt the weight of the collective stare, and knew at once
that I was being judged. There were scores of homeless young
women in Chungking — "jeep girls," Lao Chang once told me
they were called — who drove through the downtown streets
beside soldiers, and who traded their bodies for money and K
rations. I saw eyes that accused me of that. But as soon as the
corporal freed Doctor Li from his restraints and lifted him from
the rear seat, the crowd's attention shifted from me to the
doctor's scowling face and deformed body. In spite of the lap
blanket, which was wrapped about his waist and which he held
secured with one hand at his hip as he lay in the soldier's arms,
there were gasps of wonder on all sides. No one would move,
and I had to clear a path to the door by forcing people aside.

"Is Father home?" I asked Lao Chang when I encountered
him and Chang Ma, huddled in the little court between our
front door and the living area.

"No, Second Young Mistress. But if he hasn't heard yet,

he'll hear soon. The whole neighborhood saw you leave here this morning."

"Send for him right away. No, you'd better go yourself to his office. Tell him Doctor Li Chen-yu has come. Chang Ma, bring chairs into Mother's alcove. And towels and a pot of tea. Hurry!"

Chang Ma ran ahead and first calmed Mother. The sudden flurry of activity had excited her and set off a fit of coughing. The doctor, whom Corporal Hokenson set in a chair next to Mother's bed, told her not to speak. "Just rest until your husband arrives," he said in a firm but soothing voice. "I won't begin the examination until then."

Chang Ma brewed tea from the small store of special-grade leaves we owned and, as was the custom, laid out the canister in a place where the honored guest would be bound to see it. The delay lasted nearly an hour, and everyone but the doctor seemed ill at ease. Mother lay staring wide-eyed at the ceiling, unable to sleep but obeying the directive not to speak. Corporal Hokenson politely declined to sit or to drink tea. He stood beside the archway that led to the front room, just staring at the earthen floor and scraping its surface with the toe of one boot. The time passed slowly for me as well. Doctor Li's insistence on speaking with Father before beginning only served to remind me of how audaciously I had acted that day.

When Father arrived home, well ahead of Lao Chang, he was perspiring and out of breath. He looked confused by the scene in the alcove, and I realized that Cook had not dared to tell him all he knew. "Wait in the other room," he said to me, then dismissed Chank Ma just as curtly.

The next half hour was by far the most difficult part of that day for me. Though I stood against the wall of the living area, less than five feet away from the entrance to Mother's room, I could hear almost nothing for the longest time: murmured greetings; a brief discussion between Father and Doctor Li; the doctor asking Corporal Hokenson to bring him his bag of instruments; then silence. I peeked inside twice and was drawn both times to the face of Doctor Li, who appeared to have shed twenty years and all the bitterness I had seen in his eyes before.

The wait was long. But at the end, when I thought I would scream out just to break the tension, Mother herself cried, "You see? You see, Cato?" I rushed into the room. Mother was sitting up in bed, her hair lying disheveled on her shoulders and breast, her eyes alight with triumph. "Tuberculosis! That doctor was a charlatan. He would have sent me to my grave!" Her voice was clear and strong, giving the unnerving impression that a miraculous cure had already been effected.

"Please, *t'ai-t'ai*, don't strain yourself," Father said. Even as he did, Mother fell back on her pillow and was wracked again by coughing.

"What happened?" I asked anxiously. Doctor Li must have said something that only I had not heard. The fear in Father's face was gone. He smiled when I pleaded with him to tell me what he knew.

"It isn't what we thought, Hsiao-yen. It's pleurisy. And there's a medicine that can cure it."

That night I lay awake in bed, waiting for Father. I was sure he would come, but I did not know whether he would chastise me or forgive me for what I had done. For a long time I thought about all the places I had been since that morning, all the people I had seen, all the things I had made myself do. I would listen to whatever he had to say and apologize for the shame I knew I had caused him. But I would not let him leave without telling him of the sense of satisfaction I felt. I would remind him of the evening we had spent together at the opera in Peking: of the White Snake Spirit, who climbed to the top of the Enchanted Mountain and brought back the healing herb. I drifted into sleep, half dreaming, half waiting for Father, who never came.

16

FOR more than three months, well into the final summer of the war, I stayed home and helped nurse Mother back to health. On the morning following Doctor Li's visit, Father went to the city and bought on the black market, at great expense, the sulfathiazole Doctor Li had prescribed. I administered the medicine to Mother for nearly a week at four-hour intervals, night and day, making her drink large amounts of preboiled water, as the doctor had cautioned, to guard against kidney damage. By the fifth day, Mother's fever and chest pains were gone, and her coughing was significantly reduced. Weeks later, Doctor Larsen paid us an unsolicited visit, sending Father a message during work hours and arriving at nine in the evening. He pronounced Mother well on the way to recovery. "All you need now, Mrs. Yang," he said to her, and in my father's presence, "is a couple of months of rest in your daughter's competent care." I had never felt prouder of myself.

In my free time at night I wrote letters of gratitude to Doctor Larsen, Doctor Li, and Corporal Hokenson, whom I had never had a chance to thank adequately, and to Miss Peterson, whom I also asked to send me my English grammar text and a boxload of novels.

"You did well, Katherine," Mother said to me one morning

in the third week of her convalescence. "But you look troubled. Don't you believe that I'm grateful for what you did?"

"I do, Mother," I answered quickly. "That isn't it. I'm worried about what Father must have felt the evening Doctor Li came. The shame I caused him."

"Some people know there are things they have to do," she said, "regardless of the consequences to themselves or to others. I'm that way, and so are you."

"And Father?"

"He's different from us," she whispered, though no one else was in the house. She smiled in her peculiar way. "Still, he understands."

"I want to tell him why I did what I did that day."

"He won't ever talk to you about what happened. But you should know that he forgives you."

Those words made me feel resentful, but it was not until I mulled them over by myself that I understood why. I came to see that Father should have been thankful, not forgiving. I had done what it was his responsibility to do. What he had not been resourceful enough, strong enough, to do. It should never have been left to me to find Doctor Li and bring him to our house. I finally admitted to myself that Father was a man like other men, not all-powerful or all-wise. And that realization made me feel lonelier than I had ever felt before.

In July, Mother insisted that I return to the mission school and remain there until I had made up my missed classes and received my diploma. She instructed Father to call Alice home to tend to her needs, though that decision threatened to postpone my sister's graduation indefinitely.

My last months at school were different from before. The girls in my accelerated class had long since left, and every other friend I had there graduated in early August, leaving me behind to complete my studies under the tutelage of the school's entire faculty. And so on August 10, 1945, I was twenty-two miles from Chungking, sequestered in the mountains of Szechuan Provice, when the Japanese surrendered.

Every day dispatches arrived at the school, giving the particulars of the week-long spate of fireworks and music and twenty-course banquets marking the end of eight years of virtual expatriation, and celebrating that curious brand of victory that consists of the heroic avoidance of defeat.

Miss Peterson and I threw our own little party on September 2, the day of the formal capitulation ceremonies in Tokyo Bay. We cooked a feast of stewed chicken, cabbage, turnips, and rice-dough pastries, and served it in her quarters to all the teachers and staff. There were thirteen of us in all. We ate, made speeches, and sang Chinese folk tunes and American college football songs until we were hoarse. I, too, ate and sang, but I never quite entered into the mood of the festivities. Everyone there was older than I was by at least ten years, yet I knew there were other reasons — reasons that went deeper than the fact that I was to leave Faith Baptist Mission School the next morning, most likely never to see Miss Peterson or any of the others again. I felt differently about the war than they all did, I finally decided. My history and math teachers had lived for a time in occupied Nanking. And even the school's cook, who danced about and poured rice wine all evening long, had fought for two years at the Ch'in Valley front. I had never once seen a Japanese soldier. And I had only the vaguest, third-hand impressions of such men as Chiang Kai-shek, General Wedemeyer, General Stilwell before him, Claire Chennault, Mao Tse-tung, Chou En-lai, and all the other American, Kuomintang, and Communist leaders whose political maneuverings every guest at that party seemed prepared to discuss for hours on end. I found that I did not care about the causes of this conflict that had brought so much death and disgrace, nor about which faction or alliance of factions would control China's government, now that the killing had at last come to an end. In that highly educated and politically aware gathering, I felt limited, immature, even selfish, for caring only about the hardships the war had caused my family. The separations, the poverty, the sickness and near death of my mother, and a more troubling wound — one that I could scarcely let myself think about yet.

Later that evening, when everyone else had left, I was able to tell Miss Peterson how uninvolved I felt in the general jubilation, and how much I knew I was going to miss her. But I did not bare my deepest hurt. I kept to myself my disillusionment with Father.

We were going to live in Shanghai. None of us but Mother, whose decision, of course, it was, knew why we were not returning to our beloved Peking. "The Mistress still has family in Shanghai," Cook whispered to me, trying to bury his disappointment in the pleasure it gave him to impart this inside information. "She's written her sister and brother-in-law there. I posted the letter myself, Second Young Mistress. Who knows? Perhaps they'll help us."

We obtained passage on the first American warship scheduled to evacuate refugees from Chungking to the coast. In the third week of September, Mother, Father, my sisters, Lao Chang, Chang Ma, and I went one final time to the Yangtze landing at the foot of the broad stone steps. When we saw how crowded the ship's deck was, we left onshore all but our money box, Mother's remaining jewelry, and an armful each of clothing. There was great excitement in the air. Everyone — coolies, soldiers, merchants, and gentry alike — talked of nothing but their confident hopes for a prosperous, untroubled future. It seemed no time to dwell on the past, yet as we steamed out of the harbor toward the gorges downriver, all I felt was relief at leaving behind the remorseless, killing decay of Chungking.

PART V

Shanghai

17

THE engine let out a mechanical scream, and the ship jerked upward in the evening tide. We were slowing down. Mother quickly started fussing over the four of us, fixing our hair, straightening our dresses. "Move out of the wind," she said. My sisters obeyed, but I kept my place next to Father at the deck's railing. I wanted to see.

"There, Hsiao-yen!" Father cried, pointing downriver to where the city's tallest buildings rose above the Whangpoo's muddy flow. "There it is!"

The closer we got to Shanghai, the more beautiful and fantastic it became. I felt as though I were sailing into an imaginary city, a place Lao Chang might have conjured up in my youth. The buildings reached ten and twenty stories into the rose-colored sky — silhouettes of an impossible height. Blue, red, and yellow neon lights flashed crazily on the shoreline, advertising the names of stores in a jumble of English letters and Chinese characters. Even from a distance and in the pale light of dusk, I could sense a pulsing urgency all around me. In the swarm of sampans choking the junction of the river and Soochow Creek. In the narrow streets of what Father called the Native City, a teeming ghetto crammed with slow-moving traffic and lurid signs that clashed so excitingly with the staid grace of the Bund's looming skyscrapers. In the pounding and squealing of industrial machinery that, anywhere else, would have fallen silent at the end of day. Here was a city to make me forget Chungking with its bomb and fire damage and its dismal gray mists. A city that appeared to have survived eight years of occupation without losing its spirit. For the first time, I felt that the war was indeed over, that China could succeed in rebuilding itself, and that I could somehow take part in that great challenge. "Mother was right," I said to myself. "This is where we should live."

We came to rest well short of the pier, which was too jammed with boat traffic for us to dock there. Before our ship's anchor had even splashed into the harbor water, we were surrounded by a flotilla of junks and sampans from whose decks peddlers hawked steamed vegetables, oranges, fresh water, items of clothing, and, their most exorbitant offering, quick transportation to the shore.

Mother yelled so loud at the first boatman who came within earshot that he looked positively alarmed. Then she and the man screamed at each other in Shanghai dialect for a minute or so, after which the boatman smiled while Mother flung several pieces of silver at his head. Other passengers and merchants were now making deals and accommodations on all sides. "Cato, girls, Lao Chang, Chang Ma, come along!" Mother clamored above the racket. We climbed over the railing, one by one. With the help of the grinning boatman, we boarded the sampan and left behind the chaos of the ship's crowded deck.

It was not as though we were escaping to some quiet haven. The pier itself was filled with well-wishers. It had the flavor of a market about it, as vendors shouted the names of their wares and clattered their worn-beaded abacuses. How quickly Shanghai showed her face, I thought. It was a city of noise and money and, above all, speed. A city that had absorbed a multiplicity of cultures to create an atmosphere where, it seemed, almost any kind of behavior would be tolerated, as long as one kept up with the harrowing pace.

"Auntie! Auntie!" we heard from afar. It was a young man

of about twenty with four servants in tow. He smiled and waved to us the whole time he battled his way through the crowd.

"My eldest nephew," Mother murmured to Father. "They should have come themselves to welcome us."

The Ling house was a mansion in the heart of the French Concession. Everything looked fresh and different to me, beginning with the tall, black wrought-iron gate that swung out onto Rue Joffre. I knew at once I was far removed from our bungalow in the South Bank neighborhood of Chungking, and even from the elegant pavilions of my grandfather's estate. At Yenching we had had a western lawn and varnished wooden door, but nothing that compared in splendor with the garden, fountain, and marble entranceway I now encountered. My cousin showed us into the drawing room, where I counted the things I had come across in novels but had never actually seen before: a parquet floor made of four different woods, a Persian rug, a rosewood grand piano, a black-marble mantelpiece aswirl with delicate white veins. There was mahogany wainscoting, a settee covered in purple velvet, and, hanging ten feet above my head, a crystal chandelier. My first thought was that anyone who lived there must be happy.

My aunt and uncle came in and greeted my parents warmly. Their speech and movements were as refined as their surroundings, but the traditional Chinese garments they wore made them look out of place, as if they, too, were only visiting that day. Uncle looked the classic Chinese scholar — tall, serious, with searching eyes and silver-gray hair. Mother had told me during the journey east that he was a highly respected figure in the academic community. In 1938 he had resigned as Dean of Admissions at Shanghai University, refusing to follow the dictates of the wartime puppet government. "Now he's resumed his post," she had said, "and is certain to offer your father a position at the university."

My aunt was a thin, round-faced woman of perhaps forty. Her dark brown hair was coiled in a braided bun. Her complexion was very fair, her deep blue *ch'i-p'ao* and pearl earrings making her face look even whiter than Mother's. It was a pleasure to hear the words of welcome she had for each of us, for she spoke with a gentle voice that immediately conveyed self-assurance and contentment. I was struck more by that aura of security than by my aunt's obvious physical resemblance to Mother. A stranger, I mused, might not even have guessed they were sisters.

As my aunt and uncle's daughters came into the room and were introduced, I saw Mother direct a knowing glance toward Alice. Who could claim, she seemed to be asking, that her two gangly nieces were any match for the four Yang girls? But when the Lings' firstborn son next rejoined us, trailing three strapping brothers behind him, the glow in Mother's eyes quickly dimmed.

The Lings were astoundingly generous to us. Their home and most of its furnishings were ours as of that evening, my uncle announced. He was moving his family into a house on campus that the university had provided. Father thanked him profusely and explained that we hoped to impose on them only until such time as he could reestablish contact with his family in Hunan.

"You're welcome to stay here as long as you wish," my uncle said. "Also, K'ai-tao," he added with a kindly smile, "if you're disposed to head the political science department at Chung Ta College, I've arranged it so that the position is yours."

According to Lao Chang, Mother was less than totally pleased with what she saw as her sister and brother-in-law's charity. "Your mother admits that Chung Ta is an excellent school, Second Young Mistress, but she can't believe there was no opening at the university for the Master, and I confess I tend to agree with her." I felt sorry for Mother; her envy of her sister was so evident. Once I had heard her grumble to Chang Ma, "How is it, I wonder, that they did so well for themselves, even during the years of the occupation?" And I had known, from the pinched look of her mouth and eyes, that we would not be seeing much of the Lings.

The splendor of our surroundings seemed to impel Mother to spend freely, and during those first months in Shanghai we lived beyond our means. Professors' salaries had dropped dramatically from their prewar levels, and the inflation rate had continued to rise unchecked, yet Mother remained confident that her father-in-law's purse would more than bridge the difference. She entertained as often as she had in Peking, and with the same uncanny eye for strategy, cultivating only those best placed to restore my father to a position of prominence. Mother enrolled Victoria and Joan in a private Methodist school, and Alice in an expensive music academy. I too received special treatment. During the long river voyage I had given a great deal of thought to my experiences with Doctor Li and Doctor Larsen. I was contemplating a career in medicine, but had not yet gotten up the nerve to tell Mother. Still, thanks to Professor Ling's patronage and my exemplary scholastic record, I was accepted into the freshman year liberal arts program at the university, despite my youth. In addition, Mother paid the daughter of an American diplomat to tutor me in English on the weekends.

We allowed ourselves new conveniences as well, such as our first telephone. And every Sunday afternoon we went to Jessville Park, traveling in pedicabs — that ingenious cross between a bicycle and a rickshaw. We would set out at noon and snake our way through the best neighborhoods of the city, always avoiding the run-down Hongkew district, north of Soochow Creek, and always passing by the house on Rue Cardinal Mercier where Mother was born. We would ogle the well-heeled foreigners and the Chinese dandies strolling the Bund's boulevard with their walking sticks and bowlers. Week after heady week, we perpetuated the illusion that we were wealthy.

One Friday evening in February 1946, I arrived home late from school, as I often did toward the end of my first semester. Friends of mine at the university had invited me to sit in at their extracurricular discussions of social and political issues.

I had been curious enough to attend and to listen to their heated denunciations of the Kuomintang regime, but I felt too uninformed to express my own views, and too wary of arousing Mother's suspicion to stay much longer than an hour each time. That evening it was almost half past six when I hurried through the iron gate and heard Lao Chang whistle to me from the door at the back of the house. He raised a finger to his lips as I joined Chang Ma and him in the kitchen.

"Where is everyone?"

"Your parents are in the dining room," Cook whispered. "They sent your sisters upstairs and canceled the dinner party they had planned for tonight."

"Why? What happened?" The dining room was only ten feet away, yet I could not hear a sound in there.

"A messenger came . . . a messenger with a letter from Sinhwa Valley."

Chang Ma had put a cup of tea in front of me. I set it aside and went into the dining room, where I found Mother and Father sitting across the table from each other. Father was staring at the far wall, while Mother pored over the closely written sheets that lay between them. "What is it, Mother?" I asked.

"K'ai-ying has . . ."

Father glared at her and she fell silent. It was a startling thing to see. "Your grandfather . . ." he said in a faltering voice, "your grandfather is dead."

"And that isn't all," Mother said bitterly.

"That's all, *t'ai-t'ai*," Father interrupted her, rising and walking toward me. He stroked my hair as I leaned against his chest and wept.

"How did he die, Father?" I asked quietly, not wanting Mother to hear me.

"I don't know, Hsiao-yen. The message didn't say."

"*Two years* ago it happened," Mother cried, unable to restrain herself. "She saw fit to wait that long before informing us." Father shook his head and left the room. "She's sold the mine," Mother went on. She would have said what she had to say even if I, too, had dared to walk away. She pushed the sheets of rice paper toward me. "Look, Katherine. The letter is in the hand of the majordomo, Liu, but it's the work of your First Aunt. She blames the exorbitant wartime taxes. Nowhere does she mention her father's gambling debts, or the bills of the Changsha opium dealers, or . . ."

"May I be excused, Mother?"

"*Look,* Katherine. You must understand this. They're almost bankrupt — everything's gone. They want your father to go back and manage what's left. There's no chance of that," she said with a harsh smile. "Let your First Aunt run the place. That's what she always wanted to do, anyway."

That night in our bedroom I tried to talk with Alice about Grandfather's death, but it did not mean to her what it meant to me. Although the formality of our relationship had given me no chance to express it, I had felt affection for Grandfather, an affection whose depth I was just now discovering. Even Father, who had been with Grandfather for only one week of his adult life, must have grieved for a man very different from the one I had observed at such close quarters.

"Did you ever see Grandfather laugh, Older Sister? He could laugh so hard."

"I'm sorry for you, Hsiao-yen. I know you were his favorite."

It was the third time Alice had said that. Her mind was elsewhere. And there was a note of excitement, almost impatience in her voice, something she was trying her best to stifle. "What are you thinking about?" I finally asked her.

"Nothing, Hsiao-yen. I don't want to bring it up now, not tonight. Another time."

"What is it?"

"Han Liang-ming," she said after a long pause. "He's returned here, to his mother's home." Alice sighed, as though she had just relieved herself of the weight of a shameful secret. He must have come back well before today, I thought. Alice must have been meeting him and hiding everything from Mother, Father, and even me. Yet she had been right to hesitate. I was in no mood to discuss Liang-ming. I turned over in my bed and continued to think about Grandfather — who had singled me out from all the others and called me Winter Swallow — until sleep came.

We were poor again, and my parents' circle of friends must soon have suspected that was so, regardless of our grand surroundings. Father began writing political articles for a fee, as he had had to do in Chungking. While Mother managed to keep my sisters and me in the schools we were attending, she abandoned her plans to move out of the Ling mansion. She drastically curtailed her invitation list as well, and eventually stopped entertaining altogether.

Our lack of money never bothered me; I had other things on my mind. I did well in the first year of my liberal arts studies, but by the early spring of 1947 I had firmly decided to enter the field of nursing, and only looked for a favorable opportunity to broach the subject to Mother. I recalled what Miss Peterson had told me at the Baptist school, and thought at first I might apply for training as a doctor. But there were things I had seen in Shanghai — things other students had helped me to see — that persuaded me to take the quicker course.

In the academic community of postwar Shanghai, politics was an all-consuming passion. In public forums, when such debate was permitted, and in clandestine gatherings at night, young people argued the merits of the truce that the Nationalists and Communists had struck in Chungking, the breakdown of that tenuous alliance, and Chiang Kai-shek's military offensive against the Communist stronghold of Yenan. During 1946 and early 1947, that struggle in far-off Shensi Province did not impress the Shanghai populace as a full-fledged civil war, and I was of the same complacent opinion. Nor did the campus dissidents' allegations of Kuomintang corruption interest me at first. Even Lao Chang often waved me into the kitchen after the evening meal and tried to engage me in discussions of the "gossip" he had heard from sources he refused to identify: for example, that the Generalissimo's relatives were profiting immensely from each sudden shift in the government's fiscal policies. I was sixteen at the time and a year or two younger than everyone else in my class at school. I used that as an excuse for not taking an active political stance; that and my Baptist principal's convenient words of caution about not saying or doing anything in public that might reflect unfavorably on my father.

But on a winter morning in January of 1947, I accepted the often repeated invitation of one of my classmates and accompanied her to an area she called "the hidden Shanghai" — the most wretched slums of the Hongkew district.

At first I could scarcely believe what I was seeing. It was as though I had been thrown back three years to the Village of the Dying in Chungking. Just as in that foul pocket of the war capital, there were hundreds of destitute families living on the streets, some of them completely exposed to the freezing air and the filth of the gutters, others crouching beneath crude lean-tos made of tire rubber, scraps of cardboard, and flattened gasoline cans. There were people who looked dreadfully sick, and child beggars whom their parents pushed forward so that they might beg us for coins.

"It's just like it was during the war," I said faintly, sickened by the smell of human feces and so disillusioned that I had to turn away.

"It *isn't,*" my friend insisted. "It's worse than that, Hsiao-yen. I lived in Chungking too for a time, and saw the poorest of the refugees. But this is different. There are refugees here — refugees from the civil war the government would have us believe is not being fought. But most of these people aren't refugees from anything. This is the way they've always lived."

I forced myself to look again, and in the devastated eyes and sticklike limbs of a girl who could not have been older than thirteen, I saw the difference for myself.

"She's a one-dollar whore and a drug addict," my fellow student said. "If you were a man, she would have accosted you by now, and that policeman at the next corner would have turned his face away. She's probably lived on this street her whole life, a ten-minute pedicab ride from the Bund. In a year, maybe less, she's likely to die of an overdose or a knife wound, and the members of one of the benevolent societies will gather up her corpse with the others the next morning."

"That's all," I said, starting to walk blindly in the direction from which we had come. "I don't want to see any more."

That same day a group of my friends pressed me to join their growing number; to take part in public demonstrations and help them disseminate anti-Kuomintang leaflets. Though I refused, I made my decision then to apply to nursing school. From then on, too, I attended the student meetings more regularly and listened longer and more intently. For I had proof now — not that the Communist philosophy was right, but that much of the existing order was wrong.

18

IN the spring of 1947, Father received in the mail a crisp, beige calling card. On it was printed, in ornate English script, the words: *Dr. Leonard Hsu / New York, Paris, Shanghai.* "Your Uncle Leonard is back!" Father cried to me, as if I knew the man. He leaped up from his parlor chair and hurried away, actually laughing out loud, to spread the news through the household.

Father had mentioned Uncle Leonard before, but I could not remember any particulars. When I asked Mother about him, she said he was a close friend of Father's from the years before the war. Until 1929, he had been Dean of Sociology at Yenching. When he left China to go to America, he bequeathed the position to Father. Mother wrinkled her nose. "He smelled the war from a distance of eight years, Katherine." Her lips spread into a smile, and I could hear a fresh lilt in her voice. "You won't ever meet anyone like him. He has a doctorate from a famous university in America called Stanford, a wife with blond hair, and two children. Can you imagine, two children by an American wife!"

Father came in, his face still beaming. "Apparently he's given up his teaching career, *t'ai-t'ai.*"

"For something far more lucrative, I'm sure."

"Is he coming here?" I asked.

"Next week," Father replied, "according to the note on the back of the card."

"Very good," Mother said. "I'm dying to know what scheme could have lured him back from the West."

Uncle Leonard arrived in Shanghai on a Tuesday evening. When he walked into our house the following night for a family dinner, I was surprised to see how short he was. But he was a good-looking man in his prime: smooth-complexioned, strong of build, slightly balding, and possessed of a warm, ingratiating smile. In his blue double-breasted suit and gold silk tie, he looked to me like a model in a fashion magazine. His shoes were of lustrous brown leather and wing-tipped. A spanking white handkerchief was sticking out of his jacket pocket, showing the initials "L. H." in gold embroidery. Uncle Leonard embraced my parents as if it had been the day the war ended. The house was in a frenzy of laughter and tears. His arms were everywhere, flailing about. He trotted over to Alice, who was almost as tall as he was, exclaiming, "But how is this possible, Cato? She's all grown-up!" None of us knew what to say to him. We just giggled helplessly.

Lao Chang prepared an exquisite dinner that night. For all his past griping about the food in Chungking, he cooked a meal whose two main courses were Szechuan specialties: duck boiled in tea then smoked in camphorwood chips, and strips of dried beef fried with hot peppers, carrots, and celery.

The evening was a triumph for Mother. She had prompted us on how we should act. As was our guest's preference, we spoke nothing but English. And — partly because of Mother's instructions, but mostly because he was so enthralling — we listened attentively to Uncle Leonard's tales about life in California. "You know of the place, Kathie?" he asked me with a wink, using the nickname Miss Peterson had first given me. "The place where all the movie stars are?"

Even then, when I scarcely knew Leonard Hsu, I was certain I was going to like him. He was full of humor and practically bursting with energy, and he had a delightful sense of mischief that made it impossible to believe he had ever been a university professor.

Uncle Leonard announced during dessert that he would be staying in Shanghai to drum up business for Reynolds Metal Corporation. Although he had not brought his family along, he expected to remain in the city "for some time." At that point Mother glanced at Father, who immediately offered a room in our house.

"Thank you, Cato, that's generous of you," Uncle Leonard replied, "but the company has made adequate arrangements" — which turned out to be a four-room suite at the plush Park Hotel. Mother's eyes saddened at that news. As Chang Ma served the expensive cognac and chocolates that my uncle had brought with him as presents, she brushed aside subtlety and made her move.

"Hasn't Katherine grown to be a beauty?" she asked. I wanted to hide my face in my napkin.

"All four of your daughters are gorgeous," he gallantly replied, making a graceful, sweeping gesture with his hand. "In America we'd call them 'peaches.'"

"Yes, but Katherine would make an ideal goddaughter, I should think." I lowered my head in embarrassment; tonight, Mother's nerve was unbounded.

"Ideal indeed," Uncle Leonard rejoined, "for the unworthy man lucky enough to be chosen as her godfather." He smiled at me, and I thanked him silently. Before I knew what was happening, Mother had shepherded me to a carpeted area of the floor and told me to kowtow to my new godfather and future protector.

Uncle Leonard and I were to see a great deal of each other. In late May he asked Father if I might act as a kind of hostess at the weekly social functions he planned to sponsor for business and political leaders later in the year. Father discussed the idea several times with Mother. He was uncertain whether the Sky Terrace of the Park Hotel was a suitable environment for his sixteen-year-old daughter. I arrived at the end of their last argument on the subject, and saw Mother counter my father's misgivings with a peevish toss of the head. "It's what I've been waiting for, Cato," she snapped, "and that's all there is to it." My parents were taking the air in our garden at the time, strolling along the pathway beside the gray wall that surrounded our grounds. Mother asked me to wait while she and Father finished their conversation. Ten minutes later she joined me at my favorite retreat, a stone bench set under a great willow tree.

Before Mother even had the chance to bring up the matter of Leonard Hsu's parties, I asked her permission to register that autumn at the university's nursing school. Her initial reaction was a shocked silence. Then she smiled sarcastically and said, "Haven't I taught you not to adopt halfway measures, Katherine? Why don't we sign you up for medical school and be done with it?"

"I've thought about that, Mother, but I don't want to wait six or seven years to start my career."

"Your career!" There followed a tirade on why a professional career was inconceivable for any of her daughters. Young women of my class did not accept compensation for displaying their talents, she explained. "Can you imagine your sister playing music in some public hall for money?" Mother cried triumphantly. I regarded that as a fairly plausible idea, but my mother obviously thought it was a crushing point. "And to do what *you* propose!" she went on, shaking her head. "To expose yourself to strangers' diseases, and to touch their bodies . . ."

I took a deep breath. "I'll do what you came here to ask me to do, Mother, if you'll be kind enough to let me enter nursing school." The blatancy of the extortion caused a moment of silence. When Mother spoke again her voice was low and threatening.

"Are you suggesting, Katherine, that you'd even think of passing up this opportunity Leonard Hsu is offering?"

"This opportunity for what, Mother?"

"Why are you torturing me with your impudence?" she exploded. "Why do you pretend you don't know what I want for you? Is it such a terrible thing to wish one's daughter to marry well?"

"There are things that are more important to me right now, Mother. Much more important than finding a husband."

"Is that so? Please tell me what's more important than the well-being of your family? After all, it's not only you I'm thinking about here."

"It's not only me *I'm* thinking about, either," I wanted to cry out. I wanted to tell her about the stomach-bloated children I had seen in the Native City, the makeshift houses, and the empty-eyed teenage prostitute. I wanted to tell her that I intended to contribute to the healing of China's wounds, however I was able. Yet I cared too deeply about those things to submit them to her scornful laugh.

"Until you can think of an answer," she said, "I'll ask you to prepare yourself to attend your uncle's parties." Her voice became almost conciliatory. "A good number of the country's most eligible bachelors will show up there sooner or later, Katherine. You'll have your pick. They'll see that you've had every advantage and all the training you need to be an important man's wife." She continued in that vein, but I could not let myself listen.

"Maybe you're right, Mother," I said calmly. "Maybe I *am* of the age when I should be looking for a husband." She glanced at me warily. "But at the same time, it seems to me that nursing school might be a . . . safer atmosphere for me than the university's main campus, where everyone's running around, screaming about politics. And there are things one learns in nursing school that would be useful for any wife or mother."

Mother's lips formed the tight, reluctant smile I had seen the day the letter announcing Grandfather's death had arrived from Hunan. She nodded in acceptance of the compromise. The look we exchanged before she left the garden was more expressive than any words could have been. She did not have to tell me that she considered my career plans an adolescent notion I would soon outgrow. Nor did I have to tell her that I planned to decide for myself when to begin looking for a man to marry.

I spent less time than I should have on schoolwork for the rest of that semester. With her accustomed verve and determination, Mother transformed our household, during the spring and summer months, into the equivalent of a finishing school whose curriculum focused exclusively on me. "Katherine must shine," she said once to Father, "and she will, you'll see. If she doesn't stand out from the rest, Cato, I'll gladly take the blame."

Uncle Leonard presented Mother with an unlimited budget to help prepare me for his gala dinner-dances. I was to have high-heeled shoes, stockings, jewelry, coats, and a closetful of evening dresses. Merchants and tailors paraded to our house with their finest fabrics: pink and blue silks, deep red velvets, multicolored brocades, and yards of black and pastel-hued chiffon. Though I preferred the more comfortable western designs ideally suited to ballroom dancing, Mother chose for me as well several *ch'i-p'ao*s that hugged the contours of my newly matured figure. I had two favorite dresses — a cream-colored satin with gold piping at the right shoulder, and a gold-and pink-flowered brocade.

English became the official language at our house that summer for everyone but Cook and Chang Ma, who must have been made to feel like exiles. We ate with silverware instead of chopsticks, and with linen napkins that Chang Ma had to launder, starch, and iron each day. My place setting always included a crystal wine glass, from which I sipped a small portion of claret every evening while Joan and Victoria watched in awe. (That was Father's idea. "I won't have her drinking liquor with Leonard's clients," he told Mother. "Let her learn to nurse an ounce or two of wine.") Mother taught me how to shake hands "in the feminine style," letting my hand lie limply, and how to look directly into the eyes of an American or European man when conversing with him.

("Don't be shy, Katherine, it's what they prefer. They'll dismiss you as backward otherwise.")

After dinner, three nights a week, a young man named Henry Brown would show up on our doorstep, a portable victrola in one hand, a sheaf of record albums in the other. He was the son of an American military attaché who had studied with Father in the States. "Mr. Brown," as I was instructed to address him, taught ballroom dancing at the Arthur Murray Studio in the Bund every weekday. At night he was paid to tutor me. Under Mother's vigilant eye, I learned the Fox-trot, Peabody, Lindy, Viennese Waltz, and, by far my favorite, the Tango. "Don't smile, Katherine!" Mother would scold from her armchair as I stalked across the carpetless drawing room floor in my high heels, following the expert lead of the suave Mr. Brown. "It's *never* right to smile when one tangos." My instructor confirmed every point she made. It was not that he was simply toadying to her, either; she was always correct. She had read enough American magazines and seen enough movies to know.

Every night before going to sleep, I spent a quarter hour in front of a floor-length mirror that Mother had Lao Chang hang on the bedroom wall. There I preened myself in my new possessions, trying on different combinations until I had put together the greatest possible number of outfits. "Just the thing for your first day at nursing school," Alice once gently taunted. And though her remark did prick my conscience, I succeeded in blotting it from my mind. This was my first real wardrobe, and I would not be made to feel guilty about how smart I looked in those clothes, how like a proper adult. I was not unaware that our family had come full circle. Mother was reconstructing the western ambience she had first created in our Peking days, and this time I was a salient feature in her design. Yet I felt I was strong enough to keep that process in perspective. I would not forgo the luxuries being handed to me. After Chungking, I convinced myself, I was entitled to them.

∾　∾　∾

Three months later I had second thoughts as to whether I could reconcile the seemingly opposed facets of my life. Right from the beginning, nursing school was a grueling, though highly satisfying, discipline. In addition to six days of classes each week, we did ten hours of duty at a hospital on Avenue of Two Republics. While Uncle Leonard's extravaganzas were a pleasurable break from my studies and clinic work, I wondered whether I could afford the time and energy they required.

There was the dinner party itself every Saturday night, which came on the heels of a full day of anatomy and chemistry classes. The ballroom of the Park Hotel was spectacular, and at the edge of the dance floor, Uncle Leonard sat at the head of a table long enough to accommodate the sixteen businessmen, diplomats, and government officials he invited each week, as well as their wives or girlfriends. As his guests drank French wine and dined on a succession of exotic dishes (I had my first taste of lobster there, my first oxtail soup, borscht, Wiener schnitzel, and baked Alaska), my uncle gesticulated gaily in his maroon leather armchair, drawing out the quiet members of the company, dispensing free business advice, connecting people who could be helpful to one another, telling comical anecdotes about his beloved American way of life, and all the time waving the tumbler of champagne that was his trademark. At eight o'clock, a ten-piece orchestra of Filipino musicians, decked out in tuxedos, would strike up the first tune. For the Chinese guests, at least, there was perhaps never a more wonderful time or place to dance. As an austerity measure during the war, dancing had been outlawed in Chungking. And so, to move gracefully to music over the Park's gleaming ballroom floor gave one a kind of healing, liberating thrill. Uncle Leonard himself did not dance. He chatted all night long beside one of the broad red pillars that demarcated the dancing area, or in front of the magnificent wall-length window that overlooked the light-festooned harbor and Bund. I, on the other hand, never rested. As Mother had predicted, I was the most sought-after dancing partner there. "This is the daughter of Professor Cato Yang," Uncle Leonard would say to one politician or military officer after another, and soon I would be out in the middle of the floor, performing the steps that had come so easily to me in our drawing room and making my twentieth new acquaintance of the evening.

Even when I arrived home at two o'clock in the morning, I had not yet completed the weekend ritual. Seven hours later I went right back to the hotel with the rest of my family, where Uncle Leonard treated all of us to a Sunday-morning waffle breakfast. Then he would take us to the racecourse, or to the French Club for bowling, then to tea dancing at the Ambassador Hotel, ending with a round of ice cream, coffee, and pastries in his suite. It would be late in the afternoon by the time we finally got home. With most of my one free day frittered away, I would have to dive at once into my preparation for the next week's classes.

One Saturday night that winter I heard my uncle call out "Kathie!" over the blare of the band music. I turned to see him beckoning to me from his seat at the head of the table. I hesitated an instant. The tall figure sitting next to him looked so out of place there that I thought I must be mistaken. "Dr. Yang," Uncle said in the protective tone he always used when introducing me, "please meet the daughter of Professor Cato Yang."

"Would you like to dance, Miss Yang?" Father asked.

Uncle Leonard chuckled and toasted us as we took the floor and began dancing to a ballad. I felt a bit hot and dizzy, and wondered if Father guessed that I had drunk a full glass of wine at dinner instead of my usual half. I wondered, too, what he thought of Leonard Hsu's assembled guests, a few of whom were behaving less than decorously, or of the sprinkling of captivating young Chinese women in the party, whose profession might be divined by a certain eagerness to please.

It was strange to dance in Father's arms. What should have been a moment of special closeness was not. It touched me that he had come to look in on me, yet I was distracted by how different he looked from this company of revelers, who seemed oblivious to everything but music and drink. The very simplicity of his dress and manner reminded me that there were poor people living on the streets outside, and that Chinese were fighting Chinese only several hundred miles away.

"I'd like to go home now, Father," I whispered before the music had even ended.

"What?" he said in mock disappointment. "This is my big night out, Hsiao-yen!"

"Please, I'm not feeling well at all."

Father made our excuses to Uncle Leonard, who joked, "Very well, Cato. Just this once I'll permit my goddaughter to leave here on the arm of a dashing escort."

"Good night, Uncle Leonard," I said, with as much of a smile as I could manage. I would go again the next Saturday, and the Saturday after that. I would not renege on my agreement with Mother. But I was not likely to enjoy myself there as much as I once had. In the space of three minutes, and perhaps unwittingly, Father had spoiled it for me. I knew even then that I was indebted to him for that.

19

ONE morning in December of 1947, Alice asked me to meet her at the music academy at two in the afternoon, and to tell no one where I was going. She had kept to herself for months, and I had been too busy to force an opportunity to talk with her. Leaving the nursing school at that hour would mean missing a class, but I did not want to put her off. She looked anxious, almost scared. "I'll be there," I said. Even her smile of gratitude held a trace of desperation.

Following instructions she had carefully written out, I knocked gently on the door of a second-floor practice room at the appointed time. The latch lifted, and Alice eased open the door an inch or so.

"It's me, Older Sister."

"Thank you for coming, Hsiao-yen," she said, hastily pulling open the door and revealing a room so tiny that there was hardly space enough for the upright piano it housed. A slender young man was sitting on the bench, his back to the instrument. He jumped to his feet as I entered, then looked to my sister for a cue. His eyes were just as sad and as lovely as Alice had described them in Chungking.

"Hsiao-yen," Alice said with visible pride, "this is my fiancé, Han Liang-ming." He bowed his head and smiled. It was then, in the interplay between his lips and large, brown eyes, that I saw the delicacy Alice had once mentioned. I knew, before he even spoke a word, that I would like him; he had the same fineness of spirit Alice and my father shared. Yet I wondered if he had backbone.

"You're going to be married?" I stammered, thinking how unlikely a prospect that was. Mother would never accept Han Liang-ming as a husband for her First Daughter. It was clear from his frayed shirt cuffs and the sheen on the elbows of his jacket that his family had come upon harder times even than our own. Worse, judging matters from Mother's point of view, his eyes and wavy hair made him immediately recognizable as Eurasian.

"I know what you're thinking," Alice said. "That Mother will oppose the marriage." I looked down at the floor, ashamed that my thoughts were so transparent. "It's all right, Hsiao-yen. Anyone who knows her would guess at that. That's why Liang-ming and I are going to run away."

"Yes," Liang-ming interjected, before I could absorb what Alice was saying, "and that's why we need your help."

"You want . . . you want me to help you run away?"

"We're going to France," Liang-ming said with heartrending enthusiasm. "I've applied at the embassy for permission. They'll be sympathetic, I'm sure, because of my deceased father. Did Hsiao-hue tell you about him?"

I hesitated for a moment, bewildered by these foolhardy plans and by Han Liang-ming and Alice's evident belief that they would succeed without a hitch. "Liang-ming," I said at last, "they may grant *you* a visa, but they won't issue my sister one. She doesn't even have a passport, never mind a . . ."

"That doesn't matter," Alice said curtly. "If this fails, we'll go somewhere else."

"But what will you do about money, Older Sister? You can't just set out like two vagabonds."

"That's why I wanted you to come here, Hsiao-yen. I was hoping you might agree to ask Uncle Leonard to help us."

I could hardly believe what she was saying. "He won't do it, don't you see? For one thing, it would be a betrayal of his friendship with Father." Alice stared straight into my eyes, undaunted by my argument. "And what about Father?" I asked her. "Have you thought of the pain it would cause him if you were to go through with this?"

"We *will* go through with it."

"Hsiao-yen," Liang-ming interrupted once more, "if this is too much to ask, if it's something you simply can't do, we'll understand."

"No," I made haste to say, when I saw how distraught Alice was becoming, "I'll ask him, I promise."

"Thank you," Alice said, on the point of tears.

They were holding hands as I left them in that little room. Already my sense of shock had passed. Now I was afraid for my sister.

I arrived at the Park Hotel fifteen minutes early. I wanted to acclimate myself before meeting with Uncle Leonard. Since my first time there, it had always calmed me to smell the scents of leather and varnished wood that rose from the furniture and floors, to watch the white-jacketed porter's graceful economy of gesture as he opened the heavy glass doors that looked out on Bubbling Well Road. I sat in one of the mahogany chairs and collected my thoughts, gazing abstractly at the lobby's only blank wall — on which, so one of my dance partners had told me, a life-size portrait of Emperor Hirohito had hung until the last day of the war.

Uncle Leonard was passionate in his denial of my request. His broad smile faded, and he neglected the cherrywood pipe he was smoking, until the flame went out.

"You shouldn't have asked me this, Kathie," he said. "Back in the States this sort of thing is what we call 'out of line.'" He explained to me about his position as Father's close friend, as I had known he would. "Anyway," he said, relighting his pipe and shrugging, as though his stern words were to be regarded as a matter of the past and we were now speaking in special confidence, "it would be a disastrous match for your sister to make. Even as a musician, the boy has no real prospects here."

"You know him?" I asked, astounded.

"Oh, yes. At least I know *of* him."

"And Mother?"

"Now, now, now," he exclaimed, raising one hand to quiet me, and smiling reassuringly. "She doesn't know a thing about this business. Not yet, anyway." I could see in his eyes that he had not wanted to be the one to tell her.

"But how did you find out?"

"I made it my business to find out. You see . . . you see, your mother has enlisted my help in . . . negotiating a suitable marriage for Alice, and . . ."

"What?"

Uncle Leonard twisted in his chair and looked twice around the lobby, as if for an escape route. "Yes, and this news you've given me today will prompt me, I assure you, to suggest to her that matters be pushed along."

"What matters? Do you mean you've actually picked out a husband for her?"

"Well, your mother has. I'm only a go-between. It's understandable, after all, Kathie, if you'll just think about it a bit. Alice is shy and very impractical. She needs looking after. Anyway, Albert Wong is the young man's name — a godson of your mother's, unless I'm mistaken."

"Does my sister know anything at all about this?" I was almost too outraged to speak.

"I'm not sure, really."

"Do you know why Mother's doing this?" I cried, in the flush of enlightenment. "She wants Alice's marriage out of the way so that she can move on to mine — the one she's really interested in."

"I know nothing about any of that, I swear, Kathie," Uncle Leonard protested, begging me with his eyes to calm myself. "I'm just trying to be helpful."

At least my uncle never told. It was Alice herself, frustrated and at the end of her resources, who went into my parents' bedroom two nights later and threw herself at their mercy, pleading with them to let her marry Liang-ming.

Mother flew into a night- and daylong rage. Then she called Alice into her bedroom and asked, coaxed, and ordered her, in words that could be heard all through the house, to agree to marry Albert Wong. "He's handsome," Mother argued, "and extremely wealthy. His father is a banker, Hsiao-hue, you'll never want for anything. And he's leaving soon to study in the States. Just think, by summer you'll be living in America!"

"I'm going to marry Han Liang-ming," was all Alice ever responded.

Mother forged ahead. On the following Sunday she invited the Wongs and several other families to a dinner party to celebrate Albert's acceptance at an American university and to announce the upcoming marriage. She even had a date. For form's sake she had consulted the city's most fashionable astrologer; the couple was to be married the next spring, on the fourth of April. "My daughter wishes she could be with us tonight," Mother concluded with a doleful smile, "but with all this excitement . . . Well, she's feeling somewhat overwhelmed. I know you'll excuse her."

The courtship was a travesty. The Wong family, and Albert himself, I suppose, were eager to see the match through, but Alice became sullen and dispirited. She lay in bed late in the mornings, ate very little, and hardly spoke with anyone. The headaches she had not complained of in years began to recur. She sat obediently in the drawing room with Albert whenever he visited, but it was clear that she was acting a charade. Soon she had Lao Chang move her bed out of the room we shared.

"Are you angry with me, Older Sister?" I asked her, wondering if she would even answer.

"No, I'm not," she said. "I just don't want to be with anyone for a while, Hsiao-yen. Not anyone."

In the winter months of early 1948, I noticed more signs daily of an insidious fear that was spreading through the city. In some ways it appeared to be a rich man's panic. The families of my wealthier classmates were having American bills sewn into the lining of their jackets, or moving to Bangkok, Manila, or Hong Kong "to wait," as they put it, until the advancing Communist Army had been repulsed from the major eastern cities. The lines at the banks in the International Settlement often spilled onto the Bund's avenues as people vainly tried to convert their Chinese paper money into gold. And the same sense of dread had seeped into the middle- and lower-class neighborhoods as well.

"I need your help, Second Young Mistress," Lao Chang said to me one night, having called me into the kitchen after dinner. "Will you come to market with Chang Ma and me early tomorrow morning before school?" I smiled and looked quizzically at him. We had not bargained for food together since our first year in Chungking. "It's a serious matter," Cook insisted.

"Of course I'll go, Lao Chang."

"And I must ask you to keep this . . . well, to yourself."

"What are we buying, opium?" I whispered, but he only frowned and told me to meet him in the front yard at 6:00 A.M.

It was still dark when the three of us set out for the Native City. And yet by the time we reached our objective — one of the little grocery stores that sold produce and comparatively low-priced canned goods — a crowd of forty or fifty people had already gathered in the street.

"Can't we go somewhere else?" I asked.

"They're all like this now, Second Young Mistress. And this store offers the best prices. If I didn't intend to buy so much, I assure you I would've gone somewhere more convenient."

Once we finally made our way through the doors and to the counter, Lao Chang ordered as much rice as he, Chang Ma, and I could carry, then handed the merchant the six big wads of paper money he had stuffed into the pockets of his jacket and pants.

"Where did you get all that?" I asked him. It was no great amount, due to inflation, yet I had never seen Cook carry that much cash.

"Never mind," he said. "Let's just say I've been putting little

amounts aside for just such times as these. We should be buying twice this amount, Second Young Mistress. Enough to last
us until the new . . . well, until the issue is resolved one way or
the other. But the Master says we have no money to spare."

"You mean Father doesn't even know we're . . ."

"I'm doing what's necessary," Lao Chang said with finality.
With that, we lugged home our hoard and stashed it under an
old quilt deep in the servants' quarters.

From then on I paid more heed to Shanghai's uneasy mood.
As the Red Army's offensive continued to move eastward and
southward at an inexorable pace, segments of the populace
were becoming more polarized than ever before — the business community and landlords turning a watchful eye on the
coolie class; the municipal police and city-based Nationalist
troops taking arbitrary measures not only against suspected
Communist infiltrators but also against the hordes of politically unaffiliated students now marching regularly on the
avenues and streets. Everything was changing. The word "revolution" was on everyone's lips. Among those I knew, some
feared it as they would an epidemic. Some were resigned to
what they felt was now inevitable. Others awaited the sweeping
tide in rapt expectation. But no one in Shanghai ignored the
name Mao Tse-tung or the phrase the "People's Revolution"
any longer.

It was clear to me that we were not one of the rich families
that could afford to flee the coming upheaval. That we were
trapped. I felt ready to do what so many others in my position
were doing — to pressure the Kuomintang to reform. I joined
one of the student marches, and was surprised to see how
orderly an occasion it was. Though armed soldiers stood on
almost every corner of our route (Avenues Edward VII and
Tibet, leading to the racecourse), they made no arrests. Many
of the marchers carried signs protesting the government's
neglect of the poor and its openly corrupt practices, but there
was little shouting, chanting, or calling for more direct action.
That relieved me. I had feared I might be joining some band of

radicals intent on forcing a confrontation. In the main, these were young men and women who felt the way I did: in favor of preserving a democratic form of government, yet gravely disenchanted with the Kuomintang's vision of what a republic should be.

"You mustn't get mixed up in those demonstrations," Lao Chang scolded me that night.

"Who told you I was there?" I challenged him, both surprised at how quickly he had found out and annoyed at his interference.

"Never mind that, Second Young Mistress." He seemed to be in very bad health. His eyes were bloodshot and he looked pale with exhaustion.

"Are you feeling ill, Lao Chang? You look terrible."

"You think I'll forget about this if you change the subject?"

"You haven't told Mother or Father yet, have you?"

"No, and I won't. Not if you make today's little outing your last. Really, those streets are no place for you. It's getting dangerous. They've even started shooting people."

"You talk as if you were there yourself."

"I've heard things," he said.

"Well, I've *seen* what it's like, and . . ."

"All the same," he cut me off, "if you don't stay away from the marches, I *will* have to let the Master know."

"You don't care about what's happening in this city, in the whole country, do you?" I lashed out at him.

"I do, Second Young Mistress, believe me," he replied. "But student marches aren't what's going to change things. No, it's going to take more than that."

It was not long before I found out that Lao Chang had had good cause to warn me. At the conclusion of the fourth public protest in which I participated, five armed and black-booted soldiers dragged one of our leaders onto the sidewalk in front of the Asian Petroleum Building and made him kneel on the ground, facing our front lines. As I looked on in horror, a Nationalist officer shot him twice in the head. I had heard rumors among my fellow students that the young dissident was in fact a Communist. But what I saw that afternoon looked like murder to me.

As he had said he would, Lao Chang tattled, and my parents curtailed my activities. "Don't worry me this way, Hsiao-yen," Father pleaded with me. There was such sorrow in his eyes that I promised I would try to obey him. That was not enough for Mother, however, who instituted a policy of having Cook fetch me after classes each day, as if I were a child in grade school.

When spring came, matters deteriorated further still. Alice's despondency cast a pall over our day-to-day life. She never argued with Mother. Instead she said next to nothing all day, hardly ate at dinner, claimed she was too sick to see Albert when he came to visit. Mother was helpless in the face of her passive resistance. In the end she canceled the wedding. We all saw Albert Wong off at the airport when the time came for his trip to America, but my sister did not go with him.

To add to the atmosphere of gloom, Leonard Hsu announced that he would be leaving Shanghai at the end of April. "My nose itches awfully," he confided to me at one of his parties, "which is always a sign that it's time for me to take my show on the road." We were in a group, and it was impossible to talk with him then, but his words made me sad. I knew there was something mildly reprehensible about Uncle Leonard, some lack of seriousness that kept me from respecting him as much as I would have liked to. All the same, I admired the way he flouted convention, and I was grateful to him for having been so good to me.

"It's going to be dull around here if you leave us," I whispered to him, trying to sustain the playful tone he had set.

"Not a chance, Kathie," he said, flashing his patented grin. "It would take a lot more than my leaving to make Shanghai dull."

I was not at all sure that was so.

20

At one of the last of Uncle Leonard's parties, I met a man who I believe fell in love with me before the end of our first dance together. It was not Shen Chang-jui himself who asked for the dance, but his older brother, Chang-huang, whom everyone called C.H. Nor did C.H. approach me directly, as the young American officers and some of the brasher Chinese guests had no qualms about doing. He went first to my father (who had chaperoned me every Saturday night since Lao Chang had told him of my student protest activities) and made the request on his brother's behalf.

This was in effect a reunion, for the tall, ruggedly handsome C.H. had studied sociology under Father at Yenching, eleven years before. And so by the time the two of them were through with their courtesies and initial reminiscences, and I had at last been introduced to Chang-jui, the music to the tune "Smoke Gets in Your Eyes" was ending. Misreading the look of disappointment on his face, I said, "Let's dance to the next one instead," and walked out onto the floor. I was at once intrigued by him. He was not quite so tall, and slightly fairer than his imposing brother. In contrast to C.H.'s suave, polished manner, he seemed naive, even bashful.

The orchestra sounded the brisk introduction to "Tiger Rag" and Chang-jui's eyes filled with terror. "I'm afraid I'm not nearly as good a dancer as the others I've seen you with this evening," he lamented. "Actually, I waited quite a while for that slow number." I thought that was a sweet thing to admit to, though of course I did not say so. I simply swept us into the flow of the Peabodying couples. Chang-jui was as honest as he was self-effacing. He was not born to dance. As I floated backward and desperately tried to find us a channel among the swirl of more synchronized dancers, he kept smiling, never taking his eyes off mine and murmuring, "I'm *so* sorry," every time he kicked my ankle or shin.

In spite of Leonard Hsu's vigorous invitation, the Shens did not sit down with us. C.H. was the one who declined, though his younger brother was clearly in a mood to accept. He explained that they had to leave for Nanking by train early the next morning and had availed themselves of my uncle's "justly celebrated hospitality far longer than we should have." The two men bowed first to Uncle Leonard and Father, then to everyone else in our party, and left the ballroom.

"Now there go two excellent fellows," Uncle Leonard announced to the entire table. "Very promising careers in the capital, too." He took a sip of his champagne, delaying a bit for effect. "C.H. is married, but Chang-jui is another matter. In America he'd be called a 'catch,' wouldn't he, Cato?" He smiled at Father, who looked pleasantly lost in thought.

"Where are they from, Uncle?" I asked.

"From right here, quite conveniently," he replied with one of his winks. "Their father was a patriot in the days of the 1911 Revolution. His widow still lives in the International Settlement, I believe."

"Yes," Father said, reviving from his thoughts. "I've heard she stayed here through the whole occupation."

"But C.H. and his brother have jobs in Nanking now?" I pursued, wishing I could have made my interest less obvious.

"*'Jobs!'*" my uncle teased with a hearty laugh. "Yes, Kathie, you could say they have 'jobs' in Nanking. C.H. happens to be Generalissimo Chiang's executive secretary, that's all. And his brother, as you so discreetly refer to the other gentleman, serves in the same capacity to Chief of Staff General Chen Ch'ing. Not bad for a lad of twenty-seven, eh?"

This time it was Father who asked if I would not mind leaving early. He tried to conceal his reason from me, but his glowing smile could not have been more transparent. He was itching to go home and tell Mother.

When a long white box with two dozen roses arrived by messenger at our door the next morning, Mother almost purred with pleasure. "It's addressed to you, Katherine," she mused, "but who could they be from?"

I opened the card and read the message aloud. " 'To Katherine — a name easy to remember, a face hard to forget.' "

"So, he's not just handsome," Mother said, "but cultured as well."

"Oh, then you *do* know who sent them, Mother?" As she groped for a response, I excused myself and went to my bedroom, where I read the lovely phrase over and over.

It did not bother me at all that I knew next to nothing about Shen Chang-jui. I found his earnest, diffident manner very refreshing, and his face — with its high-bridged nose and deep-set eyes — uncommonly handsome. I could not understand what had prompted him to make such an impulsive show of his feelings, and I did not care. It excited me to think of myself as someone an older, good-looking man would choose to send flowers to. That was enough.

The whole next week Mother pelted me with questions and encouraging hints. Just what did I think of the younger Shen? Was it true, as she had heard, that his influential patron, General Chen, was sending him to an American graduate school? Had he said when he was scheduled to leave? I had not told him, had I, that I was a nursing student? Did I suppose, as she did, that Chang-jui was likely to show up at Leonard Hsu's farewell party the following Saturday night? Which reminded her, I might do well to have Chang Ma iron the pleats of my yellow gown. Mother had evidently embarked on an extensive investigation. By now I was sure she knew infinitely more about Chang-jui than I did.

On the morning of Uncle Leonard's last dinner-dance, which Mother, Father, and I were all to attend, a single purple orchid arrived from Chang-jui, along with a second card. At 10:00 P.M., he wrote, the orchestra would play "Smoke Gets in Your Eyes." He hoped I might save that dance for him. I told Chang Ma I would not be wearing the yellow, western-style dress, but my *ch'i-p'ao* of purple silk, to match the orchid.

Mother looked beautiful, seated at Uncle's right hand that evening. She became more radiant still when Father introduced Chang-jui to her. Her eyes showed pride and reserve, but it was easy for me to read how impressed she was. Chang-jui only bid me a courteous greeting then. However, at ten precisely, the musicians began the promised number, and he asked Father's leave to escort me to the dance floor.

No sooner had he taken me into his arms than he began whispering words that he had obviously rehearsed many times. "Katherine," he began in a shaky voice, "less than three weeks from tonight I'm to leave for America. Every day while I'm gone, *every single* day, you'll receive a letter from me. Please, hear me out," he suddenly said, thinking perhaps that I was about to interrupt him. In truth, I was at a loss for words. "I know this is unforgivably short notice, but I'd like to ask your parents' permission to let me introduce you to my mother next weekend. That is, if you don't object to the idea."

"What are you asking, Chang-jui? Are you . . ."

"Please understand. I don't want you to make any kind of . . . I mean, it would be foolish of me to expect you to feel about me yet the way I feel about you."

"How *do* you feel about me?" I was fascinated by the urgency in his voice. The song was over and we were standing alone in the middle of the floor. Chang-jui gave a start when he realized how conspicuous we were.

"I want you to think about joining me in America," he said hastily, walking me back to my chair. "I'm in love with you, Katherine."

The suddenness of Chang-jui's declaration stunned me. I would have liked just to sit by myself and think about all the things he had said, but I had no such chance. As my parents left the table to greet another couple, Uncle Leonard and I took the opportunity to tell each other good-bye. Perhaps because of what had just happened, I felt exhilarated, uninhibited. I was able to tell my uncle not only how much I appreciated his generosity, but also how fond I was of him.

"That's very nice, Kathie," he said, "and you know that's the way I've felt about you from the start." A row of wrinkles formed on his brow as he spoke.

"What is it, Uncle?"

"Kathie," he said under his breath, "you may not know about this, but I've been trying to get your father a teaching position in the United States for some time now. I'm afraid the prospects look hopeless. It's too late, it seems. Too many people trying to do the same thing, and . . ."

"I understand," I said, not knowing why he was telling me this.

"Yes, but Cato's situation . . . your whole family's situation worries me. Listen," he confided even more quietly, "you must tell your father that the authorities are aware of . . . of the 'seminars' he's been conducting in the basement of your house. And you must . . ."

"What?" I knew nothing of what he was saying.

"You don't know? He's been holding meetings with a group of his students for more than a month now. It's bound to get him in trouble."

"But . . ."

"I don't want to discuss it," he said firmly. "Just tell him what I said. And you must warn Chang Ming-teh as well. It won't be long before the police find out about the sessions he's been attending at the abandoned customs house near the Quai de France. Furthermore, you yourself, Kathie . . ." he quickly added, keeping his eyes turned away from me now. "Some of the friends you've made lately are under surveillance. You might think seriously about spending more time on your studies, if you follow what I'm saying."

Uncle Leonard looked relieved to see Mother and Father returning to their places. It had been difficult for him to say what he had. There were questions I wanted to ask him: what kind of danger he thought my father was in, and who this mysterious Chang Ming-teh was, to begin with. But I kept them to myself and watched my uncle retreat one last time into his jolly, bon-vivant self. The man in touch with everything and everyone worth knowing in Shanghai. The light-footed traveler whom neither war nor revolution would ever catch out of position. In the end he withdrew behind the smile he had worn virtually all the months I had known him — a smile in whose warmth I had always enjoyed basking, yet whose deepest meanings, I realized, I had never begun to fathom.

The next morning, I watched for a time when I might speak to Father alone. It displeased him that I had found out about his basement gatherings. Still, he reacted nonchalantly to Uncle Leonard's caution, saying that all he and his students were doing was debating the pros and cons of current government policy. "If there's a law we're breaking," he said, "it's a law that *should* be broken." I did not know how to argue with him. I could now see as clearly as Uncle Leonard that Father was playing a perilous game whose rules he did not fully comprehend. "Don't worry about me, Hsiao-yen," he added. "I'm doing what I believe is right, and that's the most important thing."

"There's something else, Father," I said in my frustration. "Uncle Leonard said that someone named Chang Ming-teh was . . ."

"I know about that," he interrupted. "That's nothing you should concern yourself with either. I'll see to the matter, Hsiao-yen."

At the noon meal I told my parents of Chang-jui's request that I meet his family. Mother was so elated that she nodded and smiled as I stressed that I was making no commitments whatsoever by going, and that the decision, if there was to be a decision, would be mine to make when the proper time came.

"Naturally," she said with a shrug. "Didn't I raise you to be independent, Katherine?"

I was surprised when I saw where Chang-jui's mother lived with her daughter and son-in-law. It was a very modest, old-fashioned house on Wuchang Road — a far less well-to-do neighborhood than I would have expected. A rich Shen cousin, our chaperone for the day, had taken us there in a chauffeured car, and accompanied us inside. We had to walk through the daughter's rooms to reach the somber chamber where the elderly, bedridden widow stayed. At once I felt I understood the entire situation. Before Chang-jui even introduced me to his mother, who eyed me from the start with a relentless stare, I recognized the scent of opium. In a better district, her habit might have proved dangerously conspicuous.

There was no servant. Chang-jui's sister served us tea and a trayful of candies and nuts. Once the greetings were completed, I became terrified. I did not know what to say to this woman, and she seemed to have decided beforehand to say very little to me. Chang-jui's game attempts at small talk fell flat, for his mother would suddenly turn to me and introduce a subject of her own in an insinuating manner virtually devoid of subtlety. "Then you were born in the Year of the Horse?" she asked once with a smile, calling attention to the ten-year difference in age between her son and me. And when Chang-jui was in the course of telling her where I had lived during the war years, she saw fit to interject a compliment, saying she had heard all about my "exploits in Chungking," and "the extraordinary ends" I had gone to when my mother was in need of medical care. After a mere quarter hour, she asked that we leave her to her rest.

"That was torture, pure and simple," I said as soon as we were back in the car. Chang-jui looked horrified, not because he disagreed with my view of our visit, I am sure, but because Cousin Ho was sitting between us and squirming with embarrassment. Had I been in any mood to examine my motives, I might have regretted my pitiless candor. After all, I was not angry with Chang-jui, who had been obliged to show deference to his mother. Nor, I felt, was the widow herself chiefly to blame. Chang-jui's brother was the one I would have liked to take to task. I could see that C.H. had given his mother a less than glowing appraisal of me, and that she was long in the practice of heeding her eldest son's words.

"Really," I seethed, "It's clear that Chang-huang's filed a complete report on me!"

"Katherine," Chang-jui said in a tone more sad than reproachful, "it doesn't become you to talk this way." I did not object to his rebuke. My fury was almost spent, and I knew that in part he was right; that I *was* speaking disrespectfully. I was even pleased by his show of spirit. I had feared he might be inclined to be too accommodating. "It isn't that my brother dislikes you," he said. "He was quite taken with you that night at the Park. But, well, I suppose he feels that your interest in political issues could . . . he just doesn't want me to jeopardize my future in government service by . . ."

"You'd think you were associating with a criminal!" I cried, angry all over again. Chang-jui searched futilely for words that might calm me. "Let's not talk about this anymore," I said after a long silence. "I don't want us to say good-bye like this." He had told me on the way to his mother's house that his flight to the States had been moved up to the following Tuesday. This was to be our last time together. Already we were approaching the front gate of my house, and the driver was slowing the car to a halt. The awkwardness of the situation exasperated me. I looked past our mortified chaperone's face, engaging Chang-jui's eyes. We smiled, neither of us turning away.

"I'm not my brother, you know," he said as he held open the car door in the street. "You'll see I have a mind of my own." Then he leaned forward and kissed me.

Chang-jui kept his word. All throughout 1948 at least one letter arrived daily at our address, sometimes two. And they were love letters. It was as though crossing America's borders had instantly given him nerve. I was not the only one he wrote. That summer Father received from him as correct and compelling a plea for my hand as Mother could possibly have hoped for. It was she, of course, who showed me the letter and entreated me to accept.

"He hasn't asked *me* yet, Mother," I responded, doing all I could to conceal how much that fact irked me. I was not ready to marry Chang-jui; in fact, the whole idea of marriage made me nervous. Still, if a proposal was being offered, I wanted it offered to me.

"But what will you write to him, Katherine?"

"I don't know that I *will* write to him yet," I answered heatedly.

"But if he proposes directly, you'll accept?"

"Please, Mother, let's wait until that happens."

"You're spiting me," she cried.

"Spiting *you?* What do you mean?"

"Then why on earth are you balking?"

"Because I don't want to think about marrying Chang-jui. Not yet, anyway. I feel as though I haven't known him long enough."

"But you *have.*"

"How can you possibly know that, Mother?"

She composed herself and said in an even voice, "Shen Chang-jui will write you a proposal of marriage. Perhaps by the time it comes you'll have reconsidered. Perhaps by then you'll realize what such a marriage would mean for all of us."

Two and a half weeks later, the time required for an exchange of airmail letters, the promised offer arrived, along with a two-carat diamond engagement ring. They were hand-delivered by the ubiquitous Cousin Ho. Chang-jui's letter moved me deeply. "I'm asking you to marry me," he wrote. "And even if you don't love me now, Katherine, I think I can make you love me."

A note, addressed to Father, was appended to Chang-jui's

message. His brother had signed it, and it bore the letterhead of the Nationalist Passport Bureau, whose directorship C.H. had recently assumed. "Esteemed Professor Yang," it began, "I sincerely regret that my duties on behalf of the Republic in these most critical times must prevent me from acquitting myself in person of the responsibility my brother recently enjoined me to take on."

"C.H. Shen has made his point!" I exclaimed, enraged by the note. "He doesn't like the choice Chang-jui has made, and so he resorts to insulting tactics like these. Get out!" I shouted at the cousin, who ran for the door. I took the velvet ring box and hurled it after him into the front yard. Mother was aghast, but there was no question of stopping me. I slammed the front door closed and stormed about the drawing room, too choked with anger to speak, then grabbed the letter and note, ripped the pages three times and scattered the fragments on the carpet. I did not know what to do with myself.

"Run after him, Cato!" Mother exclaimed. "Don't let him leave."

"No!" I said so forcefully that it made me catch my breath.

"You'll spoil everything, Katherine. He mustn't be sent away like that. Tell her to listen to reason, Cato," she implored Father, who just kept staring at the floor.

"It's your fault," Mother suddenly shouted at him. "Anyone can see that Shen Chang-huang opposes the match because he thinks of Katherine as an antigovernment protestor."

"I don't care what he thinks," I interjected, but she paid no notice.

"And you're the one who helped put those ideas in her head, Cato, I'm sure of it. If you and your students hadn't set her such a poor example . . ." Mother wept, not even holding her hands to her face. She gazed pitifully at Father and me, as if we had plotted together to ruin her life.

"Father," I said softly, "may I speak with Mother alone?" He started to say something, then only nodded and left the room.

"I've wanted this, Katherine," Mother began in a tear-filled voice before I could say a word to her. "It's as much mine as yours, what Chang-jui is offering. As much your family's as yours."

"Why do you say that, Mother?"

She started sobbing again. "He practically promised me."

"Who did?"

"Leonard Hsu. First you would go to America to join Chang-jui, then the rest of us were to follow. That's how it was supposed to work out. Don't you see, it was *arranged*. Is that so difficult for you to grasp?"

"What did Chang-jui know about this?" I asked in a daze.

"Chang-jui?" Mother sighed. "I suppose he knew as much as you did, Katherine. Just as much as you."

21

I was to have played the role of the male heir Mother had never borne my father. For the past five years she had been grooming me to fulfill the firstborn son's responsibility: to ensure the family's security in his parents' waning years. At least that was now understood.

Once Mother let me know that Chang-jui had not plotted with Uncle Leonard and her, I excused myself and left the room. It would have served no purpose to accuse her of wanting for herself the best of the new and the old social orders — the privilege of selecting not only her own husband, but those of her daughters as well. She would not have listened.

In my anger, I resorted to the kind of spite of which Mother had once accused me, and flung myself headlong into the protest movement. With hundreds of my fellow students, I marched through the downtown district almost every day, decrying the reign of terror instituted in Shanghai following Chiang Kai-shek's at last stepping down from power in January of 1949. I railed against the public shaming and, at times, execution of merchants whose only crime seemed to be that they had not contributed generously enough to the pockets of the retreating Kuomintang. The marches were now dangerous events. The Communist forces had taken Peking and Tientsin in January; Nanking would surely be next to fall. In the face of almost certain defeat, the law officers left behind began acting as they pleased. They were out of control.

I knew what I was doing, and at times I was ashamed of myself. I abhorred the regime's corruption and brutality, and felt a genuine need to demonstrate against it. Still, I also took satisfaction in the knowledge that my civil disobedience would upset Mother terribly. I wanted to punish her. For five years she had made me think I was beginning to earn her respect and affection, but all that time she had been dealing in a different currency. Now I would put her arranged marriage out of my mind and risk the lawless violence of the city streets. I felt free of the need to win Mother's love, yet enslaved in a different way. Now I was driven to make her hate me.

I was angry at Father, too. He must have known something of what Mother was up to, but he had been too weak to stop her. By his silence, I felt, he had collaborated in her exploitation of me; in her long-term strategy to barter her way to America.

Toward the end I became scared myself by what was happening to me. I had lost sight of my main objective: to earn a diploma and enter the nursing profession. Day after day I would leave school early, or not go to classes at all, in order to elude Lao Chang and join the increasingly violent demonstrations. In March, the month Nanking surrendered without a shot being fired, Father withdrew me from school. I believe I was as relieved as he was. He forbade me to venture beyond the wall surrounding our grounds. "You're hurting yourself, Hsiao-yen," he said, "and it pains me to see it."

It was difficult to while away the days at our house as droves of peasants were streaming into the city by the hour, fleeing before the triumphant Red Army, and as the citizens of Shanghai frantically maneuvered to flee South or to brace themselves for the imminent upheaval. I did not speak with Mother for nearly a week, avoiding her even at mealtimes. Our only contact came in the form of her leaving Chang-jui's letters at the door of my room.

To his credit, Chang-jui persevered in the face of my rejection and his brother's opposition. I began to consider his offer in a different light. The cast of strong-willed figures striving either to throw us together or to keep us apart were obscuring my vision with their antics. On the sixth day of my confinement, a letter arrived from him saying that he had secured me a job at the Universal Trading Company, a Nationalist Government-sponsored agency in New York City. "If you should come, Katherine," he wrote, "it would of course be with the understanding that you might or might not choose to marry me." I realized then that I would never know whether I could love Chang-jui until we saw each other for some time, and on our own terms.

From there my thoughts turned to my relationship with Mother and to three sobering realities: we were not ever likely to live together without conflict; I was too young or too immature to know why that was so; and if I did not soon escape her, I might wither, like my older sister. That very hour I told Mother of my decision to go to America. Not saying a thing, she threw her hands into the air and laughed ecstatically.

Once again our house became a nerve center of activity as Mother and Chang Ma saw to the preparation of yet another new wardrobe for me. In the meantime, Father, Lao Chang, and I braved the endless lines at the American Consulate, passport bureau, and airline offices until I had all the documents and tickets I needed for the trip. The most difficult task was getting a visa, but Father's connection with Dr. Leighton Stuart — the past president of Yenching University, who was at that time the American Ambassador to the Nationalist Republic — proved to be the deciding factor.

What worried me more than anything was the way I was leaving Alice. Since the time of her failed elopement, we had been unable to talk with each other. My political activities were as incomprehensible to her as her lingering dreams that she and Liang-ming would prevail were to me. Less than two weeks before I was scheduled to leave, Alice came quietly into my room, where Chang Ma was fitting me for an American-style dress, and asked me to meet her in the garden. "Come quickly," she whispered, "to the lane behind the oleander bushes," and she was gone.

When I got there, Alice was smiling brightly and standing beside Han Liang-ming, whose wrists and palms were flecked with blood. He must have scaled the garden wall, the top of which, as was the custom in that neighborhood, was covered with barbed wire and shards of broken glass. We nodded to each other.

"We want to thank you for trying to help us, Hsiao-yen," Alice said.

"I'm only sorry I didn't succeed, Older Sister." My tongue felt thick as I lied. Just to look at Alice and Liang-ming made me shudder with pity. I felt more than ever that they were no match for Mother, and that perhaps, as Uncle Leonard had once said, it was just as well they were not.

"You needn't worry about us any longer," she said, her voice trembling with excitement. "Liang-ming and I are going to have a child!"

My father was arrested on the second of April. Mother burst into my bedroom and told me what a Chung Ta professor had reported to her: that three Kuomintang officers had escorted Father from the college to a jail in the International Settlement, where he was being detained indefinitely for "consorting with the enemies of the Republic." "What will we do?" she groaned, shaking her head from side to side. "Whatever will we do now, Katherine?"

Father suffered that indignity for two days and nights, the time it took me to organize an informal defense. An accused man was considered guilty until he could prove his innocence, and so I enlisted the aid of Professor Ling and four of Father's colleagues at Chung Ta. Fortunately their concerted influence persuaded the authorities to drop the specific charge, which was that six months before, Father had written employment references for two of his students, who had since been convicted of being Communist spies. "This was a wrist-slap," Professor Ling said to me as we waited for Father to be released. Everyone there knew that the police could have charged him with much worse. Perhaps they had been unwilling to risk drawing the ire of the hundreds of prominent citizens who had studied under my father or been supervised by him during the war. In any case, the message was clear. By arresting him, the Kuomintang had indicated that he was not considered to be politically reliable. Cato Yang and his family would certainly not be invited to join the emigration of the Party's elite to Formosa, the exodus that was now being billed as a "temporary fallback from the mainland."

The next morning, I slipped out to join a march along Nanking Road, the city's principal commercial artery. This time it was not to spite Mother. I took my place alongside the others so that I might give voice to my own convictions about the government's abuse of its dwindling power. The militia was at its most repressive that day. At one point a young woman walking next to me was clubbed in the back by a soldier, who spat on her and confiscated the sign she had been carrying. At another, they turned fire hoses on our column's vanguard just as it reached a square in front of the Palace Hotel and, when the protestors kept moving slowly forward, menaced those in the forefront with fixed bayonets.

"You're no better than the brown dwarfs!" someone hollered, using the wartime propagandists' name for the Japanese. The soldiers did not look like our countrymen. They seemed capable of the kind of atrocities that the enemy had committed on those same streets during the occupation — the suffocation of infants who cried too loud while their mothers and sisters were being raped; the public beheadings and the nailing of the victims' severed heads to telephone poles. As many gruesome accounts as I had heard from those days, I had never fully believed them until that morning, when I looked into the face of a recruit no older than I was, and saw the animal fear and bloodthirst that could easily have driven him to kill me. A month before, that crazed stare might have sent me running home. Now I just moved to another part of the square. I would not leave.

It must have been near the noon hour when I heard Lao Chang's voice. I waved to him. We were separated by about twenty people in the crowd, but he was quickly weaving through them, shouting "Second Young Mistress!" all the while, as if I had not already acknowledged him. In the past when he had tracked me down, I had always given in and gone home with him. Just as I decided that this time I would not, I saw a tall, unarmed man, wearing a uniform I could not identify, grab him by both shoulders and throw him to the pavement. By the time I reached the spot where the assault had taken place, the officer was dragging Lao Chang through a cordon of rifle-bearing soldiers, some ten yards away. I fought my way forward, screaming at the man that he had made a mistake. The soldiers would not let me pass, and in a moment Lao Chang and his captor had vanished.

I ran to Father's college and told him what had happened. That was eight days before my scheduled departure. I insisted in a frenzied voice that I would not leave until Lao Chang was released and safe at home.

"It's all right, Hsiao-yen," Father said, though I could see the anxiety in his own eyes. "Go home and tell your mother what's happened. I'll telephone the people I know who may be helpful, then I'll go myself to Police Headquarters."

"Let me go with you."

"Go home," he said again. "I'll do all I can."

For three days Father searched the jails and courtrooms, returning each night with no news of Lao Chang's whereabouts, and lowering his eyes in the face of Chang Ma's stare. Very early the fourth morning, he came into my room and sat at the foot of my bed.

"This arrived a quarter hour ago," Father said softly, handing me an unsigned note that had been written on Kuomintang stationery. It stated simply that two days before, Chang Mingteh had been executed as a Communist supporter. I began to cry at once, and saw that Father wept too. As I turned away, wanting to be alone in my grief, he whispered to me that he was sorry, as if it had been his fault, then left the room. I cried all the harder, consumed by hatred for the cowards who had done the killing, and by a gnawing sense of remorse. Leonard Hsu's last words of warning kept sounding in my ears. The Kuomintang had made no mistake. Even if I had not, they had known the real name of Lao Chang — or, translated, "Old Chang" — as I had called my friend and servant all my life.

I left China on the twentieth of April, 1949, less than six weeks before the Communist Army overran Shanghai on its way to Canton and final victory. Almost everyone I knew came to the airport to see me off, with the notable exception of Chang-jui's brother. Shen Chang-huang had in fact attempted to stop the issuance of my passport, citing a seldom invoked technicality that prohibited citizens under the age of twenty-one from leaving the country, unless escorted by an adult. But Father had appealed to a friend of his, even more highly placed than Chang-huang. Within two days my birth certificate had been altered. On April 17, I was still eighteen years old. By noon of April 19, I was twenty-three.

The last quarter hour before my flight was an awkward time. The family, relatives, and friends who had come to see me off were not permitted to enter the cordoned area where the other passengers and I waited. Since we were not even close enough to talk, we just gazed at each other across the cavernous lobby, exchanging nervous waves and smiles.

Mother cried the whole time, as she had the evening before when we had said our real good-byes in the privacy of our house. "I sold my anniversary ring, Katherine, to pay for your new clothes," was the last thing she had said to me, restraining herself from begging me one final time to marry Chang-jui. I had thanked her dutifully, feeling no emotion.

It was painful for me now to look at Alice. I knew that she had not yet told Mother of her pregnancy, and that she had begun to realize that far from freeing her to marry Liang-ming, the revelation was destined only to worsen her plight. Failing to discuss the subject, we had taken refuge in incidentals and finished by parting as perfunctorily as I then did with Joan and Victoria. Alice gave me a present, however: a meticulous diary she had kept since our last year in Chungking. "There's nothing more I want to write in it," she said.

Father's gentle smile was what made those final moments bearable. My farewell with him had been the longest and the most comforting. We had met at his college in the late afternoon and walked home together, trading anecdotes from our days in Peking, recalling how content Lao Chang had been there.

"And if he were here with you now, and I were gone," Father had said, "would you have stories as wonderful as these to tell him about me?"

"Hundreds of such stories, Father. Lao Chang and I would never get to the end of them." He had smiled just as he was smiling now.

When the boarding gate finally opened, I ducked under the rope, ran across the lobby, and hugged Father, not caring who approved and who did not. Then I picked up my hand baggage, went to the gate, waved once more, and walked away.

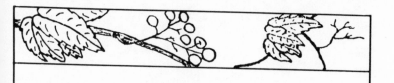

PART VI

Hankow

I was not to see my family again for thirty-two years. From the fall of 1949 until the early 1970s, no direct communication was possible between Americans and citizens of the People's Republic. Yet even after the Cultural Revolution and the subsequent political thaw, and even though I sent messages and money every month through contacts in Hong Kong, Mother never wrote to me, choosing instead to have Alice mail me terse summaries of the family news. I do not believe that was because of some private resentment, but because of fears instilled during what the Chinese themselves now call "The Great Terror."

When I saw her face to face in September of 1981, Mother was just as silent about the years we had lived apart. All along, I had heard disturbing reports from friends and relatives living in Taiwan or Hong Kong. Alice's life was a series of tragedies. To escape a violent racial purity movement, Han Liang-ming had fled to France in June of 1949, the month after Shanghai fell. Mother quickly found Alice a husband, who repudiated her three months before she gave birth to her illegitimate child. She was publicly shamed on the streets of Shanghai and sent to a western farm during the Cultural Revolution, then to Guizou Province to teach music to grade-school children. The Red Guard sentenced Father, as well, to four years in a labor camp, for being a "reactionary" and an "intellectual," later demoting him to the level of office clerk in the Wuhan library he had once directed. After a year of "reeducation," Joan was detailed to a research laboratory in Sichuan as a civil engineer. Only Victoria, a doctor, escaped *hsia-fang*, or being "sent down."

Mother would discuss none of this. "It's not permitted," she whispered the first night of my visit, and told me to keep my own voice down, since the commune cell leader's apartment was the one next door. Even when we talked about my life, it was in the most undetailed fashion. Her questions were vague and general, as if inspired only by politeness. I never took the position at Universal Trading, I explained (though I had written of all this a long time before), but enrolled immediately at the Columbia University School of Nursing. Within a year I had married Shen Chang-jui and, following specialized training at Bellevue and Mount Sinai hospitals, qualified as a nurse in triage medicine. Chang-jui and I were married for eighteen years and had three children, two daughters and a son, before agreeing to an amicable divorce. Since 1968 I had been happily married to Wei Ch'ung-ch'ing. That was all Mother wanted to know. She did not wish to be burdened with anything else.

My time with Father was troubling in its own way. On the day of my arrival, I catheterized him, since his bladder was horribly distended. His tongue was so swollen that he could not speak, but hour after hour for two full days I sat next to his bed and talked to him in a soothing voice of all things I thought he would want to hear about—his three grandchildren, my husband Ch'ung-ch'ing, my career in nursing and clinic administration. I hated to see him in such torment. He lay on his side, dressed in light cotton pants and a threadbare jacket whose sleeves failed to reach his wasted wrists. He did not even have a suitable bed but a plank of wood balanced on two facing chairs and covered with a thin cotton mattress. The skin of his face and hands was yellowish-gray. On my third day there I succeeded in persuading the Party officials to admit him to Wuhan Hospital the following morning. There the best physicians in the province would decide whether or not his cancerous prostate gland was operable. Either way, I felt, he would probably never come home again.

I wondered if my mother's friends would ever leave. For hours they scrutinized my photograph albums and jabbered with Mother about things that did not interest me. As the days had passed, the apartment had felt smaller and smaller; and since the arrival of the shipment of appliances that Mother had had me buy her in Hong Kong, there was hardly room to move about. I needed to be alone.

"Where are you going, Katherine?"

"Just outside into the courtyard for a moment or two, Mother. Father's sleeping now." I could tell it displeased her. She enjoyed showing me off.

It was hard to believe that Mother lived there — Mother, who, the last time I had seen her, was the mistress of a thirteen-room mansion in Shanghai. For perhaps the twentieth time, I strolled the length of the alleyway that ran alongside the commune's seven apartments. At one end of that lane was a splintery gate leading to the street; at the other, a partially roofed courtyard that housed all the families' common facilities: a black iron stove, a wooden-frame outhouse and, at the base of the wall opposite my parents' room, a single cold-water spigot overhanging a rusty grate.

At last the women were going home. As they filed past, we bid one another good evening. They looked at me the way everyone I had met in the last few days had looked at me — as if I were some exotic plant. It was in vain that I had packed only low-heeled shoes and plain, dark dresses for my trip. I was different from these people. In every conceivable way, we had grown apart.

When I reentered the room, Mother was seated, as ever, in her worn armchair. She had turned it away from the tea table now and was facing Father, who dozed uneasily in his bed.

"Mother," I said, "why don't we talk, just you and I." She

seemed not to have heard me, and to remain unaware of my presence even when I sat down across from her. Mother did not look well herself. Her complexion was still smooth and fair, but she seemed shrunken, beaten down by the years. "Mother?" I repeated softly.

"Not now, Katherine."

"But I have to leave tomorrow morning, after they take Father to Wuhan."

"Yes," she sighed, still gazing at Father.

"Please," I said, determined to speak to her.

She turned her head wearily toward me. "What is it, Katherine?"

"I had hoped things might be different. I feel as though we're still so distant from each other." She said nothing. "Will you tell me something more of what your life has been like?"

"I don't know what you mean."

"*Anything,*" I said. "All I've heard for three days has been banter about the running of the household, compliments on my children from your neighbors, wishful talk about how Father is sure to be cured, when we all know how hopeless his condition is."

"How American you've become, Katherine. How confident of yourself. I must say, I can't tell whether it becomes you, though." I welcomed her barbs. They were shaking me back into the realm of real emotion. "You know," she said, "I've often wondered why Chang-jui left you."

"He didn't leave me. I wrote you more than thirteen years ago about the decision we reached together to seek a divorce."

"Yes," she went on, as if I had not said a thing, "I don't imagine he appreciated this trait in you. This aggressiveness."

"No, you're right. He was too tradition-minded to see my directness as anything but a liability. But with Ch'ung-ch'ing things are different. He's not threatened by a woman's strengths." She raised her eyebrows and nodded once, then turned away again. Our visit, I knew, was at an end. Mother had no interest even in arguing with me. If I could believe all the wonderful things she had said about me to her friends, I had at last fulfilled her expectations. By marrying a wealthy and influential man, an American shipowner, I had met, perhaps far surpassed, her criteria for success. Yet sitting there with her in that desolate room, I wondered what she and I had given to each other and taken from each other, in balance. What could she show for having known me, I thought, but the six or seven machines that now surrounded her? And what of lasting value had I received from Mother? Even the drive I had inherited had been a mixed blessing. Throughout my professional life I had pushed myself too hard, often working a double shift at the hospital in addition to raising a family. With my children, I had had to be watchful, for twenty years, not to make the mistakes I felt my mother had made with my sisters and me. And I had always felt compelled to seek the approval of my friends — something I trace directly to the love withheld from me.

"Things won't ever change between us, will they, Mother?"

"I suppose not," she replied, relaxing the muscles of her shoulders and smiling wanly. "Now, get some sleep, Katherine."

Father died within the week, and Mother less than a year later. When I think back now to our final hours together, the clearest image I have is not of the look of love in my father's eyes, but of Mother's sad smile. For, what I saw in her face at that moment was no different from what I myself was feeling — a sense, at last, of deliverance.